Rex

A Mother, Her Autistic Child, and the Music That Transformed Their Lives

CATHLEEN LEWIS

THOMAS NELSON
Since 1798

NASHVILLE DALLAS MEXICO CITY RIO DE JANEIRO BEIJING

Published in Nashville, Tennessee, by Thomas Nelson. Thomas Nelson is a registered trademark of Thomas Nelson, Inc.

Page design by Mandi Cofer.

Thomas Nelson, Inc. titles may be purchased in bulk for educational, business, fund-raising, or sales promotional use. For information, please e-mail SpecialMarkets@ThomasNelson.com.

Scripture quotations are from the Holy Bible: New International Version® ©1973, 1978, 1984 by International Bible Society. Used by permission of Zondervan Publishing House. All rights reserved.

Transcript of *60 Minutes* interview with Lesley Stahl is courtesy of CBS News © MMV CBS Broadcasting Inc. All Rights Reserved.

ISBN 978-1-59555-208-2 (IE)

Library of Congress Cataloging-in-Publication Data

Lewis, Cathleen, 1957–
  Rex : a mother, her autistic child, and the music that transformed their lives / Cathleen Lewis.
    p. cm.
  ISBN 978-1-59555-150-4
1. Autism in children. 2. Autistic children—Family relationships. 3. Parents of autistic children. 4. Music therapy. 5. Creation (Literary, artistic, etc.)—Therapeutic use. 6. Autism—Treatment. 7. Autistic children—Biography. I. Title.
  RJ506.A9L49 2008
  616.85'270092—dc22
  [B]
          2008023100

Printed in the United States of America

08 09 10 11 RRD 6 5 4 3 2 1

In loving memory of my mother, Fauvette,
that you could have lived to know the blessing of Rex.

If I can love fully and completely as a mother,
it's because you loved me fully and completely as a child.

Contents

Prologue

I walked into the room holding my son's hand. He was excited and buoyant, and his springy steps showed it. As he approached the woman who stood waiting to greet him, his body was almost electric, a grin stretching across the width of his round face. She was elegant as usual—perfectly dressed and perfectly coiffed. She was smiling as he approached.

His enthusiasm preceded him, announcing before he even reached her, "It's nice to see you, Lesley. Are you having a good day?"

Lesley asked if they could shake hands. He extended his hand out limply, a notably odd contrast to his otherwise vigorous and exuberant body movements. It appeared so fragile. But the woman's handshake was like a shot of adrenaline to him, and his hand suddenly went taut in her grasp. On pulling it away, he began jumping up and down for a few seconds, and when he stopped jumping, his body seemed unable to contain the emotion. His arms suddenly bent at the elbows, his forearms moving up and down in a rapid flapping motion, while his head began shaking from side to side, like a windup doll suddenly gone haywire.

Lesley didn't appear fazed by this sudden and extreme display of excitement and erratic body movements. A consummate professional, she instead merely said, "Rex, why you've grown so tall in the last two years." Lesley Stahl had recorded her first profile on my son two years earlier when he was only seven. Now she was back to see how he was doing.

I stood behind him and laid a hand on each shoulder, applying subtle pressure, which helped his body regain control.

"How old are you now, Rex?" Lesley asked.

"*Nine* years old!" he said, as though it was a proud accomplishment. But he didn't linger there, his thought process already moving forward. "I *like* you, Lesley!"

When Lesley responded in kind, perhaps hoping to then move forward in the conversation, Rex said, "I like you *so much*, Lesley!"

"So Rex, what grade does that put you in now?" Lesley asked, referring back to his age, while ignoring what he had just said. I didn't say a word—I'd been asked to refrain from speaking as much as possible—but I knew what *not* intervening would mean.

He repeated eagerly, "I like you *so much*, Lesley," and awaited her response, like he was stuck in gear. Again, she refrained from responding, presumably waiting for him to answer her question about his school grade. I bit my lip as he said again, automatically, "I like you *so much*, Lesley." A broken record. And a stalemate.

Finally, another woman in the room broke in. Shari was the producer, supervising the cameras and sound. The CBS television newsmagazine *60 Minutes* was here in force with correspondent Lesley Stahl, who had arrived that day, heading the team. The producer had spent a few days with us prior to this interview, and she explained the situation to Lesley. "He's waiting for you to say, 'I like you *so much* too, Rex.'"

My son had his scripts . . . indeed he broke them with difficulty in everyday conversation. Until Lesley responded in kind, "I like you *so much* too, Rex," he would be locked in place, unable to move his thought process forward. It was as if he was an automated phone menu, which, not getting a proper response, loops back endlessly to the original cue. Her like response would provide the completion he needed to free him to answer her questions.

"I like you *so much* too, Rex," Lesley said, complying.

It was instantaneous. His body visibly relaxed. And though it was less noticeable, mine did as well as he began to answer her questions.

Although she had stood up to greet Rex as he entered, Lesley was now seated with him standing in front of her, putting them both at eye level. Rex had relaxed for only a moment, but now his body had turned once again to extraneous movements and excitement. She asked if she could support him with one of her hands, but he couldn't seem to hold his arms still enough for that. Again, I tried the best I could to drain some of the excess adrenaline out of him by putting a calming hand on one elbow. It would be hard today—Rex was just too amped up.

Lesley continued to interview my son in what was a labored process for him. He sometimes maintained his silence, seemingly confused by a question, or simply answered yes or no without further explanation.

"Have you ever been in a swimming pool?" Lesley asked him.

"No," he answered immediately. Shari had asked me not to jump in unless it was necessary. They wanted Rex to answer on his own, but I couldn't let this one go because I felt his answer to one of his favorite activities called for a little nudge.

"But Rex, we have a pool at home. You love swimming," I prompted him, trying to focus his mind on the question at hand.

"So, you do swim?" Lesley pressed.

"Yes," he said. His body was calm now. He was trying so hard. The cameras had caught the whole thing.

He hadn't been expecting the question about swimming pools. Maybe that was it; the context had confused him. Or maybe it was the word *ever*. Did Rex understand what the word *ever* meant? It was such an open-ended, abstract word. Surely if she'd asked him if he'd been swimming yesterday, he would have answered with a hearty, "Yes, Lesley!" Maybe even adding, "And I had a great time swimming." A question needed to be concrete, limited in time and space, in order to be answered by my son.

We were hitting dead ends with too many questions, until Lesley asked him about an autobiography he had written for some students in North Carolina who had mailed him letters. In answer, he recited the whole autobiography verbatim, unable to contain his enthusiasm. It was a script, merely rote memorization, so it was easy communication for him. As he finished by saying, "I'm learning to snow ski. I like to ski full speed ahead!" he was every bit a child who loved his life.

When the interview mercifully finished, Lesley walked ahead to the stage as I gave Rex a guiding arm. I was happy to be done with the arduous process we'd just completed. "It was an interview-issimo," he told me as we made our way down the backstage corridor. "That means 'little interview' in Italian," he explained in a conspiratorial way, like he was imparting a treasured piece of information. I wasn't sure, but I suspected "issimo" actually meant the opposite—big. I wondered if Rex had understood it was supposed to be a little interview, but for him—and for me—it had turned out to be big.

I was just glad to be moving onto the stage for the other part of the interview. This would be much easier for Rex. We had been in this theater on many occasions, but only in the audience. Today it had been reserved for our group, and the auditorium would remain empty. I was taken aback by the contrast in the clothes we were wearing, casual and colored, with the black, dramatically lit setting on the stage. But what I noticed even more was Rex's smallness against the backdrop of the massive instruments that awaited him. There they stood, side by side, twin Steinway concert grand pianos, daunting in their majesty with their sleek lacquered finish. Rex, however, wasn't intimidated. In fact, his whole body seemed to relax the moment he touched the familiar instrument.

My little boy felt the piano bench, then maneuvered his body into position in front of the keys, his small feet stretching to reach the pedals. He played middle C and then touched his belly button with the same finger. "I'm right in front of middle C," he announced, which meant, *"Yes, I'm perfectly centered."*

His piano was awash in light, but fortunately, none of the glare of the spotlights hit him in the face. I knew well how sensitive his eyes were to light. He was very familiar with this piano, although he'd never played it on stage before, only in the rehearsal room. His fingers came to life on the keys, attacking them, no longer seeming fragile; they were instead infused with dexterity, strength, and speed. As they had during the interview, the cameras caught it all. But here there were even more cameras, and they covered every angle. Nothing Rex could do would escape CBS here—the *60 Minutes* cameramen were poised to catch each nuance of his fingers and body.

"What is that you're playing, Rex?" Lesley asked. It sounded like Mozart, or was it Bach? More likely than not, it was just vintage Rex. Or, more precisely, Rex was weaving together classical influences with others, more romantic, into his own improvisations.

He confirmed my assumption with his answer, "I don't know, Lesley." That was his way of saying, "I'm making it up as I go."

"Well, it's beautiful," Lesley said as she sat down at the other Steinway. The real interview would be here. That was fortunate, since this was Rex's turf.

"Rex, I have a new song to play for you. I'm going to play it for you once, and then I'd like you to play it back. Is that okay?" Lesley asked.

"That's okay, Lesley," Rex said.

"This is called 'Try to Remember,'" she announced as she began playing. She had gotten through most of the first verse when her hands suddenly froze on the keys. Turning quickly to Rex, she said, "I made a mistake. Can I play it again?"

"Yes, Lesley," he said simply. She gave it another go. This time she got a little farther into the piece, but her hands tripped up again. Before she had the chance to acknowledge it, Rex covered his ears, exclaiming in a loud, moaning voice, "It's a mess, Lesley!"

It's a mess! He had been so floppy and chaotic himself, just moments before, as he answered her questions verbally, yet now he was crying out for precision. Indeed, anything less seemed to literally hurt his ears.

"You're absolutely right, Rex. It *is* a mess. I'm sorry, I'm not as good a piano player as you," she apologized. She decided to try a different song. With the pressure on, she played "I've Never Been in Love Before" from start to finish. But she didn't ask Rex to play it back verbatim, as she had wanted with "Try to Remember," or as she'd done for his first profile, when he'd played back "Do You Know the Way to San Jose?" after hearing it once. Instead, she threw in a twist.

"Rex, could you play that in the style of Mozart for me?" she asked.

His answer was immediate—he didn't hesitate an instant, not to reflect, not to measure, not to calculate. Instead, his hands jumped to the piano keys, filling the theater with light notes, cheerful notes, lots of trills and flourishes, Mozart-like runs up and down the keys to fill out the melody line. Lesley's piece was instantly transformed into classical Mozart under the mastery of my son's tiny hands.

It was awe-inspiring to watch, as was shown on Lesley's face as she took it in. As always, Rex clapped for himself when he finished. The rest of us on the stage applauded in sync. Instant, rote memorization was one remarkable skill, but immediate creative transformation was another dimension altogether. Now the fun began! Lesley asked him if he might be able to replay the song, but this time in the style of Chopin. Romantic Chopin!

"I'll play it like a Chopin waltz," Rex announced as his left hand began jumping up and down the piano in three-quarter time. One, two, three, one, two, three . . . his left hand made flawless leaps as his right hand picked up the melody. And there were those unmistakable liberties taken with the tempo—now speeding it up, squeezing more notes in, only to later spread them out languidly as Chopin had intended. The listener was drawn in and tantalized, only to be pushed away like a rejected lover.

Lesley began shaking her head in disbelief as she watched. The floppy, overexcited child, who seemed unable to control his body, was here master both of tempo and melody. How could he manipulate music with such ease? As I watched, I wondered why my son couldn't find that same comfort within his own body.

"Rex, do you think you could play it in one more style? Maybe like a Russian dance?" Lesley asked.

"Yes, Lesley, I will play it like a Russian dance," he answered. And then, as though *Fiddler on the Roof* was being rehearsed on that very stage, "I've Never Been in Love Before" was transformed into a choppy dance beat, romanticism replaced by driving power. Rex was having fun, and when we applauded again, he became more than giddy—he looked like he was electrically charged. His body went slightly rigid in his passion, forcing him to tilt backward on his piano bench. I could see my son's laugh building up inside him until a big belly laugh broke free. It was a sound as stunning as the music in its abandon and resonant purity. It was a laugh that caused laughter

"You're amazing, Rex!" exclaimed Lesley, chuckling herself.

"Yes, Lesley," he said. Spontaneous, guileless, joyful—Rex was every inch an innocent child.

"There doesn't seem to be anything I can throw at you that you can't do, Rex," she said.

"No, Lesley," he responded, simply.

My son had just told Lesley Stahl that there wasn't anything she could throw at him that he couldn't field—musically anyway. Not with his prodigious talent. The *60 Minutes* cameras caught it all for a second profile on my little nine-year-old boy, only two years after the first one. But why were the cameras back so soon? The world was filled with gifted children—so many child prodigies. *But there weren't many like Rex*, I thought, with a catch in my throat, not many who had been put to the test time and time again, whether at the piano, performing feats of wonder, or just going about the simple daily tasks of life. Rex was an exceptional child, no doubt about it. He was exceptionally gifted and exceptionally challenged. But why had Rex been given so much—on both ends of the spectrum? As I watched him beaming with pride at his musical abilities, I couldn't help thinking about how much life had thrown at him. It was all summed up in the opening lines of "Musically Speaking," his first *60 Minutes* profile, filmed at age seven and airing three months after his eighth birthday. Correspondent Lesley Stahl opened the segment saying, "One of the most fascinating and mysterious features of the human mind is its capacity to house striking abilities and profound disabilities in the same person, as we discovered in an eight-year-old boy named Rex."

Fascinating. Mysterious. How could Rex play music with such mastery and not be able to answer a simple question or tie his own shoelaces? How could his inability to control his body be so contradicted by the absolute control he has playing the piano? These questions, and so many more I'd asked myself since I brought him into the world, were all leading me to wonder what beautiful mystery had created the remarkable complexity that is Rex.

CHAPTER ONE

Beginning

Fear not that thy life shall come to an end,
but rather fear that it shall never have a beginning.

—John Henry Cardinal

I was pregnant—very pregnant. I looked down at my belly and hugged it . . . and him. We knew it was a he; rather, "he" was a boy. I'd get it right. We'd give him a name soon, but it had to be the perfect name. Anything less would be, well, not quite perfect. My husband, William, and I had both wanted a boy, William being South African and macho, and me being—or rather having been— a tomboy. Admittedly, I was still quite in love with sports and my husband and the world! I was giddy, that's the word. I was foolishly, schoolgirlishly giddy! Three weeks from delivery, and I was in this growing state of excitement, of anticipation that was growing with my belly, growing with the little boy who had my profile. The ultrasound had captured the image of my pug nose—it was unmistakable. That's when the beautiful reality had really struck home.

I knew that much of this euphoria was because I had waited so long to have a child. Thirty-six is not old in absolute terms, but it felt so in baby-bearing years. And it was in my thirty-sixth year that the ticking of my biological clock had begun to resound louder and louder, gripping me like so many women around my age. Fortunately for me, I was also a newlywed. After being wrapped up in my professional life in France for twelve years, I had moved home the year before and had met the man of my dreams. He had just arrived from South Africa, here for a week on business; and because I'd lived abroad for so long, it felt in a way like we were both foreigners. Meeting on a typically sunny day in Los Angeles, there had been something fateful in our instant bond. It had the smack of destiny. I knew that was the stuff of romance novels, not real life, but in a world this big and random, that kind of chance meeting had to be written in the stars.

I sighed a contented sigh and hugged my tummy again.

It had been such an easy pregnancy. No morning sickness to speak of, and my Lamaze training had me fully confident the birth itself would go just as smoothly.

That's why the phone dropped from my hand as I heard the doctor's words through the line. "The ultrasound shows the presence of a suspicious mass in the brain of the fetus." I felt a sharp pain grip my belly. Or was it just in my mind? I'd had my appointment that morning, and the doctor had reviewed the scan right in front of me and had said nothing! No, the opposite, in fact— he'd been all smiles. That's why I'd been on such a new mother's high all day! And now he was dropping this bombshell over the phone? The doctor explained that he'd wanted to look at the film more closely before advising me. That was the reason he hadn't said anything.

> The phone dropped from my hand as I heard the doctor's words through the line. "The ultrasound shows the presence of a suspicious mass in the brain of the fetus."

"It wasn't there a month ago," he went on, as though that might console a soon-to-be first-time mother about the fact that there was something "foreign" in her baby's brain. I knew it hadn't been there a month ago. What did he think, that I would have forgotten that little bit of news? That I would have remembered my baby's upturned nose but not the "suspicious mass"? I tried to calm myself down so I could just listen. But he didn't have anything more to say. He couldn't tell me what the "mass" might be. More extensive ultrasounds were needed to determine that. And they needed to be done immediately.

After a battery of more detailed imaging, a conclusive diagnosis was made—the mass was an anachroid cyst. That's what they said was in my baby's head—a gigantic, fluid-filled cyst. "It's benign," a new doctor said, this one in charge of high-definition imaging at Cedars-Sinai Hospital. The word "benign" was meant to be a reassurance. I knew that, but I was only partially relieved because I was confused by the terminology. I struggled with that word being used to describe something that filled up a quarter of my baby's head and wasn't supposed to be there. In practical, nonemotional terms, the doctors told me it meant it wouldn't endanger his life. Although I needed to deliver him quickly, the doctors could wait a few weeks to operate—critical weeks that would allow him to gain some weight, some resistance, before undergoing what would be an invasive surgery.

I consoled myself with the fact that the problem was repairable. The doctors had even told me there are adults who have lived their whole lives with cysts in their brains without even being aware of them. I was lulled into the idea that the thing really was innocuous after all. A problem that simply had to be dealt with. Once the surgery was over, we could get on with our lives—our "broken" son would be fixed, and William and I could go back to dreams and plans for our future.

Rex came into the world so easily, bypassing all the trials and traumas of labor. Delivered by C-section to avoid any potential trauma to his brain, his face had the look of an angel—bald and pure and perfect, not the look you associate with typical newborns in their ruddy, rough-and-tumble state. Tiny feet with crooked toenails—certainly they'd straighten out in time—and perfect hands. Long, slim fingers adorned by exquisitely sculpted nails. I didn't know a newborn baby could be so magnificently formed. And then there was his crowning glory in William's book—his shoulders! They'd caused quite a stir when the delivering doctor exclaimed, "Would you look at the shoulders on this boy!" as William and I awaited a first glimpse of our son. There he was, our little boy. We would name him Rex. Short, to the point, tough. A good boy's name. And it meant "king." Rex.

At eight weeks, weighing in at ten pounds, our baby was deemed strong enough to withstand the surgical procedure, which necessitated a four-inch incision down the center of a skull that wasn't much bigger than that. The neurosurgeon was going to cut holes in the cyst in numerous places so that it would drain and deflate like a rubber ball. When I asked why they couldn't just remove the whole thing, the doctor told me that the cyst was so large it was completely enmeshed in brain tissue; to take it out, they'd have to remove half of our son's brain with it!

I willed myself to be strong, as though I could counter Rex's own fragility. Our baby seemed much too small to have to undergo something so big. I tried to focus on the thought that it would soon be over, and I forced myself to keep my emotions and mind in check. And my husband was stoic—a little too stoic in my opinion. I wasn't sure whether it was a man thing, a South African thing, or maybe just a William thing I'd never encountered before

We waited in terse silence outside the intensive care unit. The procedure had gone smoothly, or so we'd been told—the cyst had been properly "fenestrated." Now we were waiting for our son to come down from recovery to the ICU where he would be interned for several days. It seemed to be taking forever. Was something wrong? Suddenly the silence was broken by the sounds of commotion as the hall door swung open, and in rushed a fleet of very *big* people, or so they seemed. They hovered over the bed they were hustling toward the intensive care unit. At first, all I could see of the occupant of that bed was a network of tubes, intertwining plastic life support for an unseen patient. Those people all but obscured their tiny ten-pound patient, but it was definitely him—Rex! My heart leaped, and so did I! I jockeyed for position to look on his face as he was hustled past us. Like a football team running their precious cargo protectively into the end zone, preventing any interference from the opposition, they hovered in a cloud of urgency that made Rex seem even smaller and more fragile. But there was no way they were going to get past *this* mother without my at least being able to look into my son's eyes. I lunged behind the bed as they hurried past, my reflexes sharpened by a potent cocktail of anxiety and love. Luckily, Rex's head was tilted backward so he was actually facing me.

That's when I saw his eyes. I felt the air being knocked out of me as they pierced right through me. Rex's eyes were frozen, transfixed on me, as though he was just waiting for an explanation. It seemed like his eyes were pleading for a reason. "There is no reason," I wanted to tell him. As I continued watching him, his eyes boring through me, I felt the steely bond of love being forged between us. For, although I'd loved Rex from the moment he was born, even from the moment I'd felt his presence in my womb, there was something new to this feeling—it was raw and all-consuming, both maternal and fiercely protective. Some mothers feel the surge grip their heart the moment they stare into their newborn child's face; for others it grows over time. With some, sadly, it never comes. For me it was in that moment, like an arrow piercing my heart.

REX'S LOOK that day would haunt me for years—the look of innocence and pleading—stalking me relentlessly at night. But I had misread the glazed stare. As a mother, I should have been able to know what was really there in my son's eyes. But I hadn't been able to see past their intense opacity and my own sense of blame and recrimination. The truth would only be revealed to me two months later by one more doctor, one more piece of information. This news would give new meaning to forever—time would shift and space would go askew. How could I have not known? Rex hadn't been staring at me that day in the hospital, his eyes pleading. The fact was he'd never even seen me. I knew that now.

I REMEMBERED how brightly the sun had been shining on the afternoon I learned the truth—how vibrantly autumn had worn its colored robe. The sun was soon to lose its gloss, and I would never again see fall colors in the same way. I had made an appointment with the ophthalmologist at Children's Hospital because I had wanted to have Rex's eyes checked. The trauma of the brain surgery had lessened by this time, and I had become concerned about the increasing movement in his eyes. They fluttered, not really fixing well on objects. Sometimes he seemed to be tracking like he should; at other times he did not, giving his eyes a random appearance. I didn't know if he needed a corrective patch or perhaps a minor surgery to fix them. Compared to what we'd been through already, my husband didn't think it would be a big deal, so he didn't accompany me.

The ophthalmologist finished the eye exam, shining a light in my son's eyes and peering in through his loupe as I stood watching. He finally asked me to sit down. As I sat facing him, he wrote some notes on a page. Waiting for him to explain what was needed to correct Rex's eyes became unbearable, the suspense forcing me to interrupt.

"So Doctor, what can we do to help Rex focus his eyes?" I asked, struggling not to sound too impatient.

I watched the doctor's face as he wrote the last couple of words on the page. A brief flash of emotion was stamped out by what appeared to be professional conditioning, and he was inscrutable as he laid his pen on the desk pad with finality. Only a sole audible breath, one of resignation, betrayed any emotion as he fixed his eyes on mine.

"There's nothing to be done," he began, then paused heavily. I wasn't following; I still didn't know where he was going. The doctor's eyes held mine, and he just said it: "Your son is blind."

I felt my body disconnecting from my mind in the most bizarre way upon hearing those words. His tone had been so matter-of-fact delivering such a brutal, unexpected blow. I felt the blow in my gut, but my mind went numb, unable to really grasp what he'd just said. He waited for a reaction. I was in shock, I suppose. I wasn't crying, but he extended a box of tissues to me anyway. Maybe he knew it wouldn't be long before the import of his words would hit me. He was probably used to the floodgates bursting.

> "There's nothing to be done," he began, then paused heavily. I wasn't following; I still didn't know where he was going. The doctor's eyes held mine, and he just said it: "Your son is blind."

I've since reflected on the best way to tell someone her child is blind, and maybe he did have to say it just like that. It seemed hard to me, like a sucker punch. But at the end of the day, there really is nothing that can be said to lighten the blow. Blind is blind. That's my conclusion, and it's so absolute that any sugarcoating is futile. The ophthalmologist told me Rex's blindness was caused by a congenital condition called optic nerve hypoplasia, which meant "underdevelopment of the optic nerves."

To me it simply meant the impossible, the unthinkable—Rex

would live his life in darkness. It meant that my child, who had survived the horrors of invasive brain surgery at eight weeks, would never see. I couldn't quite connect to the reality of it all— it was just too big, like they were trying to snuff out my baby's life before he'd even had a chance to live it. I sat there listening to the doctor's spiel about the condition, but I just wanted to flee.

"The problem isn't with Rex's eyes," the doctor explained. "It's with the optic nerves."

"What do you mean? I don't know what an optic nerve is."

"It's a nerve that connects the eye to the brain," he said. "Light hits the eye, then it travels through the optic nerve to the brain, where it's translated into an image. So, in order to have good vision, three parts have to work normally—the eye, the optic nerve, and the brain."

"Okay," I said numbly, struggling to focus on the science of it, as tremors began to seize my body. I willed myself not to break into pieces right on the spot. *I need to get the information—emotions only get in the way; hold them in check, just for a few minutes.* Miraculously, I managed to disconnect my heart from my mind.

"Well, what's wrong with Rex's optic nerves?"

"They're underdeveloped. They're much smaller than normal, healthy optic nerves. And typically, optic nerves have millions of tiny fibers that serve to convert the light of the world into images. Rex's optic nerves have far fewer fibers than normal. Even if the light makes it through, he doesn't have enough fibers for his brain to make sense of it."

"How did this happen, Doctor?" I asked pathetically, letting my emotions seep through now. "I had an easy pregnancy, then three weeks before he was due to be delivered they found a cyst in my baby's brain, and now you're telling me he's blind too? That he was born blind! This is not supposed to happen. Babies are not supposed to be born blind!" My voice and emotions rose in a crescendo, and I was wiping my eyes with the proffered tissues now.

"We don't know exactly what causes it, but we believe it happens at around ten weeks gestation since that's when the optic nerves are formed," he said. "Most of the neurological wiring is also being laid at that time. So that could also have been when the seed for Rex's cyst was laid, even if it didn't blossom until much later in the pregnancy." He told me there were other incidences of children with optic nerve hypoplasia who'd also been born with a brain cyst. "The two could be related," he said, in what sounded more like a question than an answer.

"But you have no idea what causes either?" I asked in a tone of utter disbelief that said, "I want accountability."

"Nothing conclusive," he said, launching into an explanation that sounded like he was reading from a textbook. "But we do know that there were fewer than one hundred known cases of optic nerve hypoplasia documented in the century up to 1970, then during the seventies there were hundreds of cases, during the eighties, thousands, and now it's a major cause of blindness in infants. We think it must be environmental." Amazingly, I was taking it in, as though shock had sent me into a hyper-lucid state. But then, my emotions began closing in from all sides.

Nothing conclusive, environmental, we don't know why! Blind, blind, blind! Those were the words that swirled through my mind as I stumbled out of the doctor's office, assaulted now by an unremitting noonday sun. I was horrified at the thought of telling my husband and felt like the whole thing was some sort of surreal nightmare. The world as I had known it had simply and irrevocably ceased to exist in the space of an instant. No one could even tell me why, give me a reason. It just happened! Just like that! Like we'd drawn the "blind" ticket in a great baby lottery. The doctor had provided me with a straw to grasp. "Children with optic nerve hypoplasia may develop some vision as they grow older. Some do; some don't. We don't really know why."

There was that offensive "we don't know" phrase again. He went on to explain that it was his special area of great interest and that he was conducting a federally funded research study at the hospital to chart the progress of children with this eye condition. "Children with optic nerve hypoplasia have some striking commonalities," he said. I didn't really know what that meant at the time other than the obvious—they're all blind! The irony of landing in the office of the nation's specialist in this specific eye condition was lost on me at the time. But I did agree to participate in the study before we left. I hoped it might help me understand. I also left with a number to call—to get help—for a preschool called the Blind Children's Center. As I fled the hospital, pushing Rex's stroller as fast as I possibly could, I realized the very name of that preschool made me feel sick.

CHAPTER TWO

Into the Dark

All my life I believed I knew something. But then one strange day came
when I realized that I knew nothing, yes, I knew nothing. And so words became
void of meaning. I have arrived too late at ultimate uncertainty.

—Ezra Pound

I stared out at the ocean, still stunned by the doctor's words just hours before. Rex lay at my side underneath his beach parasol waving his rattle in the air, as though to flag down the kayaker paddling past. Our blanket was in our usual place on a small patch of sand wedged between jagged rocks. I'd packed my son into the snuggly sling, toting him firmly strapped to my chest, along with our beach basket, in order to get here. The waterline was fairly high in this early afternoon hour, not leaving much sand for us to walk on. This meant navigating a few low-lying rocks in our path. But I knew the tides near our home well—high tide had been an hour ago, and the tide would be receding quickly today, leaving us an easier trek back. We were tucked away between the rocks. Hidden, and all but inaccessible to the public, this strip of isolated beach was unadorned by beach homes and was only two hundred yards down the coast from our condominium.

Since arriving at my house with the doctor's news bloating my mind, I felt it suffocating me, emotion rising in my chest like a balloon ready to burst. William was still at the office, and I had to get out. The walls of our home were too confining, closing in on me from all sides. So I went to the beach, practically running the distance, in order to breathe . . . to be able to breathe. The salt air, frothy waves, and seagulls calling out—it was nature's massage. The ocean has the power to calm me, lift me up; it always has. That's why William and I had come to this rustic Malibu cove when we married, buying our condo on the waterfront.

I was tired from the physical effort to get here so quickly, and the pounding in my head was replaced by heavy breathing as I watched the ebb and flow of the tide. Waves smashed on sand and rolled over rocks to dissolve into skirts of frothy foam and head back out to sea, leaving scattered deposits of seaweed in their wake. Tiny ripples, flirting at the waterline, hovered as the larger sets of waves gathered strength farther out at sea. The rhythms of the ocean were ever evolving, ever changing, and yet predictable and measurable.

As I sat there, I felt the sun beating on my skin as I took in the magnificent horizon, a vast, endless panorama of ocean topped by brilliant blue sky. I'd often come here to find peace in the beauty of nature's tableau—the flatness of the Pacific beyond the swells, its texture contrasted to the rise and fall of the waves as they reached the shore. The sand, coarse gray and white granules, hugged the rocks and was dotted with bits of sea life—shells strewn here and there, slimy strips of green sea grass, and tangles of golden seaweed. A seagull flew overhead, swooping brazenly down to nip the water at the top of a rolling wave, as though daring the surf to jump up and clip its flight. He cried out, high-pitched and victorious, as he rose up to freedom carrying a fish. I couldn't help but smile at his audacity, but then another sound cut in, plummeting me back to the present—shrieks of delight coming from my side, as though in imitation of the seagull. Rex. Waving his hands emphatically as he let out his happy sounds, he was the picture of joyful glee, completely caught up in the moment.

How innocent my baby boy was. Innocent and unsuspecting, he never saw any of it, not the smallest grain of sand or the sweeping immensity of the ocean. I bowed my head slowly and let the tears fall.

ON THE outside, my husband seemed to accept our son's blindness much more quickly than I did. I simply couldn't believe that Rex would never see the world. I clung to the hope that he was already developing that vision the doctor had spoken about. I certainly had the impression he was locking his eyes on my face when I held him in front of me. I would parade lights past his face to see if he would react, or I'd place him in front of the mirrors that babies normally love. Sometimes he reacted, and sometimes he didn't. Rex's responses were inconsistent and inconclusive, and yet, instinctively, I felt that stimulation was the key.

"I'm sure he can see a little," I told William. "I can just tell. What do you think?"

"He's completely blind," he said bluntly, never one to mince words.

We had gone for a second medical opinion at the Jules Stein Eye Institute at UCLA. This time William was at the appointment. He got to hear the news firsthand.

"Your son has optic nerve hypoplasia," a second doctor said, repeating the fancy diagnosis. He had waved a few toys in front of Rex's face, to which my son had seemed oblivious. "Your son doesn't react visually to anything, and he's already close to six months old."

I jumped in, desperate. "But the doctor at Children's Hospital said it's possible for him to develop some vision over time."

"He might be able to discern large objects in time," he conceded. Just as I felt a door nudge open for me, the doctor slammed it shut with a vengeance. "But will he be able to distinguish you from a horse? It's doubtful." His words seemed heartless and insensitive, but they pretty much said it all. Even so, how could I just give up?

For William, the doctor's words were a verdict confirming Rex's blindness. As we walked in silence from the building, I asked him what he was thinking. His words had become few of late. Now he merely said, "The most important thing is that he remains happy." For me that seemed impossible.

How could a blind child possibly be happy when he'd been so cheated from the start? Certainly not when he got old enough to realize! I felt such guilt about bringing a child into the world, knowing he would have such a hard fight of it. A friend had given me a book intended to help me take heart titled *When Bad Things Happen to Good People*. I wasn't sure whether to take heart from the fact that I could still be a "good" person, and that Rex's birth wasn't God's punishment for past sins, or to sink into the reality of just how "bad" things were.

IN SPITE of my pain and inability to really accept Rex's diagnosis, I did realize that information could help. So I took the first doctor's advice about contacting the Blind Children's Center. They invited us to come to the Center for an "intake" to discuss future services for our son; both parents were expected along with the child. The three of us made the long trek from our home on the coast to the small, gated complex nestled in the midst of the gray surroundings of downtown Los Angeles. A receptionist greeted us warmly and summoned the school psychologist, Miranda, who would conduct this initial meeting, along with two social workers. They commented on how cute Rex looked sitting in his stroller dressed in his preppie ribbed green pullover and rolled-up corduroy pants, complete with Docksiders he kept kicking off. It might just have been pleasantries geared to keep anxiety at bay. The staff must have known how besieged we'd felt by all sorts of conflicting emotions. Miranda asked us a lot of questions about our family and Rex's birth. She nodded each time I spoke, paying close attention to every word, counterbalancing my nervousness with her calm and poise. She had a way of looking empathetic and thoughtful while maintaining clear focus and purpose in the meeting. The goal was to determine if it would be appropriate for Rex to receive schooling at the Center. Miranda asked us lots of personal questions, but the one that left its mark was when she asked us what our goals were for our son.

I had been doing a lot of the talking, but my husband answered this one. "Cathleen and I both love sports. We just want him to be active, to be good at sports." He appeared as calm as Miranda. I didn't get it. Not his calm state and certainly not his answer, which seemed disconnected from reality. Didn't he understand our son was *blind*? I stared at him as though he was speaking nonsense, all the while being struck by hard truths I hadn't yet had time to face in the newness and trauma of all this. Rex could never play tennis as I had growing up, or golf as his father did. Yes, of course, we had wanted him to be athletic . . . before.

Don't all parents project their own hopes and dreams onto their children, making them future doctors or astronauts? The air hung heavy in the room as I felt so many dreams snuffed out before they'd even begun. Our child's life was screeching to a halt before even beginning. I felt leaden. Through all of this, Rex sat in his stroller blissfully and mercifully unaware. I was struck by the unsettling impression that my husband seemed just as unaware.

"William," I said, cutting in before he could project any other futile goals onto our child, "I don't really think that's possible now."

Miranda looked from me to William, then added cautiously,

to keep from adding even more emotion into the equation, "Rex may not be able to play all sports, but that won't keep him from being athletic and enjoying fitness, if that's what he wants." She paused, then added emphatically, "We work here to help children realize whatever potential they may have, and to discover areas of interest that will help them in life."

I had a lot to learn about blindness, and I knew that I needed to open my ears to what Miranda had to tell us. "Ninety percent of what a baby learns is through vision," she said. "That means there is little incidental learning in the life of a blind baby."

Rex wouldn't be able to watch the world like other babies and mimic it in order to acquire skills. He wouldn't have the luxury of being a passive learner. Rex would need to be engaged in life because the world wouldn't come to him through vision. He would need to reach out through touch, through active engaged learning. Rex would have to be "hands-on." Miranda used the words "purposeful" and "methodic." That's what the teaching would be for Rex, and it would need to begin as soon as possible. That was the reality of our son's life, if I understood the gist of what Miranda was telling us. The task of filling in that 90 percent blind deficit seemed monumental—from where I sat it seemed all but undoable. To make up for what amounted to a horrendous, inexplicable birth defect, Rex's life would require nothing less than endless work and absolute commitment from all of us. But even with that, how could anything make up for not being able to see?

It was the tour of the Blind Children's Center facility and playground that provided me with some desperately needed encouragement. We glanced into classrooms where children seemed to be actively engaged in activities—the classes were all hands-on, colorful, and full of life. In one classroom of four year olds, children were busy unscrewing caps off bottles and then locating coins on a table to put into the bottles. "They're working on finger and hand dexterity, and tactual discrimination," Miranda explained. In another classroom, some younger kids were intent on a finger-painting activity. "The paint has granular Jell-O in it to create texture they can feel," the psychologist said. Then, as we were watching some babies in high chairs sweeping their hands across their trays, our guide explained, "They're learning to locate Cheerios on their trays." The bell for recess rang.

Miranda led us into a yard as colorful as the classrooms. A couple of older kids walked across the playground with their long, white canes stretched out in front of them, guiding them, until they reached the stairs of some playground equipment. They seemed to accomplish the task so easily. "They know the route well," Miranda said. "They use the edge of the grass meeting that spongy surface under the structure as a spatial indicator."

Both students climbed the stairs of the structure in turn, turned to the right, walked across a bridge, and finally turned to the left to a big, winding slide. Just as the first child completed his snaking descent, my attention was drawn to a little girl standing by herself in front of a big pile of fallen autumn leaves—it looked as if they had all been purposefully raked into a pile. They were a mountain of varied orange and brown hues.

Miranda had been providing program information through-out our tour, and as we stood on the playground she told us, "Our goal in the Center is normalization. By that, I mean providing skills so that the blind child can eventually integrate into a sighted world. In order to help us do that, we have what we call a reverse mainstream child in each classroom. That means a sighted child, who serves as a sort of benchmark, an example if you will, for the other kids."

Suddenly the girl in front of the leaves bent down and picked up a big armful, tossing the colorful leaves skyward. As they fell back on her head, she laughed as though she were having the time of her life. I turned to Miranda and said, "That's obviously one of the sighted children you're talking about."

She smiled, clearly gratified by my assumption, and said, "No, actually, Abby is completely blind!"

But she looks so happy, I thought. It was a flicker of light that hit my heart—brief, but unmistakable.

REX BEGAN school at a mere six months! This was none too soon when you think of a "90 percent deficit" looming above his head every waking moment. He was placed in the "Mommy and Me" class, which meant he would learn at school while I was being shown how to work with him at home. The philosophy of the Center is to work with families, not just with children. Their efforts at school were only as good as the parents' ability to carry through at home. Thus, Mommy and Me—and, theoretically, that would include Daddy at some point. The staff also worked with parents outside the classroom in a forum that was just as vital as learning techniques and methods. It was the critical psychological and emotional forum. They were aware that "new" parents of blind children had just had the fabric of their worlds ripped apart, and they embarked on a mission to mend them, to put them back together, to put *us* back together. The staff knew the statistics— our children had little hope of overcoming such mind-boggling odds without strong parents at home to support and defend their interests. Broken parents are no good to their children. That's why Miranda and three social workers were on staff—to help us cope, to help us understand. For me, coping was one thing, understanding quite another. In time, they might help me cope, but I would never be able to understand. How could I understand something so senseless and incomprehensible?

Rex's first few months at the Center were very successful.

Much better than my own. He had the flexible brain of a baby, while mine was rigid and patterned. He was about getting on with this thing called life, while I was trapped in all my lifelong conditioning about how things were supposed to be. My boy began picking up skills, learning to feed himself with his fingers and explore objects in age-appropriate ways. While this gave me some hope, it still seemed too inconsequential in the overall scheme of things. The big picture—meaning the whole sighted world—just seemed too big and unobtainable. How could Rex ever learn about the immensity of an ocean he'd never see? Or develop sensitivity and harmony in a colorless world?

At the same time, I was struggling with my own issues—the emotions of severe trauma. The big four, as I learned from Miranda and the Center's social workers, were grief, anger, guilt, and fear. I was grieving the huge loss of our "perfect" child we'd dreamed of. At the same time, I was angry. Miranda told me that anger was normal because we'd been robbed of something so precious. "Senseless" and "arbitrary" were the words I used, and the phrase "it just happened" filled me with rage. I wanted someone to tell me why it happened. And so entered guilt—guilt that it had somehow been my fault. Did things this bad *really* happen to good people? At the very least, I felt I'd failed to protect my innocent, defenseless son against something that "just happened." I suppose the sum result of the whole situation was an overwhelming fear of the future.

It was a daily battle to make headway against such heavyweight internal stuff, all the more so because Rex's dad seemed to be able to just go on with life, like nothing of consequence had happened. Of course, work and professional worries insulated William from the day-to-day life I shared with Rex. I had decided not to go back to work. It didn't seem to make sense anymore; the financial markets I had worked in before with such passion only confused me now. Buy, sell, buy, sell—it all seemed futile and purposeless.

Endless repetitions that yielded nothing of worth, not when compared to what repetition would yield for Rex.

To listen to the staff at the Center, the keys that would open up the whole world for our son were work and repetition to build concepts and gain life skills. Even the simplest task, like feeding himself with a spoon, couldn't be taken for granted as one might with another child. I learned that without vision there were numerous steps in any process—locate the spoon, locate the plate and its edges, locate the food on the plate. And endless related questions: How do you know what you've scooped up with the spoon? How do you know it hasn't spilled onto the table or the floor, that the spoon hasn't tilted in midair if indeed it had scooped anything in the first place? How do you differentiate mashed potatoes from peas without touching them with your hands? It went on and on. And that simply meant that Rex needed his mother. I needed to be with my son. So my "workplace" was an emotional battleground. On some days I was buried under the weight of it all; on others, I just allowed myself to love my child.

It was in this context that Rex turned one. I was determined to bury any conflicting emotions for this day. His first birthday would be a celebration! It was a day for children, and adult "stuff" had no place in it. I ordered my one-year-old the most beautiful, colored cake with streamers he could touch and a big candle that played "Happy Birthday" when you rotated it. The event took place at the Blind Children's Center. I had come to appreciate that their specialty was normalcy. Their goal really was to help these kids acquire skills and patterns of behavior early in life so they could be integrated into mainstream schools later on. They worked hard to make every blind child feel normal, and they emphasized celebrations and daily activities that sighted children took for granted. I suppose when Rex grabbed the streamers from his cake and tried to eat them instead of play with them, that was probably a one-year-old's age-appropriate reaction. And, perhaps, when he took a big bite of rich, sugary cake and then promptly threw it up, that was also a normal reaction!

All of this was a powerful and wonderful counterweight to the psychological stuff I was dealing with. In spite of myself, I was beginning to feel more normal as well. It was a fact—Rex's first six months at the Center were very successful. No one could deny that! As I watched him standing beside his birthday table, I felt pride in my child, who would most certainly be walking far before the two-year-old average walking age for a blind child. There was Rex, already standing strongly. Our broad-shouldered boy would soon be on the move! The teacher smiled as she put her hands over Rex's hands, helping him rotate his birthday candle to make the candle play "Happy Birthday" again. Cause and effect—everything was a teachable moment. Giddy upon hearing the tune, Rex broke loose with a long string of animated babble. He was "a talker"; that's what the speech pathologist said, referring to his daily babbling. I couldn't wait until he would begin to pronounce real words in a few months, so we could begin to really communicate.

It was very tough to think of my child being deprived of sight, but in the months since Rex had come here, I had to admit that I was beginning to feel blindness really could be overcome. My son would not only be able to enter into the mainstream, to be "normalized," as they described the process here, but he could even excel in the "real" world. Signs were certainly looking good, and by now I'd read about Helen Keller, who had lived an exceptional life being not only blind, but deaf too. I believed Rex would be like that, blind but a high achiever even by sighted standards. Indeed, he had gone about his first year of life with energy and enthusiasm, like he was grabbing at possibilities. He was curious and pretty good at just being a child. His joy in living was contagious. When he laughed with pure abandon, it could light up a whole room, as it did now, with his teacher helping him turn his birthday candle one last time. A sign, a very good sign indeed.

"HAPPY . . . BIRTHDAY . . . to . . . you." Three days later I could still hear the refrain trailing out in my memory, fading with the remnant giggles in the classroom as I waited with my son for the doctor to read the MRI scans he'd just taken. "Routine status check of brain cyst at one year of age," had been the doctor's order.

The eminent neurosurgeon walked into the room, holding the scans. "The cyst is growing again," he said without preamble. "Looks like we're going to have to put a shunt in it."

I stared at him, mute, my vision beginning to blur, my head spinning. Growing again? A shunt? All I could hear was my son's birthday song, his laughter. I was back at the party, not here.

"It's a very easy operation, Mrs. Lewis, and it's the only way to assure that the cyst won't scar over again and begin to reinflate."

The doctor looked distorted; his words were senseless. He kept talking at me, but I wasn't there. *Let's twist that candle one more time, Rex!* Ah, the giggles.

"A shunt is a drain, which will allow the cerebral fluid to circulate normally."

He wouldn't stop talking! Why wouldn't he stop talking? Operation? Drain? Not another invasion into my baby! Did he realize I hadn't said anything? I wanted to scoop Rex up in my arms and run.

"Believe me, it's the best way to safeguard against hydrocephalus," he added.

The word was a jolt to my own brain, and it broke my silence. "Hydrocephalus?" I mumbled feebly.

He nodded, his eyes dead serious. A look of terror must have crossed my face as reality struck full force. The party was over. Cake and streamers had no place here, and "Happy Birthday" just mocked us now. I turned to look at my little boy, who would soon have a shunt in his brain! There was no choice, because I knew what hydrocephalus meant. It meant water on the brain—swelling. And that caused—I bit my lip—brain damage.

CHAPTER THREE

A World Upside Down

> *When the world says, "Give up,"*
> *Hope whispers, "Try it one more time."*
>
> **—Author Unknown**

R ex didn't have much appetite again today," his Mommy and Me teacher said as I walked into the classroom from my parent support group. She was sitting next to Rex trying to spoon-feed him. He was sitting in his high chair, tapping his fingers on the tray, ignoring his teacher and a bowl of puréed peaches in front of him. His teacher set the spoon back into the bowl. "The only thing he would eat was graham cracker bits."

"Seems like all he wants to eat is finger foods these days," I said. "Graham crackers for lunch and dinner, and Cheerios for breakfast." His teacher looked concerned, so I added, "But, it's only been three weeks since the surgery. Maybe we just need to be patient. At the rate he grew last year, he's gotta get his appetite back soon." I smiled a smile of confidence I didn't quite feel. There was something different about my son. Of course, he was weak from his latest operation and was probably adjusting to having a permanent foreign object in his body. (That's what the shunt was, even if it was helping drain his brain.)

"I'm sure we'll see him get his old energy and appetite back soon," said the teacher, who was as aware as I was of how apathetic and lethargic Rex was these days.

THE FIRST real clues that something was seriously amiss came about six weeks after Rex's first birthday. He had become a picky eater, that was true, but I knew that children could be like that. They went through food phases. What made me really take note were his hands. There was definitely something different about Rex's hands. I could never forget the perfection of his tiny newborn fingers. They were still the beautiful, exquisitely formed hands he'd had at birth, but he now seemed really hesitant to use them as he'd done before to explore his world. He would still feed himself bits of dried food with his fingers and hold his cup of milk to drink, but that was about it. When offered an object or toy, he would now pull his hands back, squeezing his fingers into a ball. You'd have to peel his hands open as well as use a lot of coaxing to get him to take the toy. In addition, he seemed unable to hold on to things anymore—even if he grasped an object, he'd then drop it almost immediately. That really unsettled me, since it was his hands that had to replace his eyes!

"It's called tactile defensiveness," explained the occupational therapist at the Blind Children's Center. "Many blind children have overly sensitive hands. That's why we have the kids explore things like whipped cream and spaghetti. To desensitize them." She spoke to me about sensory integration, which is a therapeutic approach to combat this abnormal sensitivity. "We could start him on an intensive program immediately." Her reassurance only helped calm my concerns for a short period.

In addition, Rex was becoming increasingly irritable. At first, the main cause seemed to be his hands and the things they came in contact with. But now, I also struggled to get his socks and shoes on. If I couldn't get the socks on in one fast, unbroken motion, it would inevitably set him off screaming, as though in pain. He also seemed not to enjoy standing anymore and had begun suddenly collapsing his legs. They could go from taut to limp at any moment. The sensory integration specialist we'd begun seeing said it was probably due to increased sensitivity in his feet as well as his hands.

Then there was all the extraneous body movement Rex had begun to develop. He had always had a few "blindisms," as they called them at the Center, which are the repetitive body movements many blind people have to varying degrees. Due to the absence of vision, the blind seek stimulation in other parts of the body by rocking back and forth or tapping their feet or hands repeatedly. I had learned that these gestures and movements normally lessen as the child develops and his brain matures. But now the opposite appeared to be occurring. Like a cancer, these blindisms were spreading to new areas of my son's body previously not involved. They were beginning to include rapid hand flapping and chin tapping, side-to-side head shaking as though he was watching a tennis match at warp speed, and bicycling his legs when he was sitting or lying on his back.

"Give him time," William told me one evening, when I was obsessing about everything that seemed to be going wrong with our son. "He'll get his old character back." I wanted to believe that was true but was having a hard time being patient. I wanted it all to go away now.

The next morning, William left for work as I was trying to get something more than dried Cheerios into Rex's stomach before heading off to the Center. In a hurry to get away from what had become a morning feeding war, my husband closed the front door a little too forcefully. Rex jumped and screamed at the sound. That was the first time I noticed a new sensitivity—he began startling more easily than before. Soon it became apparent it wasn't even particularly harsh sounds that set him off. At the Center, the sound of running water began upsetting Rex so much he'd cover his ears every time someone went to wash his hands, accompanied by the ever-increasing screams of what had to be pain. Next it was light switches; the barest click was torture to his fragile ears. It was like my son's little sensory system had lost any capacity to modulate. Normal sounds had become like fingernails screeching on a blackboard. Touching everyday objects was as upsetting as if he'd stuck his arm into a hornet's nest. And his emotions had become excessive, swinging erratically and at breakneck speed from one end of the spectrum to the other. He could be laughing hysterically one moment only to start screaming the next. Conversely, tortured crying could switch instantly to runaway laughter. It was frightening to watch the swing; it was as if some outside puppeteer was working the controls of my child's body, whipping him around at will.

> *The sound of running water began upsetting Rex so much he'd cover his ears every time someone went to wash his hands, accompanied by the ever-increasing screams of what had to be pain.*

By the time Rex was eighteen months old, his reactions to sensory stimuli were out of control, a daily assault to his body and mind—and to my own. I'd had no training in all of this. Indeed, life never gives training beforehand on what to do if something goes wrong in the brain, especially in the brain of your child. What do you do when the wiring suddenly goes haywire? How do you unscramble it? None of those smart and elite college classes I'd taken as a Stanford undergrad explained any of it. Nor had there been even the smallest clue in all my life experience abroad. And to top it all off, I had no time to think. The six months since a shunt had been inserted into Rex had placed me in a frantic state; much of my time was now spent on damage control to his newly sensitive body rather than helping him make developmental gains. Rex and I (and William when he wasn't preoccupied, or was it avoidance?) had become hostages to his sensitivities—to his hands, his ears, and his mouth because he had begun to require almost liquid nourishment. Moving forward in life was relegated to second place, after the sheer effort it took just to hold our own on a daily basis against the tide of sensory onslaught.

The world had become a hostile place from morning to bedtime, where every part of life was a potential attack. It was an upside-down battleground where things didn't make sense anymore. Not to my son, and not to me. This was made crystal clear on one dark, cloudy morning in January. A storm was brewing outside—and inside.

I was getting Rex ready for his morning at the Blind Children's Center. Just back from Christmas break, he was eighteen months old, and his Mommy and Me teacher had invited me to confer with her while aides covered her class. I was hoping she'd have some advice, because we couldn't go on like this. I'd gotten Rex's pants on and pulled the neck of his T-shirt so wide it didn't even graze his fragile head. So I was ahead of the dressing game when I started to put on his first sock.

Bunching the sock up so the whole thing would fit onto his toes with minimal impact, I said, "Rex, I'm just putting this sock onto your right foot." I stuck the thing on, and he reacted, but then relaxed. I pulled it up quickly. Another startled reaction, but again, it passed. We were doing well today. Confident now, I said, "And here's the left sock." Onto his toes it went. One more tug of the sock, and we'd be home free. But then, as I was trying to pull the thing up in another smooth, noninvasive motion, disaster struck! It twisted and stuck at his heel!

High-pitched screams of pain hit my ears. He wailed like he had an open wound or like I was burning him with coals, not passing soft cotton over his foot! My hands were shaking as I quickly tried to undo the mess I'd made of his sock, straightening and sliding the thing "painfully" over his heel. Both of his feet began kicking full throttle, back and forth, like he was pedaling a bike, anything to avoid wearing shoes.

"It's okay, sweetie. You're okay," I assured him, all the while sensing how far he was from okay. "Your socks are all on now. We won't put your shoes on yet." I rocked him in my arms to calm him. Once Rex was calm, I hoisted him into his high chair and handed him a cup of milk.

"Here's a nice, big cup of milk to get your appetite going." He loved milk, and the cold liquid soothed him further. I wouldn't even try to force anything more than dried cereal into him this morning. "And I'm pouring some yummy Cheerios onto your tray. When you're ready, you can just pop them into your mouth." But today the sound of the dried bits hitting the tray made him wince. Imagine, it was just Cheerios dropping on a tray! I berated myself for not placing them there quietly. He set his cup down, but instead of reaching for the cereal like he normally did, sweeping his hand slowly across the tray to find the round pieces, he curled his fingers into fists and batted them away with the back of his hand, flinging them onto the floor. He grabbed his cup back like it was a life preserver, drinking voraciously. Thank God he would still hold that. But then the phone rang, and it hit him like a bolt of electricity. Screaming, he dropped his cup, and the milk spilled onto his tray, dripping down to the floor, making a soggy mess of the Cheerios.

"Rex, honey, it's just the phone!" I said as the phone call routed to the answering machine.

Rex rammed his fingers into his ears, his body beginning to shake as did mine. I lifted him out of his high chair and hugged him tight, singing in his ear. Physical pressure seemed to help his nerves as did singing, even if my voice was wobbly. Gradually, he calmed down. I set him back in his high chair with a new cup of milk, and then I went into the bathroom to wet a towel to mop up the floor. I carefully avoided running water in the kitchen so the sound wouldn't destroy him further. I shut the bathroom door, ever so softly, to block the water sound.

I mopped the floor while he finished his drink. He placed the cup down and began drumming his hands on the high chair tray. The rhythm calmed him further, and he now seemed content. On the other hand, my nerves were already shot, and we'd barely begun the day. Not daring to upset him further, I threw his shoes and jacket into the bag, put him in his stroller, and headed for the car.

The dark clouds opened up as we pulled out of our garage, and light rain began falling. I love the soothing sound of rain and hoped it would calm both of our nerves. But our world was upside down. We hadn't even gotten out of our driveway when Rex's head started shaking like he was trying to fling something off his head. Then the movement seized his shoulders as well, and his hands shot to his ears, like he needed to get outside his body.

God, no! I screamed in my mind. *Not the rain! He can't be reacting to the rain falling on the car roof.* Yet I knew that was exactly what was going on. "Rex, we can't get away from the rain," I pleaded. But reason had no place in our car. Not with my son's dysfunctional brain. I tried a different tactic, cajoling, as he began moaning loudly. "It's rain, Rex, and it's a beautiful sound. The rain, falling on the roof." I began a rhythmic chant. "Pitter-patter, pitter-patter goes the rain on the roof." His body calmed slightly. "Pitter-patter, pitter-patter . . ." He was pulling his hands slowly from his ears, intrigued by my chant, but just then thunder boomed, as the sky opened up, pouring sheets of water onto our car roof, causing his moaning to escalate into screaming. Desperate now, I fumbled with the radio, trying to find something, anything, that would pull his attention from the torturous rain. Only static. Rex screamed even louder. I slapped the radio with my hand, as if that would somehow tune the thing. One preset button after another, until I came across a station that was static free. It was a classical station, playing Mozart. Just as I was ready to flip to another station, fearing classical music wouldn't make a dent in Rex's consciousness when pitted against the torrential downpour on our car roof, I realized my son's body was calming down. His shaking abated, the tremors ceased, and suddenly he sat contentedly, serenely listening to a Mozart sonata, completely oblivious to the rain outside. Thank you, Mozart.

With Rex now calm, I allowed my body to relax. My shoulders loosened, drooping slightly, but then I suddenly realized my hands weren't steady on the wheel. The car jerked to the right as I was beginning to spasm myself. I pulled left on the wheel, struggling to keep in my lane. *Steady on, grip firm!* My eyes twitched, blurring, and I knew Rex had passed his shaking off to me. *Eyes on the road!* With the downpour virulently assaulting the windshield, I began shaking my own head, trying to cast off my nerves, to get outside my own body. The battle raged on while my child sat completely absorbed by the music, cocooned in the notes.

I pulled the car haltingly into the Center and breathed hard. One breath, then two; I sat for a moment, breathing deeply, trying to collect myself before my conference. Rex was contentedly tapping his hands on his car seat, a smile playing at the corners of his mouth. I leaned over and kissed him tenderly on the cheek, then hugged him tight, allowing the touch to calm me this time.

I had to hustle Rex out of the car to avoid a soaking, but I managed to get him to his classroom relatively dry. I left him there and, with my body moving on autopilot, headed off to meet with his teacher, Linda. I sat down more heavily than I intended, and I barely had a chance to shift gears when she announced, "I'm concerned about Rex." No beating around the bush or banalities, she just cut to the chase.

"Well, I'm concerned about Rex too," I said defensively, still jittery from the morning battle. When would he be back to his old self again? "I've been brushing him and doing all that joint compression Jill recommended around the clock," I said, referring to the technique his occupational therapist used to counter sensory defensiveness.

"I know," she said, but repeated, with emphasis this time, "I'm *very* concerned about Rex. He's so apathetic in class; it's difficult to engage him in anything."

"Of course he's apathetic!" I said, agitated. "His poor little body has to spend all its energy defending itself against things like *running water* or *rain!*" I was getting worked up because I wanted answers, not more questions. Why is he apathetic? Why wouldn't he eat anymore? Or stand? Or touch anything? How long was this going to last?

Linda didn't say anything immediately, perhaps out of respect. I added, "He does perk up when you sing, and have you noticed how rhythmic his clapping is?"

"Yes, it is," she admitted. "And he loves tapping objects," she offered, but then added, "just not touching or holding them like he needs to." Then she said, in a voice that was filled with empathy but was nonetheless frightfully direct, "I'm afraid Rex is autistic."

> Then she said, in a voice that was filled with empathy but was nonetheless frightfully direct, "I'm afraid Rex is autistic."

"Autistic!" I repeated in disbelief, thinking of the bizarre, detached behavior I related to autism. "That's impossible. Autistic means unable to make social relationships; Rex is completely attached to me." There was no denying that. His personality shone through one-on-one with me.

Linda admitted that was true but said his extreme sensory

issues were typical of a child with autism, as were his flapping arms and other repetitive body movements such as hitting his chin or the table in rhythmic patterns.

Autistic *behaviors* didn't mean autistic! No way! Because it was obvious Rex could have social relationships. I'd read all about autism, and he wasn't distant and removed like the literature described those children—except, of course, when he would crawl into his protective shell. But that was caused by external stimuli, not a result of his permanent state.

"He's not autistic," I said, as if I were stating a fact, leaving no room for discussion. "He just needs time for his brain to mature." I left the conference in a huff, refusing to give merit to the teacher's rash and uncalled-for assessment.

I couldn't deny the obvious, however, that Rex seemed to be crawling more and more into a protective shell, not the opposite. Why weren't classic therapies working to rebalance his sensory system? Sometimes I'd look at his face, and yes, it was completely empty, as if the child had receded so far inside as to be invisible from the outside. One afternoon I sat in the living room watching my son mindlessly tapping his chin with a blank, removed look on his face. The day had been hard for him, so I understood. But I *knew* my child was in there—even if he was hidden.

Autism? No, it couldn't be, because I got to see the real child, a different Rex entirely, when he didn't have to confront the world at large. That Rex was joyful. I got to hear the laugh, see the light in his eyes. It was there, but only when I made sure his environment was filtered, which was only really possible at home. Especially now that his sensitivities included things like rain! How could this beautiful child who existed only in a completely controlled environment, be brought into the world? And not just survive, but thrive? Would he ever be able to embrace the sounds and beauty of the world, or would they always be tragically distorted for him? How could God have allowed this to happen to a child? Rex was innocent; he'd done nothing to deserve the life he had.

My son hadn't gained a single ounce since his first birthday. He'd begun the year at twenty pounds; two months before his second birthday he tipped the scale at the same weight. Almost a year and no weight gain for a soon-to-be two-year-old! Rex was now subsisting mostly on liquids and the small bites of puréed food I could manage to get into his overly sensitive mouth. We faced all this with the ongoing threat of a feeding tube looming over our heads. In areas of development, the news was even worse than his zero weight gain. Rex had lost skills he had acquired before the age of one, such as finger feeding and pulling himself up to stand. The fact was our lives had been utterly ripped up, torn to shreds by Rex's sensitivities over the course of the year. In the beginning, my husband had left the entire emotional and psychological task of raising our son to me. Over time, the distance between us had grown. Now it was cavernous, and he said he was leaving. He "couldn't do it anymore," was the way he put it when he asked for a divorce.

It was the story of so many fathers—that's what the statistics confirmed. Seventy percent of married couples with a severely disabled child end up divorcing. I knew of the division of roles in our household, and apparently we were the statistical norm. The father earns the living while the mother copes with the rest. The psychologist at the Blind Children's Center, Miranda, had explained how that leaves fathers insulated from the day-to-day intense stuff mothers live with, which leads to isolation and ultimately alienation. The father didn't forge the same bond with the child, that fierce love bond so necessary to deal with extreme disability.

My husband's sudden departure left me more thankful than ever for my solid career experience in Paris before my marriage. Rex and I would be okay temporarily. Though a world away from trading stocks and the money markets now, success in that world would provide shelter for a time. It would allow me to escape becoming a financial statistic along with everything else. How many other mothers in a similar situation would have to face the heartbreaking choice between earning a living and devoting critical time to their special-needs child? I'd have to watch our financial situation, but we'd be okay for a while. However, the same could not be said of my emotions.

There were days after my husband left when my knees would just buckle or my mind would become confused. One day I came home to find the specialist from the Foundation for the Junior Blind pulling her car out of our driveway. As I flagged her down, I said, "Ana, what are you doing here on Tuesday?" When she told me it was Wednesday, her normal time to work with Rex at home, I stared at her blankly for a moment, unable to connect her words to reality. *Was it Wednesday already?* One day blurred into the next.

"Are you okay?" she asked.

"Yes, of course," I answered. But was I?

The fact was my own nervous system had become as fragile as Rex's. I would cry at the drop of a hat. I was terrified I'd just tumble over. As if I were standing on the edge of a great precipice, the more I tried to back away, the more the ground crumbled under my feet. Sometimes Rex could manage to keep me on solid ground just with a smile, but the weight of our lives had become too heavy now. Rex and I were alone.

It was as mother and son, equally fragile, equally broken, that we made our way up the hill to Malibu Presbyterian Church a month before Rex turned two. My older brother Alan had come up from San Diego a few days before, and I had been sitting with him in my living room. Shaking my head, I said, "I just don't get it. I don't get what it's all for." Meaning Rex, his condition, our lives, *everything*.

My brother looked at me intently, his eyes boring in. He had the resolved look of someone who had just made a decision, and his voice took on a soft-spoken and solemn timbre. "It's simple. It's to glorify God." His answer surprised me; it was not at all what I'd expected, if indeed I'd been expecting anything. I had no idea what he meant. Our family hadn't gone to church when I was a child, except for special occasions, and my big brother had grown up alongside me. So what did he know that I didn't?

"I don't know what you mean," I answered feebly. I certainly couldn't manage the connection between glory and God and a child who was obliged to live like Rex. It sounded as disconnected and surreal as the life I was living. Had I not been so tired and confused, it would have made me angry.

Alan grew quiet, contemplative. I knew this meant my usually gregarious brother, whom I'd been so close to growing up, was full of real emotion. He said, "I've been wanting to talk to you about something for a while now." There was meaning attached to each word, which drew me to attention.

My brother had lived a good life. That I knew, even though we'd only been close through the high school years, since afterward I'd gone away to college and from there moved abroad until shortly before Rex's birth. Alan had been the most popular kid on the block, Little League baseball hero, remaining the big athlete on campus up through his high school years. He had even been voted Best Personality as a senior. Now he was married to his college sweetheart, Jenine, with whom he shared the parenting of two beautiful children. It all looked pretty good from where I was sitting, so I didn't immediately grasp what he was saying.

"I realized I was still stuck in the glory days," he said. "Yeah, I thought I was pretty hot stuff back in high school—big athlete." He paused and shook his head, full of emotion. "I was pretty full of myself." Then he spit out, "Prideful!"

It had a heinous sound to it, as if there was venom in it, as if pride was a thing to be loathed. I'd never heard it used that way before, since I'd always thought taking pride in oneself was a good thing. Pride helped you achieve, and being a "high achiever" was a thing to aspire to. I know how much I'd loved the label growing up. I'd worked hard hoping to make my mom and dad proud. My throat caught as I remembered that brief moment of pride I'd felt in my own son—my little blind son facing down the world on his first birthday. But here was my big brother, whom I'd so admired growing up, describing that very emotion, *pride*, as an obstacle. An obstacle, not a vehicle to achievement.

"Big-time pride," he said. "Yeah, I think it was bigger than me," he added, chuckling, "but I realized how empty I was outside of it." He shook his head softly, his eyes going back to what was obviously a painful time for him. "How empty I was," he repeated in confirmation. "And I asked myself the same question you just asked. 'What's it all for?'"

My mind was struggling to catch up as my big brother went on to describe how he'd discovered faith. Not faith in *himself*, like he'd had in excess when we were growing up, but true faith in God.

His words had definitely taken me by surprise, not at all what I'd been expecting on a Saturday afternoon, but there was something in what he said that made me feel close to him in a way we hadn't been since those high school years. And yet I could not, by any stretch of the imagination, describe my own state as emptiness. In fact, it was the opposite—crammed with daily crises, my state was more akin to overload and sheer desperation.

That night, before going to bed, I was washing my face when I glanced in the mirror. I was shocked to see the face that was staring back. That couldn't be me! What had happened to the confident and joyful young woman I used to be? Where was Cathleen? Where was the girl who had gone off to live in Paris, to seek adventure, to see the world, to experience life? Where was she now? I saw the lines of fatigue around my eyes, the pallor in my skin. I tensed my facial muscles, but the set in my jaw and brows became too tight, too rigid, making my face look harsh. Yet when I relaxed the muscles again, the vision staring back at me looked slack—unnerved and undone. There was no in-between, no relaxed softness left in my face or my being. That's when I realized how tightly I'd been holding the reins, and for how long. I'd had to, just to keep from breaking. Now the undeniable truth was staring back at me in the mirror, etched in the dark circles under my eyes—I was on the verge of a nervous breakdown. I'd been living in this state for too long—twenty-four hours a day, seven days a week—to go on without rest. I didn't know whether God would have anything to offer Rex or me, but I did know we had nowhere else to turn.

> *I didn't know whether God would have anything to offer Rex or me, but I did know we had nowhere else to turn.*

So here we were, entering the sanctuary of "the church on the hill," as I'd always thought of it. I was scared and apologetic that Rex had to stay with me, seated in his stroller. "He can't go to the nursery," I said to the usher at the suggestion. "He's blind." As if that should explain everything. The usher was an older gentleman with white hair and a kindly look, which put me at ease.

"It's okay. Don't worry—we're used to having kids here," he told me when I looked mortified at some of the strange sounds Rex had begun making even before the service started. But, thankfully, once the worship music began, he was pacified and listened quietly, intently even. I don't know whether it was the kindly words of a stranger, Rex's look of contentment at the music, or God's holy presence that caused me to relax in a way I hadn't done in months. How good it was to just sit there. I could feel the tightly coiled knots in my stomach begin to unwind, releasing the constant pressure. I looked at Rex in his stroller. There was an expression of peace on his face, a calm that was far removed from his frequent apathy. Could this be, at long last, a moment's respite from the storm? Suddenly, the tears I hadn't allowed myself before began falling softly, silently, but uncontrollably.

Over the next weeks, I realized I was going to church to petition God on behalf of my son. Maybe it was spiritual naïveté to think I could either bargain with God or dictate to Him how to be glorified, but that's exactly what I was—spiritually naïve. It seemed logical enough, at the time, to think God would heal Rex in exchange for glory. And so I began praying for my son. I didn't know whether God would listen to me, someone who had been so conspicuously absent from church throughout my whole life, so I enlisted the church to pray for Rex as well. Make him walk, Lord! Make him talk! Show Your power! For Your glory! Day after day, week after week, it was the same prayer.

With Rex's second birthday just days away, he had still not taken his first step, which had seemed so imminent a year before. Nor had he begun to speak; his incessant babble of the previous year had all but disappeared in favor of sounds that didn't resemble speech at all. Still, there was something I had come to observe in Rex that had become a constant since that rainy day in January. It was amazing to watch him listening to music, notably classical music, ever since he'd discovered Mozart. Oh, I knew the theoretical link between such music and brainpower, but this was more direct. When my son was listening to the music of the great classical composers, there was a look on his face that seemed to say, "This I understand." Like he was leaving us mere mortals here on earth, to stroll for a while in the heavenly realms with the likes of Bach and Beethoven, as if he somehow had direct access. It was an even sharper contrast, given the rest of the world, which he'd been denied. There were his rhythmic skills too. He loved "the clapping game." I would clap out patterns that were so complex I could barely remember what I'd done myself. But he'd inevitably clap them back, flawlessly. All done with a twinkle in his eye that again said, "I get it."

We turned the page on Rex's second calendar year without William. When Rex's father came to visit some time later, he was bearing a present. I was pleasantly surprised to find he'd actually been listening when I'd described Rex's affinity to music. For here was a forty-eight-key Casio piano keyboard and stand. William set up his proud offering, and we stood Rex right in front of the instrument. "Rex, look, I've brought you a piano," his dad said.

Rex's hands balled into tiny fists and shot straight back to his shoulders the moment his tummy came in contact with this foreign object. That was his typical reaction to touching something new. Usually, it would be a matter of literally peeling his hands open and forcing him to touch. Then, one of two reactions would ensue: either he'd pull his hands away with no verbal response, or he'd begin screaming like he'd been scalded.

"It's a *piano!*" I said with excited emphasis in my voice, trying to draw Rex in, distract him. At the same time, I took his hands without opening his sensitive palms and brought them down on the keys. They shot back up immediately in a conditioned response as the notes floated through the air. We watched Rex, and as I was wondering what to do next, a strange look slowly came over his face, like some kind of internal light. I didn't dare breathe for fear the look would disappear. But it was there, unmistakable and absolutely breathtaking! Rex was intrigued. As I continued to hold my breath, I felt a huge lump rising in my throat, and I watched my son's tiny arms relax as he brought his hands down to strike the piano keys with closed fists. But this time, they stayed on the keys as though glued in place by the tones rising up to his ears, and a look of wonder consumed him as his taut fingers slowly uncoiled. Gradually, he played one note, then another, then both hands intermittently like a kind of drum roll.

"Look up here, Rex," I said as I hit a note at the upper extremity of the keyboard. Since he couldn't see, he didn't know how far the piano keys extended in either direction and was striking only the keys in front of him. *What was that? A new sound?* his face seemed to ask. Now he wanted those high notes and reached for them, but he couldn't extend the whole distance without toppling over. Instead, he came down on the keys in between. A look of comprehension dawned on his face. *These are new tones.* Then he took both hands (playing in sync), made a rhythmic pattern of six notes going up the keyboard, and replicated it. Same pattern, same notes.

William and I watched Rex lay his hands fully on a mass of keys to combine notes, dissonant but a blending nonetheless, as if he was seeking a more complex sound. Then he continued his exploration, enraptured, just as we were. Since the day we'd learned of Rex's blindness, the divide between William and me had been ever broadening. The result was our recent separation. But we were back together on this afternoon, as if to bear witness to something extraordinary. In that singular moment, we were bonded in our little boy, who'd spent his first two years fighting a losing battle in a hostile world. I even caught a trace of mist in William's eyes as he realized how absorbed his son was in every note of the

> *For those brief moments, it was as if the piano had freed him from the constraints of his body. It became his eyes, and the notes became his voice.*

little keyboard. It was like our boy had been transported to a friendly world, one he understood, where the pain of his daily existence was held at bay. For those brief moments, it was as if the piano had freed him from the constraints of his body. It became his eyes, and the notes became his voice.

All too soon, the spell was broken. Rex finally tired of playing the little keyboard, and we were rudely jolted back to real life. With the music gone, the usual awkward silence once again filled the room, splintered only by emotions that again seemed forced. "Wasn't that amazing!" William said in a voice that had gone flat. All of a sudden in a hurry, he announced he had to go. He called Rex a "clever little guy," threw him up in the air a couple of times, which always brought giggles of delight, and then was gone. As the door closed with resounding definition, I knew it was final; the separation would indeed be permanent. Rex and I were alone, alone with a little piano keyboard.

But something else had happened, as obvious to me as the finality of William's departure—an extraordinary event had taken place. Had the same door that closed on the father allowed an opening for the son? Had Rex just been given a lifeline?

OVER THE months that followed, it became apparent that that little piano hooked Rex into life in a way nothing else had. It wasn't just a fluke or my desperate mind exaggerating reality or a passing fancy; it was a passion! He could play that little piano until he dropped from pure exhaustion, and he did just that, day after day. There were days when he'd stand at the piano, which strengthened his legs. When his legs would tire, he'd plop down to the floor. Even then, I'd watch him reach up, arms extended over his head, needing to play on. At other times, when he played sitting down, he'd go at the keyboard until he would eventually topple onto his side, but he still continued to reach for the instrument as if it were a magnet— drawing him, holding him, possessing him—until, sapped of all strength, his little arms would fall, deadweight, to his sides.

My spirit, on the other hand, was quite the opposite of dead-weight. In fact, it was downright light, at least in comparison to what it had been. Rex's endless hours at the piano provided a respite for both of us and began to lift the oppressive yoke of his second year. Normally abrasive-to-Rex sounds like running water and a ringing phone didn't affect him at all when he was at the keyboard which provided a temporary override to dysfunction. Playing that thing was what he wanted to do first thing in the morning, and it was what he wanted to do even when his body couldn't do it anymore. I wasn't a musician, but I knew what he was playing was musical, rhythmic, and full of life. After the darkness, the absolute desolation of that second year, it was like a bright light shining down into our lives, like a rebirth. Gradually, a new sound began to resonate through our home along with his music—it was Rex's laugh. It was as if he was defying his condition. I thought it was like a touch of grace.

As the months wore on, his days at school were still hard work even as his home life was one of ever-increasing lightness. I suppose you could say there was now a growing divide in his life, a dichotomy between the ease and harmony he felt at the piano at home and his struggle to overcome all the rest. He would use his hands beautifully at the piano, developing a rhythmic dexterity, but he still wouldn't use them much elsewhere. He had made gains in a number of areas, but progress was slow and labored and still filled with upset for him, his teachers, and me.

It was June, shortly before his third birthday, and he'd had a mixed day at school, meaning tough but manageable. The finger-painting activity his classmates had reveled in first thing in the morning had set him screaming. I watched as a little boy named Manuel voraciously rolled and swirled his hands in gooey wonder, and I hoped Rex could do the same thing, praying on the spot for a miracle. Rex's teacher helped him find the finger paint in a sort of drumming pattern. "Look, Rex, it's not finger painting. It's just drumming!" Up, down, up, down, *rat-tat-tat-tat*, over and into the goop! It worked; he hadn't balled up his hands. Music could be used to get him to do things that were otherwise impossible. I used the technique at home, and now his teachers had begun using it here as well. But as soon as the drumming pattern was broken, and he discovered his hands in the paint, it was as if his whole nervous system was once again being assaulted.

Mercifully it was music time, and he was able to recover. As usual, he excelled in his clapping patterns to the songs and humming the tunes. It wasn't real humming, but a sort of chorus of "ahs." He couldn't pronounce any word, but it seemed he could voice a chorus of "ahs" to any song, and in perfect pitch.

I still carried him around most of the time, or the teachers did, but—inspired by the music—he had managed a couple of steps. But then he would immediately collapse his legs in what I had come to call his "spaghetti-leg" mode. Six months before, I had believed that God was answering my prayers when I witnessed Rex taking his first miraculous, independent steps. I had celebrated, throwing my arms around "my little walking boy" and doing my happy dance! But the celebration had been premature because Rex's first steps didn't develop into a consistent walking pattern like most kids, but instead into an on-again, off-again pattern. One day I would believe he was building strength and balance, but then the next he'd be back to square one, his legs buckling the moment I'd stand him up. On the bad days, I tried not to let it get to me, focusing on the fact that I'd witnessed his ability to walk, even if it was still hidden much of the time.

Rex's school day was capped by lunch; for him it was a "good food day," laughable by any standard but his own. "Good" meant he'd managed to consume about an eighth of a cup of puréed sweet potato, but only when the occupational therapist smeared it on his lips, obliging him to lick it off to clean his mouth. Rex would not eat voluntarily and would normally jerk his head away from any spoon that would dare to touch his lips. It was like he was "threatened" by food. To counter that, the therapist would put the food on her finger and rapidly smear it on his lips before he could dodge away. Once on his lips, his tongue would sneak out slowly, testing, licking bits off. A labored process, but on a good day, like today, Rex would actually consume the food he "found" with his tongue. As a scene on TV, it would have been humorous, but as a mother watching her son fighting a life-sustaining process, it was hard to take.

His days at school were intense; there was no denying that what seemed like child's play was work for him. But now I watched him in our home, content at his piano, oblivious to the inspiring ocean view out the living room window. The sun sparkled in allegro on the surface of the water and seemed to mirror Rex's light notes as they cascaded up the keyboard. I so enjoyed living beside the ocean, with its unimpeded horizon. Only the island of Catalina was out there sticking its head timidly through a translucent skirt of mist. No June gloom today, just the leaves of palm trees flickering in a gentle spring breeze. Rex had extended his arms to the very extremities of his keyboard, like he was embracing the world, a world as vast as what I could see out the window. He kept his arms spread with one index finger at each piano extreme, playing them back and forth—high, low, high, low—over and over again, a look of rapture on his face. Then he slowly lifted each finger to touch the edge of the piano, as if to verify it really ended there. He often made piano runs up and down to the ends of the instrument, and I wondered whether it was to fix boundaries in his own mind or to test them. I had noticed his intrigued look the day I played a Chopin nocturne for him on the stereo—it clearly had notes not contained on his own miniature keyboard. Where were the missing keys?

Chopin's sky-high trills were clearly nowhere to be found on his little forty-eight-note piano! Testing limits, pushing back limits. Wasn't that the essence of childhood? And order! Rex seemed to be creating order in a brain that was otherwise filled with chaos and dysfunction. Endless runs, methodology, intervals. He went about playing his piano with the same absorption I witnessed when he was listening to Mozart.

His fingers were still stuck to the ends of the keyboard, and I said, "Beautiful music, Rex." My voice startled him out of his absorbed state, and his fingers darted back into motion. On a typical day, as I watched the ebb and flow of the ocean tide, he would create endless musical tapestries. Sometimes playful, sometimes majestic, always rhythmic and constructed, which stood in stark contradiction to the disconnected and random child I'd see at school. Rex was creative—it could be seen all too clearly in his music. He was curious, and he could learn. He would learn!

I looked back at him, as his hands opened up on the keyboard, moving once again to its edges, its limits, as if he wanted more. More notes? Or just more? Why couldn't we push past those limits? Crash through those boundaries? Extend outward to the world?

CHAPTER FOUR

The Meeting

All journeys have secret destinations of which the traveler is unaware.

—Martin Buber, biblical translator, philosopher, and interpreter

We rushed through the gates of the Blind Children's Center complex, once again late, in spite of my efforts to get us there on time. The other children, who didn't have as far to commute, were all seated on blocks in the green, grassy playground, shaded from the already-scorching sun by a couple of large trees. It was summertime, and there was a feeling of lightness in the air as I watched the kids singing their good-morning songs.

The teacher made room for Rex next to one of his classmates, and I carried him to his seat as the children continued singing. I studied my blond boy, looking so handsome in his black polo shirt and khaki shorts, clapping with impeccable rhythm, never missing a beat. Suddenly, two of the older children, Ellen and Carson, stood up. They held each other tightly by the shoulders as the next song began. They circled round and round to the tune of "Ring Around the Rosy"—preschool rock and roll! Both were blond and beautiful—older versions of Rex.

As they came to the lyrics "ashes, ashes, we all fall down," the kids dropped to the ground to Rex's drumroll clapping. There were giggles from the children, and I turned to go inside. Time for my meeting; I had been "invited" to meet with the educational

director of the school to discuss Rex's progress. Just as I was step-
ping into the hallway, a familiar sound hit the airwaves. Like a
thousand-megawatt bulb, it lit up the playground—the laugh!
Rex's astonishing, infectious laugh probably brought on by escalating giggles. I turned to see my boy, full of life, his face still
wreathed in a beatific smile special to him. I couldn't help but
smile myself as I left him with his schoolmates.

I stepped inside the schoolhouse, which was as bright as the
outdoors. The office of the educational director, Miriam, was at
the far end of the brightly lit corridor. On one side of the hallway
sat a big stuffed bear, more voluminous than most adults. He was
perched on a softly cushioned bench in front of a window, through
which streamed the brightness of this summer day. The bear,
dubbed Barney the Bear, felt like a friend; he was a sort of cuddly
greeting card welcoming visitors to this entrance hallway. He was
an expensive animal, not because of exquisite design or exclusive
fabric, but because each year he was purchased at auction by some
generous benefactor of the school, who was willing to exchange
hundreds, even thousands of dollars, for the right to say "I care."
Buying this particular bear didn't confer ownership, but it did buy
the right to have your name sewn onto the belly of this oversized
guardian alongside all those other caring people's. Annually auc-
tioning the bear was an institution in this private preschool for the
blind, which only managed to keep its doors open due to such
financial generosity. We, the parents, were not asked to pay a
dime for the right to be here. This was very fortunate, since most
of the families had taken quite a hit financially. Like any severe
disability, blindness hits families in every area—emotionally, practically, and financially.

Facing the bear were three classrooms, shielded from the
curious eye of the casual observer by relatively opaque windows.
If you wanted to watch the kids in these classrooms, you had to

practically glue your face to the window. This was not at all a discrete posture, mind you, but I had personally been known to do the face press on numerous occasions—no withering violet, this mother. Being faint of heart was not a luxury I could afford, having Rex for a son. Now, however, the doors to these rooms were open because they were empty. For once, I could gaze casually inside as I walked past. The room had bright colors as a backdrop, with multiple varied textures on the walls and floors. There were real objects to touch and to be used to teach themes, and in the corner of Rex's classroom, a little piano keyboard. I had brought it in for him to use if he needed a "collect yourself" break. I also wanted the teachers and specialists to see how nicely he used his hands on the piano keys. I hoped the skill would be transferable.

While children were outside, the bear was keeping a silent vigil awaiting their imminent return. In spite of the brightness of the décor, the absence of the kids' joyous voices caused the place to seem oddly hollow, a body without a heart, something unsettling as I listened to the sound of my own footsteps echoing off the walls. What was the matter? I was only going to meet with the educational director of Rex's school, who had asked me to come see her to touch base on his progress. This was something Miriam and I had both agreed would be a good idea from time to time. And, since it was the beginning of summer school, what better time to do it? Far from being unsettling, for me this meeting promised the opportunity to share ideas concerning Rex's day-to-day education and my visions for his future. A child his age needed consistency, which meant synchronizing my own efforts at home with those here at school; working together was the key.

The door to the office stood ajar, and as I approached, I could hear hushed, subdued voices within, which seemed out of place here at the Center, where each word was always so clearly weighed and enunciated for the children. As I pushed the door open, I was surprised to see not only Miriam's face but also the director sitting among five other members of the school's mostly female staff, each an expert in her field. As I looked around the room, I noted the familiar faces I'd known since Rex was barely six months old. They were my friends; they were his friends, his teachers in so many different disciplines. They'd known him from the time when we'd first come to the Center.

I entered the room to face these educators, who had become the substance of our lives for these last two and a half years. Though it had been an association forged by necessity, they'd been there to help when there was no one else, had helped me cope with a broken heart and a broken child. They'd provided a safe place for my son and me, where we could both recover and grow. I felt I was in the company of friends. All eyes were on me, and we all murmured greetings as I found my way to the sole seat that had been left vacant. They had saved me a chair facing everybody else.

Still, I was relaxed, although surprised by so many participants in this "routine" meeting. I did, however, question the reason for Miranda's presence. Why would the school psychologist be at an educational meeting? On that first visit I had been impressed by the idea of a school having a psychologist for preschoolers, and I vaguely remembered even having joked about it. But, of course, Rex wasn't the one who needed psychological help in all this. He'd been just a baby then; now he was but a child, with a child's expectations. He was innocent, blameless. No, Miranda had been here for me, on that first day and on all the days since. The school psychologist was there to teach parents how to lift our chins, to get on with life, to reestablish eye contact with the world. Being in charge of all the parent-related issues, I could only assume she was here today for me. What that meant, I wasn't exactly sure, but I refused to give in to old feelings of anxiety, and remained calm. Eyes up, straight ahead. My breathing remained even. In and out, in and out, it felt so comforting in its predictability.

Once seated, I took out a small notepad, which was more a security blanket than a means to jot down points under discussion. Miriam focused her whole attention on me, with one of her signature melt-the-iciest-of-hearts smiles, which always seemed to say, "You can trust me; I'm on your side," or "I truly know how you feel." It was a smile of empathy, sympathy, and compassion, and Miriam always seemed to exude warmth and understanding. She was highly organized and ran the school with precision, and yet she always managed to carefully dose her efficiency with a large amount of heart and caring.

Her calming presence massaged away any residual tension I might have been feeling, and I was at ease as she spoke directly to me. "I've asked everyone who is involved with Rex to come to this meeting," she said. Holding my gaze, she went on. "As we decided before, I feel it's a good idea to touch base from time to time about his progress at school. So, each person who works with him will explain to you how she believes he is doing."

I allowed her words to soothe me, reassure me. I knew full well how my son was doing. He had finally stabilized. Things were turning around at long last—his piano had been the key. I mentally checked the image of the keyboard in his classroom—progress, slow, but the process was beginning.

As Miriam spoke, everyone was completely silent, watching me tentatively, expectantly. All the while, Miranda's attention was focused on me. Her look was attentive, but noncommittal. She was a listener, a trained professional, who knew how to read a parent's feelings merely by the way he or she sat or held her hands, or by watching any eye movement. Miranda missed *nothing*, said or unsaid.

I spoke before anyone else could. "I'm so happy to be able to meet with you all like this. It's important for me to know that what I'm doing at home is right—that it will support what you're all doing here." Not waiting for a response, barely stopping for breath, I continued. "I know how much we all need to be working together to get Rex on track. And I have to say how excited I am about how he's changed since he got his piano keyboard last year."

I glanced around the room, expecting them to mimic at least part of my enthusiasm. Instead, what I felt was their discomfort. Maybe it was their body language, the uncertain shifting as I spoke, the eyes filled with sympathy, all focused too intently upon me.

I was Miranda's pupil; indeed, I'd come to call her "coach," as life with Rex was oddly akin to a competitive sport. She was here at the Blind Children's Center to teach us parents how to hold our own in a world made scary by our children's births, how to come to terms with frightening emotions, and how to deal with complex medical and educational situations. Simply put, she had taught me about the subtleties of true survival in the world of "special needs." It was from her that I'd learned to read situations in much the same way she could: by going past the spoken word and paying attention to body language, giving importance to all those little external clues people give off—their posture, the sideways glances, eye contact or lack of eye contact, telltale fidgeting. I had learned to glean information that way. And here in this room, on this sunny summer morning, my internal alarm was suddenly sounding.

"Yes, we do all want to be on the same page," Miriam said hesitantly, a dubious validation.

So what page were *they* on? Each person present, except Miriam and Miranda, sat with notes on her lap and probably with many pages of observations stored in each of those specialist heads. I had a sudden urge to run, and yet my body felt leaden. I somehow knew how potent their words would be. Huge words, with huge implications. Lethal and unforgiving words. I braced myself for the impact.

His classroom teacher was the first to speak. "Of course, we're happy Rex's piano allows him to relax. Given the complexity of his sensitivities, that's very important for him to be able to get through the day." A slight pause, and then, "But we have quite a few other concerns about him. We're concerned there's not more progress." I had no external reaction, although my insides were churning.

Miriam cut in, relieving the teacher. "He hasn't had a single operation or hospitalization this year, and he's still not progressing," she said. My eyes bored into her as no one in the room dared to breathe. Everyone was still, surely in deference to the assessment they all must know to be forthcoming. "He's still inconsistent with his walking. So it doesn't look like his overall lack of mobility, and his periodic regressions, are linked solely to his medical issues."

I was being stripped of my armor of denial, of explanations, of excuses. Was that it? Had I just become adept at making excuses? I knew his progress had been slow in the making. I knew that Rex had started walking only to stop several times in the space of six months. And of course I knew all about his "spaghetti legs," my great nemesis. But each time he had started walking again, I had renewed hope that he would continue. He would outgrow sensitivity in his feet and any childish obstinacy thrown into the mix. It had to end. There was no other option, since he would soon be too heavy for me to carry. He was now three years old, and though he hadn't gained an ounce in his second year, his third year had been different. In spite of his ongoing resistance to food, patience and ingenuity during feeding, along with lots of protein powder added to his milk, had set his growth back into motion this past year. But suddenly I felt the weight of each of his hard-earned ten pounds. "It's just a pattern," I threw out, grasping at straws. "It can be broken."

The occupational therapist responded. "We've seen this pattern of behavior continue on into adolescence." I heard the words but didn't immediately grasp their import—they were mere words banging on my brain, devoid of meaning, disconnected from reality. "Rex is getting heavier by the day." Her implication should have been obvious, and yet it still escaped me until a single word hit me head-on—*wheelchair*! Rex could end up in a wheelchair! I locked on the phrase "getting heavier." It was true. Rex was getting too heavy. As I pictured myself struggling to carry my son, refusing to give in to using a wheelchair, the meeting was moving forward.

I was just going through the motions, nodding to signal understanding, acquiescence, all the while pulling myself inside, hiding behind a protective layer of cloudy consciousness. They were education professionals—clear, concise. They knew their stuff, and they were moving on with the meeting, reading from a painful script. Now the speech pathologist was discussing Rex's communication skills. My mind was drowning; I couldn't keep up as I heard her say, "Rex isn't speaking yet; he hasn't pronounced a single word."

"Not *yet*," I jumped in, half affirmation, half plea. My voice had cracked with emotion. His piano had become his way of communicating. His voice would soon come too.

"Yes, but Rex is three years old," she said gently. "He needs to begin to communicate in some way." She paused heavily. "In whatever way he can, even if it's nonverbal," she added. For me, her voice rang with dissonance, as though trying to infuse hope into a hopeless situation. I remained silent, once again struggling to follow the gist of her words. "We'd like to work with him on using his hands to speak, teach him some sign language."

Nonverbal, sign language, wheelchair! They were concepts broached with care, but the words themselves were not cautious words, and to me it felt like a barrage.

"Teach him sign language?" I asked in disbelief. "But he's not deaf!"

"But he is nonverbal at this point," Miriam said, then added, "and three years old."

Just the beginning of his life, I thought. This time my own thoughts were dissonant as I heard her go on. "Three years is a very important stage in child development." *Patterns could be set for a lifetime by this critical age.*

Miranda had her eyes glued on me as I sat there mute, as though she thought I might crumble at any moment were she to look away. And with good reason, because apparently the jury was in. Here. Now. The developmental alarm clock had just gone off. Three years! Was Rex's die cast with the verdict that had just come in? Part of me wanted to cradle my head in my hands and cry, "Why me? Why Rex? What had we done?" And part of me wanted to stand up and scream, "Foul!"

But I only reacted in the deep recesses of my mind, and I didn't counter their dire prognosis. Instead, I listened numbly to their reports of their research into optic nerve hypoplasia. Children with this specific eye condition had some shocking commonalities—a whole slew of kids with spaghetti legs! Walking was invariably an issue with these children who had the condition. Rosemary, the vision specialist, said, "I've been reading about a lot of case studies documented on the Internet. Parents of kids with optic nerve hypoplasia like Rex hoped and hoped and hoped until they finally gave in. Ultimately, they admitted and accepted the inevitable." I understood the inevitable would be a child too heavy to carry, a child in a wheelchair. And more. But then she couched it in a subtle nuance, attempting somehow to soften the blow. "I'm not saying Rex will necessarily be like that, but I want you to know what information is on the Internet, in case you come across it yourself."

I'd been running a race against time for three years, a life-or-death race; that's what it felt like. *Patterns are set for a lifetime.* Never stopping to take a breath, for fear Rex would lose critical time. Since the day my baby had come into the world, I'd been trying somehow to bring safety to his unsafe world, exhorting God, pleading on Rex's behalf. But now the specialists were telling me I'd been running a losing race against *patterns*! A losing race against his brain structure because Rex's brain was stuck in a rigid *pattern* of nondevelopment. His wheels were spinning in place, going nowhere. Was that it? I was swept up in a current of violent, uncontrollable despair. I was babbling in my brain, and yet managed to respond coherently.

"Thank you for being so honest and forthright with me," I told the group. "Having all the information is important," adding a comforting banality, the simplicity of which acted as a counterbalance to the growing wave of complex and confusing emotions that had just caught me in their riptide.

"As far as Rex's placement here, we will definitely have a place for him next year as we've told you," said Miriam. "After that, we'll have to see." It meant his final year in preschool at the Center was at risk. If his development didn't take off, he'd be out by the end of his fourth year of life.

The Center didn't have the staff to work with children over three who were nonambulatory, and so normally kids didn't even receive placement in their fourth year if they couldn't walk. Rex had somehow managed to make the cut this year—perhaps due to the fact that he would sometimes walk. "There's no physical reason he's not walking," I heard his physical therapist say, not so long ago. "His muscles are fine, a little hypotonic, but all in all, they're not keeping him from walking." But what *was* keeping him from walking? I wanted to scream. What was making his muscles collapse all the time if they were strong enough? What was keeping him from talking? No one ever seemed to have any answers.

As the meeting concluded, Miranda told me she would be available anytime I needed to talk. "Thank you," I said woodenly.

The others had already rushed off to their other duties, perhaps purposefully avoiding any potential emotional fallout, leaving me there with the psychologist and educational director.

I stood up to go but I wasn't sure exactly where to go, as frantic thoughts began pouring in on me. I just knew I needed to get out of that room, fast. I put one foot in front of the other and just moved, until I pulled myself together.

I walked out of the office, murmuring my good-byes and thank-yous. Miranda uncertainly watched me go. I approached the stuffed bear, feeling the brightness of the day streaming through the window. The classroom doors were closed now that class was in session. Life goes on—a continuum—at once insensitive and reassuring. For once, I didn't press my nose up to the window to spy on Rex. I had to keep going, one foot in front of the other, eyes up toward that window. I needed to get some air, to figure things out. I would have liked to float away, shed the weight of responsibility, be a child again.

BE A child again . . . I stared down at my sleeping son's face, so unaware of the high-stakes meeting that morning to discuss his future. But I was aware of it in every fiber of my being as I collapsed into the rocker next to his bed. Far from feeling like a child, my body was deadweight, drained, like I'd aged ten years in a day. How do you go on when even a monumental effort seems it is for naught? When everywhere you look it's pitch-black darkness?

I shut my eyes and massaged my temples to relieve pressure pounding there—an imminent migraine was building. I gradually became aware of a sound—like a barely audible tapping on a door slammed shut—soft, gentle, but insistent. It was there to stay. Rex's breathing! In and out, so calm and even. As my fingers applied more pressure to the sides of my head, I began rocking slowly in my chair, like I was hypnotized, allowing his breathing to soothe me. The most primal rhythm of life goes on. I remembered his gasping, labored breaths in the first weeks of his life before his operation—how he'd slept at my side, how I'd been scared to fall asleep for fear he'd stop breathing, for fear he'd just be gone. Inevitably, I had to let go each night when my body was overcome by fatigue, falling asleep against my own will. But each morning I would awaken to find him still alive. A force infinitely more powerful than his mother had protected him. I knew that, somehow.

As I allowed my mind to relax, I heard another sound, a new rhythm to layer upon my son's breathing. This time it was coming from outside. On the beach, waves rippled against the shore in a gentle caress. It was another of life's rhythms—its own soft lullaby. Suddenly the distant cry of a seagull called out, cutting in. Was he flying solo, somehow separated from his flock? His high-pitched cry resonated strongly with some internal cry of my own. I opened my eyes to see Rex's face aglow as moonlight streamed through the parted curtains and softly embraced his cheeks. The essence of innocence.

I still didn't know what the future held. Would Rex be like that seagull crying out solo in the night, or would he rejoin the flock one day? The questions were still there, maybe even bigger now. Surprisingly, I didn't feel assaulted by fear. Against all odds, my mind was taking refuge, finding rest even, in the one absolute in our lives—the love I felt for my son, sustaining me now in the darkest hour, by what I knew could only be the grace of God.

> *Against all odds, my mind was taking refuge, finding rest even, in the one absolute in our lives—the love I felt for my son, sustaining me now in the darkest hour, by what I knew could only be the grace of God.*

CHAPTER FIVE

Searching for Understanding

Not until we are lost do we begin to understand ourselves.

—Henry David Thoreau

The sanctuary was empty and silent as I sat with Rex by my side. Scant wisps of late-afternoon sunlight resting on the pews to my right provided the only illumination in the otherwise darkened room. I'd never come here during the week before, but upon returning from our day in town, I had felt the need to be in this holy place. I wanted to sit in silence with no pastor's words filling the room, with no Sunday congregation lending a social presence. I just wanted to tune into the spirit of God directly, thinking that perhaps I could hear His voice more clearly this way, by filtering out intercedants, interpretation, noise.

Turning to Rex, I smiled and said softly, "Noise. Just like you sweetheart, gotta filter out the noise." I'd had enough "noisy" interpretations at the Blind Children's Center meeting, the sting of those words still ripping away at my insides when I thought about them. What I needed was to get those awful words out of me. So I would speak them here, out loud, and in doing so, share them. In essence, I would hand them off in the hope there would be solace in that.

"Rex is still not walking, Lord . . . or talking . . . or . . ." I paused heavily, then just let it out, "or doing much of anything." Sighing audibly in release, I bowed my head, hoping to hear a voice other than mine, beyond my own thoughts, a voice of guidance. But nothing came.

As I sat in silence, my mind was forced to consider thoughts of the week since the meeting. We had gone about our lives as usual, in part from not wanting to disrupt our routine and in part for not knowing *what* to change. But in spite of keeping to our normal schedule—mornings at the Blind Children's Center; speech, physical, or occupational therapy in the afternoon; and piano for Rex in every free moment at home—I knew that something needed to be done. We couldn't just go on as before, as if nothing had happened. But I was at a loss.

What I had been observing in the wake of the meeting was my own emotions. These were the emotions I'd lost track of for some time, immersed as I'd been in all of Rex's stuff. But the meeting had jarred me, and the trauma of it had caused me to look inside myself. I was beginning to see there was an internal divide. It wasn't as obvious as Rex's own dual nature—between the child who played the piano with such absorption and creativity and the child who moved so randomly everywhere else—but it was definitely there.

My duality might be defined as how I dealt with Rex's disability—between how I felt at home with my child and how I felt when we were out in the world. Alone with Rex, I rarely experienced the weight of his disability as I had in the beginning. That was the love he inspired, like on that night after the meeting. Yet the old pain came back frequently when we were faced with other people doing the normal things of life. Daily triggers reminded me that the world at large remained a painful place. Painful for Rex, certainly, with his sensitive ears, I knew that all too well. But now I was beginning to realize how emotionally painful it was for me too. My emotions were just too sensitive, too fragile.

A child's hand reaches out for a brightly colored box in a supermarket; the child smiles up at his mother. I see it and my insides knot up as I rush off down the aisle with my son, whose own unseeing eyes remain oblivious and downcast. Children are building castles in the sand or trotting along the seashore searching for shells as I push Rex past in his jogging stroller. When I compare Rex's situation to theirs, it only serves to amplify the divide between Rex (and me) and the rest of the world.

The other morning it had been kids on a playdate in the park running between the slide, swings, and the monkey bars, while their moms sat on the park bench chatting.

"I'm exhausted all the time," said one mom. "If I turn my back, Tommy's off and into some new mischief."

"Lisa likes to hang around me, so she doesn't tear things up," replied the other mom sharing the bench, "but I never knew a three-year-old could talk so much. 'Give me this. I want that.' And the questions! She always wants explanations for everything."

That was enough for me. In fact, I knew that generic conversation by heart—the same words spoken by the other mothers I used to meet in this very park, before I had given up on the concept of the "playdate," at least for the time being. Back when we used to accept them, these dates had always consisted of the same thing—the other mothers sat around comparing child stories while their kids played together, kids who always seemed to be fast and curious. The world was made for the fast and curious, and the world certainly had them in abundance. Rex was neither. So on those get-togethers I would always be with the kids, not the moms, helping my son to play, to swing, or to slide, helping him to interact with his environment in the most basic ways.

On that day, the oh-so-familiar, tinny voices of the young

mothers faded away with their complaints ringing in my ears as I carried Rex over to one of the secure baby swings. My blind child's playdate was once again with his mother, as it had always been. He couldn't play without help. I could never experience the joyful normalcy of being a mom who sat on a bench watching her child.

I opened my eyes and raised my head to the altar. "I know You must have a plan for Rex; I do," I said simply but resolutely, letting the impact of the words settle into myself. *There must be a reason for all of this*. "I just don't know what it is. I just don't. So I'm going to need Your help." I paused in reverence, humbled, knowing only that this was where I needed to be. "Help me to see, Lord." *Help me to see*. It was the first time I'd prayed for anything other than direct healing for my son.

OVER THE next month, I found myself returning to the academics that had been so important to me before Rex was born. I felt if I got to the bottom of it all, then there would be a scientific explanation, a reason, to guide me. My quest for knowledge resumed, sparked by desperation and fueled by my need to see, my need to know.

The logical place for me to start was the medical world, with the doctors, in the hopes that their expertise in the brain and body would give me some answers. Since Rex was part of the Children's Hospital study of optic nerve hypoplasia, a study that was geared toward finding answers about its cause and future consequences, I went to see his ophthalmologist there, Dr. Michael Bryant.

Dr. Bryant was busily jotting down notes on a notepad as I walked into his office, reminding me of the day I had first learned of Rex's blindness. Surrounded by the tools of science, assorted lenses and lights, and the inevitable ophthalmoscope, the doctor seemed in his element. He was immaculate and preppie, wearing a dark suit, a striped shirt, and his trademark bow tie and spectacles, his hair carefully combed. He looked every inch the intellectual he was reputed to be. The doctor looked up briefly as I sat down, but then he held up his hand, a gesture for silence, as though imploring me not to interrupt his thoughts. It was a request to give him one last moment to jot down one last vital note before he had to shift gears to focus on Rex and me.

He pushed the notepad to the back of his desk and stood up to shake my hand. "It's nice to see you, Mrs. Lewis and Rex," he said. His manner was professional and polite, but I felt it was a bit rote, with his mind still caught up in his own important thoughts. As I searched his face, I held out hope that this man of science, of such seeming intelligence, would be able to use that gift to provide me with the answers I was seeking. I briefly explained my concerns and handed him a folder full of Rex's brain scans. The MRI imaging sheets had been on file in the hospital since Rex's earlier surgeries.

He clipped the sheets to an illuminated board beside his desk and moved his head closer to the most recent scan. "The cystic area is there," he said, pointing, with the pen in his hand, to an area that appeared nothing but blotchy to me. "But there are other abnormalities as well," he said, clinically surprised, as though he were recording notes into a Dictaphone. He didn't do any pointing this time or speak directly to me, but I saw the puzzled look on his face, like one who'd been blindsided and didn't like it, or like a scientist who'd allowed an omission in research data under his watch.

"What do you mean, 'other abnormalities'?" I asked.

"He has no septum pellucidum," the doctor said, still looking at the scans. "And his corpus callosum is smaller than normal." He recited these facts in a way that seemed automatic, rehearsed, like he was reading from a script. As it turned out, he was reading the script of a diagnosis. Glancing briefly at me, his head remained fixed on the sheets as he told me it was a pattern, that these specific types of brain malformations happened frequently in children with optic nerve hypoplasia (ONH). But the presence of the brain abnormalities changed the official diagnosis from ONH to septo-optic dysplasia. And therein lay the offensive error in the doctor's research, or at least that's what his attitude seemed to imply.

"But I didn't know about that before," I said, disbelieving. "I didn't know there were *other* abnormalities in Rex's brain besides the cyst. He's my son for heaven's sake; I have a right to know," I said, beside myself.

Reluctantly, he turned to face me. Then he said, "Apparently there's been some miscommunication among physicians." Just as quickly, he retreated back into his professorial style, avoiding further explanations about the "miscommunication." Before I could ask if he was referring to Rex's neurosurgeon, he launched into a tutorial. He explained that the septum pellucidum was a thin membrane located at the midline of the brain, which separates the left and right brain hemispheres. He continued by describing the corpus callosum as a bridge of white matter joining the two different sides of the brain.

I felt my own brain rattling as I tried to follow the scientific mumbo jumbo, my insides beginning to shake. I wanted to grab him by the shoulders and just shake him! Rattle him! Bounce those spectacles and knock that bow tie right off him to get to something real. But all I could do was blurt out, "But what does all this mean?"

The doctor sighed in resignation, like I was forcing him to come out from behind his protective shield of science, forcing him to be human. He took a breath, as though it were real effort to shift down so many gears, then said, "Simply put, Rex has no divider in his brain, and the bridge linking the two sides is smaller than normal."

I felt tears of frustration beginning to sting my eyes. "But what does all this mean for Rex, for his life?"

The doctor leaned forward, sliding his glasses down to the tip of his nose to peer at me, indulging me. "Mrs. Lewis, I'm just two years into my research, but what I'm finding is that there's no real difference between the children with septo-optic dysplasia and those with optic nerve hypoplasia." This time he tried to translate even without my asking but seemed to be reaching the limits of his patience. "Or, if you want, no difference between the children with those particular brain malformations and those who don't have them." And finally, in a tone that implied I was a child needing everything spelled out, he said, "It doesn't change anything. It won't make any difference for Rex." And that was that, tutorial over, class dismissed.

As I put Rex into his car seat, something didn't set right with me. My instincts told me the septum pellucidum, there to divide the brain in half, had to have a function other than a mere physical presence, or it wouldn't be there. And if it had a function, why could nobody tell me what it was? *Was the human brain such a mystery?* Could it be possible that this little three-year-old boy in the car seat was leading us into some sort of uncharted territory? It was hard to believe that such could be the case, in the age of modern medicine and technology, but that seemed to be our present reality. With that gnawing sense of unease in my gut, I wondered where to go from here.

Maybe Rex's neurosurgeon could throw some light on the matter, help ease my own frustration. I wrote him a letter and got an appointment for just a week later. While waiting with Rex for the busy surgeon to enter the office, I realized that this place always made me anxious. It had at once the feel of waiting and foreboding. I suppose that's what pediatric neurosurgery is supposed to feel like.

The surgeon entered in a flurry. This time his uniform was a white lab coat over blue hospital scrubs. This man always seemed to be on the move, and his lean, agile build and features added to that image. His hair was completely white, a testimony to years at his trade, but his face was unlined and smiling. In spite of the brusque aura that surrounded this eminent doctor, he had the ability to focus his eyes right on you and disarm with a smile, like an elder statesman. He looked me straight in the eye now, with an indulgent smile, and said, "I've read your letter, and I understand your concerns, Mrs. Lewis." However, he went on only to explain that Rex's cyst remained under control and the shunt was functioning properly. That was certainly good news, but it was not the information I was looking for. When I moved on to my real concerns, trying to elicit clues as to what Rex's potential brain function might be, he said he really didn't know. Then he hit me with that smile again. But this time it didn't disarm me. It just seemed to say, "End of accountability." There would be no projection as to how the current structure and state of Rex's brain would impact his life. He was a surgeon, a cutter, and that simply wasn't his responsibility. And, to be fair, he probably really didn't know.

That second hospital visit had upped the ante, both in expectations and in final disappointment. I couldn't believe that doctors of such eminence could be like that—seemingly so myopic. How could the system of medical specialty be so compartmentalized that ophthalmology and neurology didn't even seem to communicate? Was this supposed to build highly qualified specialists? If so, I asked myself, at what cost? Because from where I was standing, it made their vision restricted and rendered them both incapable of helping with any sort of global brain diagnosis. How would the different pieces of the Rex puzzle fit together to define his being? What could we expect from his life? And *why* couldn't anyone tell me?

The whole hospital experience made me feel as though I was turning in circles and going nowhere. Finding more questions than answers in the medical world, life hadn't gotten any simpler than when I'd begun my search for information. If doctors couldn't help, and there'd been no word from God, I hoped the therapists could help. In frustration, I turned to Rex's weekly therapy schedule.

First came occupational therapy on Monday afternoons. The purpose of the occupational therapist (OT) was to help Rex use his body and hands in appropriate ways to carry out his daily activities. They worked on developing the muscle movement of each individual hand and coordinating the use of his hands to make them a team. They called it "bilateral coordination."

Rex's OT, Jane, began the session today, as she often did, by bouncing Rex on a therapy ball. This was to "get his motor running," in addition to working on balance and strengthening his stomach muscles. She held him securely at the hips, bouncing him up and down, forward and back, side to side, as he laughed and flapped his arms to each side of his body. I told her of my recent discovery that Rex's brain had a smaller-than-normal bridge between the two sides, to which she responded, "He does have extreme difficulty crossing midline. Could be the reason." She explained "difficulty crossing midline" as "lacking fluidity of hand movement on the opposite side of the body." When I looked confused, she said, "Just think of midline as his belly button. He doesn't move his right hand past his belly button to the other side. Same with his left hand."

Well I knew that! I just didn't have a label for it. On his own, Rex was like a robot with toys or objects, batting the ones on the left with his left hand while tapping those to his right with his right hand. If he wanted his hands to change sides, instead of crossing them over his belly to the other side, he would spin on his bottom. He had even perfected the movement. I called it the "butt spin": half circles, full circles, and on occasion the "double twister." And it was effective because if I placed a musical toy to his left, and touched his right hand, saying, "Play it with your right hand, Rex," he would execute a clean half circle, and voilà, his right hand would play the toy that was now at his right side. I was aware that he wasn't crossing over in a normal, flexible way, but had attributed it mainly to his blindness and lack of visual information to imitate. I had believed that with training he would learn more "normal" movements. But suddenly, I was beginning to see that it was more, much more—a new reality was dawning. Rex's body was more rigid because his brain was more rigid, and he lacked the connectors necessary for normal flexibility.

Jane geared the OT session to address that issue. She helped Rex slide down off the ball onto the thick, cushioned therapy mat and assisted him into a side-sitting position. That meant he had his legs bent at the knee and both calves on the left side of his body. This position allowed his left hand to rest on top of his right leg and even cross over to his right side. Thus, he was "crossing midline." He didn't whine or fight the position, which she applauded, "You're doing a great job, Rex."

Indeed, he sat playing with the toy she'd placed there. It was his favorite therapy toy, a little xylophone, which he could tap with a baton to make crystalline notes sing out. He was having a good old time, and he was not only holding the baton firmly in his left hand but was using it to play the toy instrument on his right side. Such a simple thing for almost any child, yet here it was something to be applauded. After a couple of minutes, Jane removed the toy, signaling it was time to change activities. This routine told Rex he needed to get himself out of the side-sitting position. But a confused look crossed his face as he tried to move his body. He didn't know how to do it. Jane had put him into the position, and he didn't know how to unwind his legs.

"Rex, you're stuck!" I said, loudly voicing the obvious, which partly masked the growing sense of unease I was feeling. Then converting internal tension into action, I repeated, "You're stuck, Rex," but this time it was in a playful tone, which I hoped would stimulate him. "Come on, honey," I urged. "You can get yourself unstuck. You can do it." Exuberance could incite Rex into action when it was focused directly on him. He soaked it up like a sponge, like now, and his face lit up feeling the pulse of energy. It sparked a spurt of adrenaline, causing his legs to straighten at the knees, as he took the challenge to get back into a normal sitting position. Unfortunately, his excitement had gotten out of control, and he'd been too quick, too jerky. His body didn't compensate by shifting his weight in order to maintain balance, and he toppled onto his right side. He laughed as he tumbled, thinking it was fun. Normally that laugh was impossible to resist, but today it made me want to cry.

That night I sat wearily on the living room couch replaying the day's therapy session in my mind, reliving the therapist's words, hearing their negative bent—*lacks fluidity of movement, difficulty crossing midline.* It was exhausting for me and for Rex, in spite of the moments of fun he'd had. Why should life be such hard work? I was sipping a glass of wine, trying to unwind, while watching Rex doing his own unwinding at his piano keyboard. His hands were moving more rapidly than usual on the keys, like he was releasing the day's tension. We were clearly each using our own coping methods.

As the minutes slipped past, I remained caught up in my thoughts, each one more confusing than the next. Why was God letting me be so confused, when it was clarity I was so desperately seeking? I glanced at the wine glass in my hand—just a few drops left. Then I looked over at my boy. He was still playing, but his tempo had slowed down, becoming mellower, and he looked at peace, his face at ease. Weaving notes to form his own little made-up melodies with his hands that were so rhythmic, so . . . fluid.

There was the very word the therapist had used today—*lacks fluidity in his hand movements.* "But look at their fluidity here," I wanted to shout.

Then, like he was reading my mind, he suddenly threw his right hand across his body to hit piano keys to the left, then pulled it back again, only to throw it over once more in what became a series of effortless leaps to the far left extremity of the keyboard—over to the left and back to the right, repeatedly—while his left hand played notes directly in front of his body. Crossovers! He was using his right hand to cross over, again and again, meaning he was "crossing midline." Repeatedly and effortlessly! Rex *could* get his hand across his belly button on his own—easily! I almost dropped my wineglass as I realized his brain had the capacity; it was right there in front of my face, like an answer to prayer. I couldn't wait to show his occupational therapist. I asked myself, *Does Rex know what he is doing?* As though answering my thoughts, he began squealing in delight.

The following day was Tuesday, which meant physical therapy, not occupational therapy. His physical therapist (PT), Tam, worked with him to get his entire body to move better, not focusing primarily on his hands like his OT did, although there was some carryover. Tam often worked with him on different swings, from platform to bolster swings, getting him to climb on and off and then working on Rex's balance once he was on the swing. I told her about the piano crossover and, being well aware of Rex's "crossing midline" issues herself, she was thrilled to hear what he'd done at the piano.

Seizing the moment, she tried to get him to demonstrate the skill by grasping the left hand rope on a platform swing with his right hand while she held his left hand. She even put a little musical box by the rope to entice him to reach for it with his free right hand, but his hand just extended out in front of his body. After trying unsuccessfully for a couple of minutes, Rex became frustrated, and my own sense of letdown was palpable. He couldn't do it. Or wouldn't do it. I confess, in that moment, I didn't know which it was. I was even beginning to doubt the reality of what I'd seen at the piano. That child seemed so far removed from the child who was in front of me here. After what seemed an eternity, Tam took Rex's hand and drew it gently across his body to grasp the rope.

"It's okay, Rex; you're doing fine," she said, in an attempt to relieve the tension she felt surrounding her. She then helped him into his usual "climbing on the platform swing" position. He began to raise his right leg onto the big swing in a slow, labored movement, as I repeated to her the news from the scans regarding the two sides of Rex's brain. From her point of view, Rex's main difficulty was not in his muscle strength, but in his inability to use that strength to accomplish a specific movement. "He can't motor plan when he has to execute a series of different body movements."

Motor plan? I didn't get it and said so.

"It just means he has the strength to climb on the swing and all these swings," she said with a sweep of her hand. "He just doesn't know how to do it."

I watched in growing discomfort as Rex struggled to get each leg in succession onto the swing. Tam explained how movements that most of us do with absolutely no thought are actually complex patterns of smaller steps. Right knee up, hands forward, shift weight forward, then left knee up, twist torso onto bottom, and so forth. It should be as natural as breathing, right? If not, there must be a serious breakdown in the brain's wiring.

Rex finally finished his task. It had taken him monumental effort to climb onto the platform and grasp the ropes. But now he was ready to swing. It was his reward for pushing his body and brain to the limit. As I watched Rex flying through the air, he seemed so free and unfettered. Yet once the swing stopped and he was required to climb down, the tortured process began once again. It seemed endless! That's when Tam hit me with the kicker: not only could Rex not motor plan movements he had never done before, but once he was taught how to execute them, he had trouble doing them again. "It's called apraxia," Tam said.

Another new word she was applying to my son; another neurological disorder supposedly afflicting him. In essence, it implied his brain couldn't remember how to accomplish even the simplest movements. That seemed impossible, certainly unthinkable. How could you forget how to climb onto a swing? As I listened to her explanation, I realized this thing was getting out of hand. It was becoming more than I could handle; I thought information would be the key to unlock the mystery of my son, but I was getting buried under the weight of it all. How could brain parts doctors said were "insignificant" wreak such havoc in my son?

The next day was speech therapy. The physical body is one thing, but speech touches at the very essence of a human being, the ability to communicate. For me, it represented the ability "to be." I needed desperately to cling to hope as I entered the familiar speech therapy room, but I felt fear gripping my insides even as I set Rex down at the table where he normally worked. Without preamble, I asked his speech pathologist what she believed his issues were. Why wasn't he speaking yet?

Suzanne hesitated just a moment, and then to my shock and horror said, "I think it's because he has speech apraxia." Speech apraxia! She believed his speech was impaired by the same disorder affecting his body!

No God, not that! I screamed in my mind. Not that word again. But it was out there now; Pandora's box had been fully opened. His brain was unable to tell his tongue and the muscles in his mouth how to formulate the sounds that normally develop into speech. A new brain/body breakdown, or in this case brain/mouth breakdown! But Rex *could* babble. He could get indiscriminate sounds out of his mouth. But, she emphasized, he couldn't do it on command, and that was what made her believe he had apraxia.

All I could do was repeat the words in my mind and rage at the Creator. "No, God, not that!" It simply couldn't be true, because I wanted more than anything to have a conversation with my son, to just hear him say, "Mama." He needed a voice to speak, and I needed to hear him speak.

Rex's speech therapist, perhaps sensing my disbelief, said she would demonstrate what she was talking about. She set a spinning top on the table in front of him. The top played music as it spun, and she knew this would normally cause Rex to make happy babbling sounds. And sure enough, it did. At the sound of the tinkling music, Rex squealed, clapping his hands in excitement, and spurted out a string of "bas,"—"ba, ba, ba, ba, ba, ba." She then silenced the toy and said, "Let's hear you say 'ba,' Rex, like you just did." She mimicked the pronunciation several times, exaggerating "bb-aa," so there could be no doubt as to what he was supposed to do.

Rex put his lips together as he should to make the "b" sound, and I was willing him to do it. With lips pasted together, he twisted his mouth in various directions, as if that would make the sound. His face went taut then and his lips pursed, as though the "b" sound was going to burst out. He was trying with everything he had, and I leaned forward as if that might pull the sound out of him. I jumped in. "Say 'ba,' Rex, you can do it, sweetie," and waited, feeling it would come, praying it would come. Another second . . . two, three, an eternity, and then suddenly his face went slack, his voice still silent.

Rex's head drooped like a broken doll as he sat there listlessly. The effort had drained him, like a rubber band that had been stretched to its limit and then snapped. It had drained us both. The therapist didn't immediately break in, presumably out of respect, or perhaps because she felt the strain as well. Silence weighed heavily in the room, broken only by the faintest metallic humming, as though its length was a measure of our exhaustion. Rex made me notice sounds I'd never noticed before, lost as they were for most of us in the crush of life. But his sensitive ears heard everything, often making me seek out the source of potential offenders. I looked up to see what was making the sound, and I realized it was the wall clock, used to keep time for the therapy session. A large round face, with big numbers and a sweeping hand, mechanically ticking away the seconds, keeping the beat of life. Time wouldn't stop. In that instant, it seemed to be the only certainty I had.

Nearing the end of my rope, I had nowhere to go but back to the beginning where this whole frantic, confusing search had begun. Back to the Blind Children's Center and the very room where we'd had the meeting that had set this whole process in motion. Between noncommittal doctors with their business-as-usual attitudes and therapists all seeming to demonstrate endless areas of severe dysfunction, I couldn't seem to put it all together, to make sense of it. I needed someone to help me connect the dots. I knew the best people to do that were at his school.

Rex had been coming to school every day, but I hadn't been back in the educational director's office since that meeting. Mercifully, thoughts about wheelchairs and sign language were subdued by the adrenaline of the moment. All my energy was focused on my current mission—to make sense of what seemed to be nonsense. Miriam was poised as usual and greeted me warmly. "How are you, Cathleen? How have you been?"

After exchanging a few niceties, I cut to the chase. "The doctors at Children's Hospital say one thing. But then the therapists seem to prove exactly the opposite," I said, my annoyance obvious. I explained to her the new findings in Rex's brain scans, and how, as a result, he now had a new eye diagnosis. "But according to Dr. Bryant, that won't make any difference." I was speaking quickly, venting, in a tone that let her know just how fed up I really was. "I think he said 'no functional impact.' Can you believe that?"

Miriam smiled at me, trying to take the edge off my anger. "I see it with doctors all the time. It's unfortunate, but they have their domain and we have ours." She shook her head slowly and leveled her eyes on me, trying to support me with the intensity of her gaze. "Dr. Bryant doesn't work with the kids day after day like we do," she said. "So I don't see how he could know what impact the absence of the septum pellucidum might have." She was leading me with her logic, confirming what I'd learned in all of Rex's different therapies. "The fact that Rex's diagnosis is now septo-optic dysplasia changes a lot in what our expectations for him might be. In our experience *working with the kids*—children with the brain structure abnormalities like you're now telling me Rex has—it is much more involved than children with just the eye damage." She stressed "working with the kids" as the essential qualifying criteria and paused to give me a chance to respond. When I remained silent, she drove her point home in a calmly professional voice. "Cathleen, there's a big difference between septo-optic dysplasia and optic nerve hypoplasia!"

There it was! Was that what I'd been trying so desperately to find through explanations, through science? As I sat facing Miriam and heard those words, distraught as I was, I felt an odd jab of irony. I'd just given her validation for Rex's severe developmental delays in a label: septo-optic dysplasia. They'd handed me their verdict at the meeting, but now I was the one providing the proof, like a double whammy. What a twist! She'd caught the irony too—I read it in her eyes—but there was something else there as well. Her face had softened to an almost maternal look, which said "compassion" to me. Her tone had clearly been professional, but I couldn't miss the empathy I heard there as well, as if she knew the road ahead would be a very hard one.

Arriving home, I phoned my son's babysitter. "Is there any

way you could come over and stay with Rex for an hour or so right now?" I asked in a voice tinged with desperation.

"Is something wrong?" she asked, worried.

I assured her that everything was fine, but that I needed to air out my brain, to sort out "some stuff."

The young lady arrived, and I left the two of them there. I didn't take the elevators to make the descent to the beach today. That would be too confining, and confinement was the last thing I needed with my head about to explode. I would climb down the steps to the waterline today, all eighty-nine of them, and hope the exertion would help take the edge off the emotions all knotted up inside me. Upon reaching the sand, I was breathing heavily, but I knew I couldn't stop here. Glancing to the right, I saw the tide was in too far to allow me passage past the rocks on that side. So I took off running to the left, where the sandy beach was wider. As the waves lashed at the shore, my feet were ripping through the wet sand. I ran on and on into an afternoon head wind that slowed my pace but couldn't stop me. There were no seagulls shrieking overhead today, but I heard them in my mind, egging me on, as my chest began to burn. "Don't stop! Don't you dare stop!" And I didn't, not until nature blocked my way. The tide was just too high this afternoon, and I reached a narrow strip of beach where a mass of rocks blocked my route. I briefly considered scaling them, but saw that, like life, they were too many, too high. I threw myself down, right there in the sand, burying my head in my hands. My breath was gasping and irregular as my jaw clamped tight.

I just couldn't get the frustration out, couldn't get away from it, no matter how hard I tried. It was still all twisted up inside me as I lifted my head from my hands, looking upward in a rapid motion. The wind had swept the sky clean, leaving it a deep, vibrant blue, free of any clouds that might have marred its brilliance. But instead of calming me, the flawlessness of what I saw overhead only served to make me madder.

"God, I don't want to see any more blue skies!" I screamed. "Don't You get it? I'm tired of it." I paused for just a moment as I felt the tears surging in my eyes. I took a deep breath, held it for a second, and with tears of rage spilling down my cheeks, I let the dam break. "And how many perfectly normal kids do You think I need to see every day to get the message? I get it! Rex isn't normal! But why? I want to know why. And I want to know what he is. Who is he? I thought that by getting information I'd find out, You know. It was supposed to help me *see* . . . that's what I asked You for. I want to get it, to get what his life is all about!"

My eyes were blurred from tears rising from a well of rage I hadn't acknowledged before. As I shouted up to God, who seemed deaf to my pleas, I suddenly knew how deep my anger ran. First of all, I was angry with myself for the whole mess. I was definitely angry with the doctors and therapists who had led me nowhere. But I was also angry with the other mothers, all those mothers who *dared* to have normal kids. And if I really wanted to admit it, I was angry with the kids themselves who *dared* to be normal. But my anger didn't stop there. It suddenly seemed so clear to me—I was angry with the president, too, and the postman, angry with friends, certainly at strangers in the street. But most of all I was angry at . . . "You, God! You are ignoring my pleas; You won't listen to me."

Apraxia . . . crossing midline . . . bilateral coordination . . . corpus callosum . . . septo-optic dysplasia . . . brain membranes . . . connectors . . . dysfunction, and on and on. I spit the words out like a poison I had to get out before it killed me. My fists were clenched in utter fury. "And autism, God!? I'm blinder than Rex right now!" I shouted, my voice cracking in intensity. But it didn't stop me as I delivered my last desperate punch, throwing my voice into each word to make it rise up over the waves and linger.

"DON'T . . . YOU . . . CARE?"

CHAPTER SIX

Miracles

A mother understands what a child does not say.

—Anonymous

I t was Saturday morning in the park, and I felt as if I had a hangover. No headache, just a feeling of disconnect, like I was watching the kids running in the playground through a haze, hearing their chatter through a filter. Ever since I'd spilled out my heart on the beach two days before, I'd been oddly out of sorts. The information overload followed by the resultant meltdown had left me in this listless state. Then there was Rex. He was anything but listless, bouncing up and down in my arms as I carried him to his swing. I might have seen it as an ironic reversal of roles if I'd had my wits about me, but today there'd be no deeper analysis. All I saw was his excitement, and nothing could dim his expectation that in a moment he would be flying through the air! He loved to swing more than anything except playing his piano. The fact was, he craved movement—all the movement he couldn't get from his own legs. He loved to be thrown in the air, spun around at high speed, bounced up and down, jostled, thrown over my shoulder and carried like a sack of potatoes, and a variety of other surprising movements when you considered his lack of self-initiated mobility and other sensitivities. His therapists called it "vestibular," or movements that stimulated his inner ear, giving him a sense of balance and well-being. I just called it "being a child," especially now. That's what I needed to hold on to. The rest had quite simply become too much.

Rex's face beamed the moment the swing began its gentle arc. I always pushed from the front, so I could talk to him with each push. We played conceptual games wherever we went—I never let up trying to get his brain wires to connect. And for him, the games made everything more fun. So, today, in spite of the general apathy I was feeling, conditioning took over once he was seated, and I began chanting, "Back and forth, back and forth, Rex is swinging back and forth. Oh, so slowly, back and forth."

As the swing gained some momentum, Rex's face sparked with excitement, knowing that soon he would be really moving. "Shall we go high, high, high, way up to the sky?" I asked, like I'd done so many times before. I watched his eyes light up, barely able to control his anticipation. He said nothing, but I knew what he wanted, and so I let rip with a couple of strong, though admittedly robotic, pushes. My thoughts were still in a muddle as I heard my son's squeals of delight. In spite of myself, the sound drew me into the game, and without warning, I grabbed the swing in mid-arc, stopping his flight with a jerk, surprising him.

"Uh oh, Rex is caught in a trap!" I held him prisoner there as his squeals turned to deeper, more vibrant laughter. Then I gave an extra-big push. "Rex just got out of the trap." As he flew backward to the height of the swing's arc, I added, "With a swoosh!"

That's when laughter really took over his little body and, with a power that cut through numbness, it took over me as well. Swooshing and laughing! So, there we were, laughing like we hadn't a care in the world, caught up in a joy that was attached to nothing but itself and the immediacy of that moment, joy that was oblivious to time and circumstance.

It was there in the union of our laughter that I finally felt His presence, heard the voice I'd been seeking. It was clearly and unmistakably the voice of God imparting His message. And it was as simple as my son was complex. He was asking me not to lose heart. He was asking me to walk—to live—by faith and not by sight. *Walk by faith, not by sight.*

REX WAS still giddy when we arrived home. I was on a high as well, going to the stereo to put on Beethoven's Ninth Symphony, feeling its "Ode to Joy" was the perfect cap to our morning. It was the masterpiece Beethoven had written toward the end of his life, after he'd become deaf, and Rex was instantly captivated, listening enthralled to the work he had never heard before.

I watched my son tapping his fingers on his legs, as though he was playing his keyboard, so, when the piece finished, I knew where he wanted to go. Leaving him at his piano, I went into the bedroom. I could hear him play a few notes, then stop, then play a few more, then stop again. Normally he would just let fly with his own melodies and rhythms he created, but today he was oddly tentative. Wondering what was going on, I walked back into the living room. Rex's face had a faraway look as he picked out notes on the keyboard. That's when I realized what those tones were when strung together to form a melody. I gasped! It wasn't a melody of his own this time, a new improvisation. Instead, Rex was picking out the tune to "Ode to Joy" right there in front of my eyes. He'd heard it, and now he was playing it back! Beethoven! My three-year-old, nonverbal, blind son was playing Beethoven's "Ode to Joy" on the piano! There was mischief in my boy—I could see it in the slight smile that played at the corners of his mouth and the light shining in his eyes as the notes fluttered hesitantly at first, but then rose triumphantly to fill the room. It was in that timeless melody that had spanned almost two centuries that I realized I was not hearing the master Beethoven. I was hearing the voice of a little blind boy singing out. It was Rex. And it took my breath away, filling my heart, filling my soul, with hope.

How could he do it? I asked myself in the days following his miraculous musical feat. But then I answered my own question—it didn't matter. The important thing was that he was telling me to believe in him, to not give up. *Walk by faith, not by sight.*

Two days later, I had Rex in his high chair, music playing on the stereo to distract him from the feeding process, or the feeding "battle," as was usually the case. I was diving in with a spoonful of puréed sweet potato in mostly unsuccessful attempts at landing a bit in his mouth, while he shook his head from right to left dodging the

It was in that timeless melody that had spanned almost two centuries that I realized I was not hearing the master Beethoven. I was hearing the voice of a little blind boy singing out. It was Rex. And it took my breath away, filling my heart, filling my soul, with hope.

invasive spoon. I was worn out physically from the battle, but my heart was still so full from the "Ode to Joy" memory, I thought I'd keep at it a while longer. Today, Rex was so fast, with his head jerking, flat out refusing to open his mouth. Finally, as I sensed he was tiring from the process himself, his head slowly stopped shaking. He seemed wary, on guard, lest I try a sneak-swoop move with the spoon, which would force him back into action. Then, suddenly, to my surprise, he began opening his mouth. I thought I was about to witness a feeding miracle, and that he would actually take a bite of food voluntarily. But just as I was going to push a bite home, I heard a guttural sound lurching from my son's throat. My spoon froze in midair, as the throaty "c-c-cu" sound came out, with a pop at the end to form the word *cup*. My jaw dropped, and so did the spoon in my hand, splattering his high chair tray with the orange goop. I was stunned, but then recovered quickly to grab his milk cup and hand it to him. This was not a feeding miracle; it was much more than a few free bites of food in his mouth. This was Rex breaking the chains of his silence—this was his voice. His voice!

Over the next few weeks, Rex proved he could say "cup" whenever he wanted to. This meant he was overcoming his speech apraxia by demonstrating he could form a word when he wanted to. It also meant he'd found a new power in communicating his needs or desires. In this case, he used it to avoid being forced to eat. Just say the magic word "cup," and you will be instantly drinking instead. I have to say he became a little cocky, armed with the power of his one word. You could see it in the glint in his eye, as he would instantly throw out his command, "Cup!" And lo and behold, he had instantly halted that menacing army of spoons, loaded with puréed peas or carrots.

I found his antics amusing. Even if he was foiling my labored attempts to feed him, I knew how important it was to give him a sense of control through the use of language.

Clever boy that he clearly was, he soon realized there was another word that was part of "cup," which he could use to avoid being forced to walk. It was "up," meaning, "Pick me up, Mommy." Rex's first two words became the tools that allowed him to escape what he must have perceived to be torture—eating and walking!

Several weeks passed with Rex flaunting his new power, but no other verbal communication emerged. This made me wonder just how much he understood of the spoken language. He was almost three and a half, and he'd never answered a question. He only used his two words when he wanted to avoid a negative consequence. His speech therapist didn't really know what to think. She was thrilled with his ability to voice words, but instinctively, I think she had been hoping for more. At the Blind Children's Center, the concern was focused on his extreme sensitivities and on his new use of language to escape attempts to push his development forward in other critical areas. The doctor said Rex had to eat or he would end up with a feeding tube in his stomach. That meant he would have another tube in his body along with the tube draining his brain. He couldn't live forever off the scant bites of purée and Carnation Instant Breakfast that had long been the mainstay of his diet. I refused to even consider it for the time being. I'd just spend more time to work more food into his mouth. *Walk by faith, not by sight.*

In the meantime, there was another concern that made me feel the passage of time even more acutely than his extreme feeding issues—those infernal spaghetti legs. At three and a half, he was getting heavier by the day, too heavy to carry around, and he was outgrowing his stroller. Why did he keep collapsing his legs? He had the ability to walk, he had shown us all—his physical therapist, the staff at the Blind Children's Center, and me—that he could, and yet he wouldn't, especially now that he had the word *up* in his "control and defend" arsenal. Maybe I hadn't been tough enough these past few weeks, caught up as I'd been in the joy of hearing him use language, his two grand words. The scary reality of what we were facing struck in his physical therapy session, when his therapist Tam pulled out a catalogue and showed me some lightweight wheelchairs. "He doesn't need anything heavy-duty," she said, as if that might soften the blow, "but he is going to need something soon." Her words felt as if she'd doused me with cold water, and I couldn't get the thought out of my mind all week.

Walk by faith, not by sight. I could hear the words at night and clung to their promised hope during the day, because I felt letting go would be the end for us. And yet a question began to arise in my mind. How do you have hope without getting lost in it? Without leaving yourself open to letdown or eventual heartbreak? I wasn't sure I could find the answer by myself.

It was Friday afternoon, the ending to what had been a very long week. Arriving home after therapy, I needed some air. I was hoping Rex would be up for a walk down to the beach. I wanted to catch the sun setting over the water, such a beautiful sight these days. The golden hues, slightly tinged with red, reflecting off the ocean and framing the horizon, had never failed to inspire me with that sense of hope I so needed right now. We were deeply into autumn, the air crisp and clear, but the days were becoming shorter. In spite of the unmatched beauty of a November day, it was a period of the year that normally didn't set well with me, filling me with angst, merely because daylight was giving way progressively to nighttime. Darkness stealing light. It was an irrational fear, I knew, but still ever so real when added to the reality I was living with my son. But this afternoon I was hopeful that the life-affirming beauty of Creation would prove hope is stronger than fear. I blocked out images of lightweight wheelchairs, feeding tubes, and any other artificial support for Rex as I told him how fun it would be to walk down to the beach so "we could listen to the waves going crash." Normally, when I said the word "crash," I would pretend to throw him down, a game he loved. As I did so now, he laughed in spite of the end-of-day tiredness, so I knew it was a go. Our "walks" to the beach consisted of me coaxing him to walk a short distance and then giving in to his cries of "up," which would normally get louder with each step he was forced to take. Then I would carry him the rest of the way.

But today I did things a little differently. I began by carrying him, and then stopped midway to the beach along the sloping entrance driveway to our condominium. Instead of heading directly toward the sand, which would take us down the sloping driveway, for some reason I looked in the other direction. Had it been a bird calling out from over there that had drawn my attention? The sound of a car behind us? Or just the silent whisper of a brisk autumn day? I looked up to the top of the driveway. There was an outdoor parking lot, the tarred surface buckling and cracking in several places, begging for repair. There were also planters brimming with pink and red geraniums skirting the road, adding spots of color at the base of the predictable palm trees. But today, all I really saw was the driveway itself, its slope, and how steep it became at the top. Suddenly, I had an idea. I carried Rex all the way up, then quickly set him down onto the tarred pavement, facing him down the slope. His legs were rigid as he stood there, stiff as rods, which was normally the way they got right before they went "spaghetti." Going from one extreme to the other—*hyper*tonic to *hypo*tonic mush. Before his legs had a chance to buckle, I gave him a slight nudge on his back and said, "Go, Rex, go!" I jumped in front of him, poised to catch the inevitable fall, as he took the first faltering steps I had forced him into. But he held himself up as the slope made his legs move faster. Gaining momentum, he began walking faster than he ever had, while I backed up in front of him, guiding him with my voice, egging him on. "Rex is walking faster and faster! You can do it, Rex!"

Then, as though a Divine hand touched my son, I felt something infinitely higher supersede my own efforts as a sort of ecstasy swept over him. Gone were spaghetti legs. Instead, his legs were infused with vibrancy and strength as he walked faster and faster, until he was walking *too* fast for his own legs. But he didn't stop; he couldn't! And he didn't pitch face-first into my ready arms either. Instead, with his motor all revved up, he began running! My child began to run! His face registered disbelief, having never done anything remotely like this before, but he ran faster still, veering right, then left. He tottered, his arms flailing like a novice skier. Yet he had no fear, and his balance held as he ran faster and faster. His face was alight with surprise at what he was doing, the discovery of what he could do, and I gaped in awe myself. His disbelief gave way to overwhelming joy in the thrill of intense movements in his little body, the body that had been barely mobile for so long.

"That's running, Rex!" I shouted. "Isn't it fun?" As he broke the chains of his body, his legs spinning full speed, he began laughing as he ran. It was infectious, a laugh straight from his belly, its resonance testifying, like nothing else could, that God was on high and all was right with the world.

> *As he broke the chains of his body, his legs spinning full speed, he began laughing as he ran. It was infectious, a laugh straight from his belly, its resonance testifying, like nothing else could, that God was on high and all was right with the world.*

That night I lay in bed floating on my own high, full of the joy of the day and full of peace. Rex had gone to bed easily and was sleeping soundly, his body exhausted. This time it was the peaceful exhaustion of good physical exertion. If I could etch a picture in my mind that would endure throughout eternity, it would be Rex's arrival at the bottom of our driveway that day, his look that of an Olympic runner breaking the tape at the finish line to win the gold. It had been a perfect moment. As I lay in bed, I acknowledged how few moments in life touch us to the core of our very being. Moments that make the rest of the world fade into nothingness. Moments when the past is a distant memory and the future remains far away and irrelevant. It's in those moments that you know what you need to know and you forget what should be forgotten. You have a brief glimpse of eternity, as time is suspended as though God is looking you straight in the eye, with a smile that leaves you clear in the knowledge that all is right and good and is as it should be.

In the days that followed Rex's miraculous run, he was like a child who'd been given a bite of sugar. He wanted more. Now he knew what it felt like to really move, flying through space for the first time on his own, and the great way it made his body feel, all that adrenaline coursing through him. The problem was that his brain still had some defective motor wiring and conditioning to overcome. That's where music stepped in. Every time he appeared to be frozen on his legs or ready to buckle in spite of himself, I (or his teachers) would begin to sing a catchy tune. That was our "control switch" that allowed him to bypass conditioned response, and he would begin to walk or run, fueled by his memory of what fast movement felt like. I prayed that over time this musical "jump start" would help my son's brain create new conditioning in his motor responses. Interestingly, Rex seemed more at ease running than walking, almost as though fast movement took fewer thought processes, less control. I've since equated it with the game of tennis; it's easier to hit the ball hard than it is to hit slow finesse shots. But then, too, speed of movement gave him positive sensations that were clearly powerful motivators.

As Rex was finding increased freedom in his body movements, his piano music became infused with faster tempos, bolder tapestries, and new, more vibrant melodies. It was during the Christmas season in his third year that I came to understand that Rex's duplication of Beethoven's "Ode to Joy" was definitely not a singular phenomenon, a musical miracle never to be repeated. Instead he began filling our living room with not one but several songs of the season, such as "Hark! The Herald Angels Sing," "Joy to the World," or his seeming favorite, "The Little Drummer Boy." Anchoring his left hand on a single note, marking rhythms, he created melodies with his right hand. As he played "The Little Drummer Boy," he would hum along to the melody, hypnotized, with a faraway look in his eyes, almost as though he were gazing down on the Savior child in a bed of hay. How I wished his humming would somehow miraculously become words so he could sing along with the piano. Because for us, Christmas wasn't frosted cookies or other sugary treats. It wasn't brightly colored Christmas decorations or finding the perfect tree. Nor was it toys, most of which were meaningless to Rex. It wasn't even Santa Claus. Christmas was music.

I witnessed this on the most festive day of the year at the Blind Children's Center, the day when the LAPD arrives in force, its sirens sounding a salute. The police chief himself came bearing gifts for the students, and the entry parade provided a sort of VIP escort for the guest of honor, jolly old Saint Nick. As police chief Bernard Parks spoke to the directors of the Center, the real celebrity was being mobbed by the kids. The teachers were allowing one child at a time to sit on Santa's lap, and it was almost Rex's turn. A little girl named Maria, just a month older than Rex, who'd been in his class from the first day we came, had just jumped onto Santa's ample lap.

"Hi, Santa. How are you?"

Maria's mom, Claudia, raised her camera to take a souvenir shot, while Maria began reciting her Christmas list, not even waiting for Santa to respond. "I'd like a CD player, a Raffi CD, and a new doll and some clothes for her."

Claudia smiled at me and said, "Rex is so cute. Maria always talks about his laugh. She says it's so happy, it makes her laugh too."

"That's nice," I said, distracted, since what I was really hearing was the verbal onslaught Maria was delivering to an amused Santa Claus.

"Do you really go all over the world in a big sleigh, Santa? My sister left a whole bag of cookies for you last year, but the dog ate them instead. Would you like some milk this year?"

Claudia looked at me as I gazed intently at her daughter. She laughed. "I think Maria just loves to hear her own voice, you know, like a lot of blind children. But as chatty as she is, sometimes I wish she'd *stop* talking."

I forced a smile, thinking of other moms in other places I envied so. I'd known Claudia since Rex began school there three years before—we'd both been in the same boat then, devastated and grief stricken by our children's blindness, trying our best just to cope. Back then we'd had similar battles to fight, tough emotions to work through, but now, only three years later, our respective kids seemed to be living in different worlds. In spite of all of Rex's recent breakthroughs, I couldn't help feeling a deep, longing tug at my heart as I watched Claudia snap one last picture of her daughter talking Santa's ear off. It was Christmas, and Christmas was the season of wishes.

As Rex took his place on the jolly man's lap, Santa's jiggling belly and hearty "Ho, ho, ho!" made Rex laugh. Otherwise, my son remained silent. When Santa asked him what he wanted for Christmas, he giggled at the deep resonance of his voice, which was almost musical, but said nothing. Santa Claus didn't mean anything to him, and he didn't have his own wish list. But I did. As Rex began jingling Santa's bells, I jumped straight to the top of the list, asking in silent prayer. I wanted a true Christmas miracle and nothing less than the big one. *Let Rex answer Santa's question.* Yet, not wanting to seem ungrateful in my innermost desires, I hastily added my silent thanks. *Rex's piano music is amazing, miraculous. Thank You for filling our Christmas with it.* I paused, feeling real awe at my son's recent piano feats, certainly the hand of God at work. Yet I couldn't hold back the truth in my heart. "But what I really want is to talk to my son!" I'd blurted it out loud this time, and Father Christmas looked up from Rex to me and gave me a benevolent smile.

But Father Christmas isn't Father God, and the holiday season came and went without that prayer being answered. December turned to January, then February, and my moods mirrored the increasingly gray and cloudy skies. I began to wonder more and more how much language Rex even understood, since he never answered questions. He used his two words when he wanted but never in response to a question. For example, at feeding time if I asked him what he wanted, he would maintain his usual silence. It was only when I would try to put food in his mouth that he would say, "Cup."

Was his communication ending after barely beginning? His teacher at the Blind Children's Center was becoming increasingly concerned this was the case. At least that was the feeling I got when she gave him a daily choice of activities, only to be met with a blank response. And his speech therapist wasn't making any progress either. I struggled to hold on to God's words during these months in spite of the evidence to the contrary. *Walk by faith, not by sight.* But it was a real battle because I had prayed desperately for a Christmas miracle that hadn't come. I didn't know that God might just be planning on delivering on a different holiday altogether. *In His time, not mine.*

Spring was now upon us, and Easter was days away. The "Beeping Easter Egg Hunt" had been a fun event at the Blind Children's Center, even for Rex, who was often overwhelmed by the noise at parties. He had gotten a kick out of the musical quality of the Easter eggs. But now I was happy to have a week of vacation from school and all of his therapies. That way we could disconnect from the expectations that swirled around us and just "be" for a few days. That's the only thing I was praying for during this new holiday week.

It was early morning, and I had just gotten Rex out of bed. He was wearing his blue-gray pajamas adorned with little sailing boats and was still groggy as I carried him to his piano. Playing the piano was the first thing he wanted to do every morning, and I knew any sleepiness would be gone the second his fingers hit the keys. Crossing the living room, I described the world and our movements to him, as you would for any blind child. "We're passing the big fluffy chair now, Rex, and it's a beautiful day. The sun is shining bright."

"Rex, sweetie, what would you like to do this morning?" I asked my usual question, again expecting nothing back. I was beginning to set him down, even as I was asking the question, when all of a sudden, I noticed his face was all scrunched up. With his lips pasted together, he seemed in the midst of some monumental effort. I pulled him back up to my eye level, asking, "What is it, Rex? What is it, honey?"

After twisting his face this way and that, his lips finally popped open, and like a firecracker exploding, he said, "Pp-pp-aaa-ooo!"

I gaped! It was an important moment, I knew that, but I didn't understand the word, and I desperately needed to get it. "What is it, Rex?" I asked again, practically begging.

He repeated the same extreme effort, trying with his whole body this time, his head dipping low, before snapping back up with another popping sound. This time it was a little clearer. "PPPaaaano!" His face lit up from his own sound, like he'd just been struck by a bolt of electricity. He'd done it this time, and he knew it! He balled his hands into tiny fists, knocking them together, and repeating with each knock, "Pano! Pano! Pano!"

It was in that instant that I got it, and I didn't know whether to laugh or cry, so I did a little of both. I danced a jig, twirling my son round and round, shouting, "Piano, piano! Yes, my sweetheart. That's it! You want to play your piano!" What a curious sight we must have been—a little blind boy knocking his hands together in excitement and his crazed mother, tears streaming down her cheeks, whooping for joy and dancing a jig, all because of one little word.

One little word, *piano*—it was the answer to my question.

What would you like to do? He'd clearly understood me. But more than that, it was the answer to my prayers. Because this word "piano," which tapped in so directly to Rex's musical soul, had the power to break through any remaining wall of doubt and open up the floodgates of lots of words. Language. Unlike when Rex said "cup" or "up," uttered in isolation and driven by avoidance, "piano" was a bridge to more. Almost immediately, he began to put words together into short sentences, which were musical at first. The singsongy cadences seemed to make language easier, more accessible to his brain. It was clear that music, with its order and rhythm, had opened up a big door for Rex. Only time would reveal where that door would lead.

Walk by faith, not by sight.

CHAPTER SEVEN

The Ripple Effect

*If you don't like something, change it; if you can't change it,
change the way you think about it.*

—Mary Engelbreit, artist and entrepreneur

Rex had always loved the water, as befitted any child who grew up near the beach. Pools, the ocean, his bath, he loved it all. He'd only been ten months old when I got my courage up, blew sharply into his face, and dunked his head under the water in a pool. Since then, he'd been fearless in the pool; using his inner tube for buoyancy, he'd flap and kick his way from the shallow to the deep end of the pool.

At the beach, I would hold him, as rippling baby waves hit his legs, gently massaging them. The rhythm and movement of ocean waves became a game that sent him into peels of laughter. When he'd feel them hit him from the front, I'd say, "The waves roll into the shore." Then, as they flowed at him from behind, I'd say, "And then they get *sucked* back out to sea!"

And then, there was his bath. It was alternately soothing, soaking sensitivity out of that little body, and exhilarating. At times Rex would flap his hands into a wild splashing frenzy, soaking the floor and me, along with his own face and head. He didn't use the toys I'd put in the bath much, normally plucking them from the water and then dropping them out of the tub to get them out of his space. The water itself was his preferred plaything.

Tonight we were playing a new game in the bath. I took a large marble (about an inch in diameter) and dropped it into the water from about a foot up. There was a sharp plop as it hit the surface, ending with a thud as it struck the bottom of the tub. He clapped at the *plop-thud* sound, giggling. "More, Mommy, more," he said, already into the game. I retrieved the marble, dropped it once more, and then put the marble in his hand to show him how he could make the sound himself.

"Just hold the marble way up high." He raised his hand a little, but not high enough. "Your hand's gotta be higher, higher, higher, sweetie," I said, and he extended his hand as far as it could reach this time. "Then just drop it with a plop and a thud!"

He dropped it, then found it in the bath and dropped it again, over and over, loving the *plop-thud* sound effects. As I watched the water rippling out from the marble's contact point, I thought back to my childhood home and our old square swimming pool, where I used to sit with my own mother, tossing stones up into the air. We wanted to see who could make the biggest splash as they plummeted down. Water rippling out from the contact point. I had begun to witness a similar process unfolding in Rex's life, as the miracles that had touched him resonated outward, touching others as well.

Entering into my son's fifth and final year at the Blind Children's Center, his language development was moving forward, with his voice echoing through those hallways with increasing frequency. He was a child breaking out of the prison of his body, with his personality opening up along with his voice. He still had his sensitivities, to be sure, but through music, the beginnings of language, and increased freedom of movement, he'd gotten a critical foothold in the world. As Rex continued to push back the borders of his existence, I watched him help others do the same thing with their own lives, gaining respite from their daily burdens. Water rippling from the contact point. It was there at his preschool that I first began to witness that effect.

Rex had a soft, little voice when compared to other loud four-year-olds, but it was bright and cheerful. It was also musical to the ear, made up of singsongy cadences, with a bit of echolalia (repeating phrases rather than answering them) and scripted speech patterns. He often repeated conversational sequences the same way, like there was only one way of communicating. If one changed the phrasing, he was at a loss as to what to do. For example, the question, "Rex, how are you today?" couldn't be changed to "Rex, are you doing okay today?" The rigidity in his brain wasn't allowing that yet. He seemed to need rhythmic cadences, treating words in a sentence as though they were beats in a measure, in order to comprehend the spoken word. Ask him, "How are you today, Rex?" in a monotone, and you'd likely get a blank look. But repeat the same question with each word highly intonated, and he'd promptly answer, "I'm fine, and how are you today?" Rex needed routine and order to make sense of things. He also needed music the way the rest of us need air. Breathe in music, and breathe out comprehension.

Fortunately his new teacher at the Center grasped that critical link, and she proved to be a godsend. Not only was she creative and capable of thinking out of the box in order to make Rex's curriculum more effective by making it "more musical," but she loved to sing. It wasn't kids' songs that interested her, which was good, because those songs only went so far with Rex. She liked popular music, or maybe I should say music that was popular in the '70s. That seemed to be her era. So when she saw how my special boy could be motivated through music, and understood his easy grasp of her preferred genre, she plunged him into the world of 1970s vocals!

I came to pick him up at the end of class one day to find him playing the '70s classic "Lean on Me" on his classroom key-board. The next day he was singing it: "Lean on me, and you'll feel strong . . . if you need somebody, you can lean on me." Among laughter, his classmates would take turns leaning on him to see how strong he was. Music became a learning tool for Rex and for those around him. His soft speaking voice gained clarity and strength when he sang, and his ability to memorize complicated lyrics was almost as astonishing as his piano-playing ability. Soon he was also singing "Leaving on a Jet Plane," "California Dreaming," and his favorite, the Simon and Garfunkel hit "Feelin' Groovy."

It became a common sight to see a delighted little boy tromp-ing down the hallway or out on the playground swing singing, "Slow down, You're movin' too fast . . . I've gotta make the morn-ing last . . . I'm kickin' down the cobblestones . . . Looking for fun and . . . FEELIN' GROOVY!"

Inevitably, someone would be watching, captivated, whether it was a teacher, the parent of another child, or an outside visitor to the Center. It was as if they wanted some of what Rex had, some of that magical something that seemed to override limits, that seemed to take him outside his disability. As though Rex had a magnetic pull, anyone watching would normally struggle to tear himself from the sight, reluctantly leaving the child, the joy, and the song.

THE EFFECT my child began having on people wasn't limited to the Center but began rippling even farther. Rex was four and a half and needed his yearly blood test at Children's Hospital to check his endocrine status. Children with septo-optic dysplasia are often beset by problems with their endocrine system—everything from growth issues (necessitating daily growth hormone shots) to hypothalamus problems, resulting in such things as an inability to regulate body temperature. I'd even read an article written by a mother who had been devastated by the sudden death of her five-year-old son with septo-optic dysplasia when he'd spiked a fever of 108 degrees! Then there were the adrenal glands and the thyroid, which were also at risk, not to mention the threat of premature puberty (meaning really premature, like five years old!), or the possibility of not going into puberty at all (necessitating shots in order to continue physical and mental development). Thankfully, Rex didn't have any major endocrine dysfunction yet! But he continued to be at risk, and his endocrinologist said he could develop more serious issues at any time. Again, the research was too recent to know definitively, but that's why his condition needed to be monitored.

My boy often had a sort-of musical gait when he moved, which matched the bouncy tone in his voice. That was the way he was moving as we reached the front of the hospital. As for me, I was rigid, as I always was when I came to Children's Hospital, as though that would help keep things in control in the place that had thrown our lives so utterly out of control. Hospitals represent the stuff of a mother's nightmares. As if on cue, my pulse began to race the moment we passed through the front doors. There had been too much pain here, and it was that memory of suffering and trauma that invaded my whole being as we headed down the long, stark entrance hallway. Rex normally became extremely agitated as well, once the loud, painful sounds of this place hit him, with his own memories of being restrained in order for someone to poke or jab him or otherwise inflict "torture." I was prepared for the worst.

But this time a different scene was to unfold, one filled with healing. We were sitting in the laboratory waiting room, waiting for the nurse to call in Rex. The room was full of people deep into their own thoughts, filled with their own pain. It was always the same at Children's Hospital, where the patients were the innocents. Everyone seemed to be really hurting: the kids, the parents, and even the staff.

Nobody in that waiting room comprehended what they were suddenly witnessing, least of all me. A beautiful little boy, with silken blond hair, had stood up from his seat and, oblivious to anyone's worries, began to sing. Rex! His voice was pure and sweet, like his face, and the clarity of the tones began drawing the people in the room out of themselves. I watched furrowed brows soften and clenched jaws broaden in wonder. They could see he was blind, indeed it was impossible to miss by the way he'd stood up with his hands feeling for support and by the way he stood there with precarious balance, his eyes seeming to focus only on the unseen. So the spectators were all the more stupefied as they witnessed something akin to true sight when his voice sang out, angelic and in perfect pitch, "God is so good. He's so *good* to me." As he finished, the whole room broke into applause, amazed and spontaneous, while Rex beamed and clapped for himself, as he so loved to do, pronouncing, "'God Is So Good' is a beautiful song!" When he heard more clapping, he repeated for emphasis, "'God Is So Good' is a beautiful song!"

I knew from the reaction in the room that I didn't need to tell Rex quietly, "Sweetie, we need to wait until we get to the car to sing." I also knew he was in the mood to sing, which meant he'd inevitably launch into another song. Not wanting to impose religion on the room in the form of our church songs, I whispered "Feelin' Groovy" as a suggestion. But not this time, not in this place. Rex clearly had ideas of his own, and apparently it wasn't a 1970s carefree kind of day. Ignoring me, he announced decisively, like he was a singer on a stage, "This Little Light of Mine." Without a moment's hesitation, he broke into the sweetly moving song, which was one of his Sunday school favorites. As he finished the refrain, "Let it shine, Let it shine, Let it shine," the applause was renewed, even more vigorous this time, from patients and staff alike, while Rex smiled broadly, loving it. I glanced around the room to see the most astonishing mixture of smiling faces and moist eyes as his captive audience shook their heads in amazement at this beautiful and unexpected scene.

And with that I knew I'd received the unexpected myself—an unexpected healing. My old ghosts were finally being laid to rest, as my heart that had been battered and bruised in this hospital, on so many occasions, now soared on the light of Rex's smile.

Let it shine, Rex!

THERE WAS going to be a special musical event held at the Blind Children's Center a couple of months before graduation day in June. All I knew was that it was a concert for kids only, and I assumed that whatever it was, Rex would enjoy it. Since parents had not been invited, I dropped Rex off in his classroom and then left to run errands. But out of curiosity, the unavoidable curiosity one experiences when being specifically excluded, I returned to the Center to see if I could "accidentally" catch the end of the "kids only" concert. As I entered the lobby, I could hear strains of guitar music coming through the closed door to the reception room where the concert was going on. It sounded like a Barney song, but I'd never heard Barney sung and strummed like that before. It was smooth and jazzy, in a pop jazz sort of way. Suddenly, like the songs Rex had been singing of late, the singer's voice snapped me back to 1980 and the unmistakable voice of Kenny Rankin. All my college friends had listened to his light, airy pop jazz, which had captured the mood of that era so perfectly. Back then, it had been "date music." But today, Kenny Rankin was using the power of his voice, his music, in a different way. Not to warm the hearts of young lovers, but to put smiles on the faces of blind preschoolers.

I sat there through another song, wishing I'd been invited along with the kids, when the door opened. The concert had ended, and as the kids started heading back to their classrooms, the executive director of the Center saw me and beckoned for me to come into the "concert" room. She was effusive. "Cathleen, I told Kenny about Rex's music, and he'd like to hear him play something. Would that be okay?"

My son, playing for Kenny Rankin! It would certainly be okay with me, but Rex might be disturbed by the change of routine, routine being so important to his sense of balance. It was recess time now, not staying-inside-with-Kenny-Rankin time. Predictably, he began whining as I detained him at the door, while his classmates headed outside. Kenny saw him then and rushed over.

"Hi, pal," he said. "My name is Kenny, and I hear you're a little musician."

Rex didn't answer, so I did. "This is Rex."

"Well it's nice to meet you, Rex," Kenny said. "You want to play some piano for me?" Rex's face was blank. Kenny led him over to his guitar, which was positioned on a chair. He took Rex's hand and placed it on the guitar strings. "How about the guitar? You want to play the guitar, Rex?"

Pulling his hands away immediately, still defensive, Rex said, "Don't want to play the guitar!"

"Okay, well how about if I play the guitar?" Kenny asked, strumming a few chords. Rex relaxed instantly, as though he'd been tapped by a magical wand, all tension seeming to melt from his body into the richness of the chords. I was kneeling down to be eye level with my son as he stood leaning against me, when

Kenny began strumming a familiar song. It was his own version of the Beatles' classic "Blackbird," with the words from the past fusing into the present—haunting and prophetic. I felt a lump forming in my throat as Rex stood spellbound listening to words that could have been his own: ". . . take these broken wings and learn to fly."

The image of the blackbird crying out into the depths of darkness in lonely desperation hit me in the heart with a longing so intense I had forgotten the whole point of this encounter had initially been Rex playing the piano. But Rex hadn't forgotten, and using his name in third person as he always did, he said, "Rex wants to play the piano."

"Great pal let's hear it!" Kenny said.

I led Rex to the piano. His fingers struggled to depress the keys of this acoustic instrument, since he was used to the electronic ease of his piano keyboard at home. At first he wasn't getting any sound, but then he struck harder with his fingers, determined. Notes at last! He knew what he had to do now to make the notes, and they began filling the room. I immediately recognized what he was playing, as did everyone else in the room—Kenny, the executive director, and some administrative staff members who'd come in as the first few notes had been struck. It was the ultimate song of God's transforming grace, "Amazing Grace." It didn't matter that he was missing a note here and there on those stubborn keys as his sweet vibrato voice hit the final:

> I once was lost, but now I'm found,
> Was blind, but now I see.

I looked to see Kenny utterly speechless, his eyes brimming with tears. This brilliant musician had come to share his gifts with the children at the Center, and as I watched him rub his eyes with a hand, I knew Rex had given him a special gift back. Was Kenny's song like my lifelong prayer for my son? I didn't know, but what I was sure of was that Rex was answering that prayer through grace, as had God when He sent His Son.

IN THE weeks leading to Rex's graduation day, I had become more and more emotional. This was more than preschool graduation; it was graduation from the Blind Children's Center. Since all parents get choked up and nostalgic when their children reach big milestones, I knew that part of the reason for my increasingly frequent crying spells was a normal reaction to "my baby" growing up, but I also knew that my emotions ran much deeper.

The big day came and there was a buzz in the air at the Center. Emotional parents, excited kids donning blue caps and gowns, and media cameras rolling to capture the event for the evening newscasts. The mayor was even there to present the diplomas. Colored balloons floated in the air, attached here and there, with rows of tulips adorning the stage. As I sat in my front-row seat, my older brother, Alan, poised with his camcorder and tripod off to the right to capture the event, I knew all the fanfare was to say to a group of blind five year olds, "You made it! Now you're ready for the real world." That was a pretty big message. I also knew how close we'd come to not making it, how close we'd come to being broken in this place. I shuddered briefly at the thought. Like one tottering on the edge of a cliff, it would have been so easy just to topple over. Rex's life might have ended before it had even begun. But it hadn't, and here we were! This morning I had wondered about so many details surrounding this day: Would the sun be too bright, bothering Rex's eyes? Would the ceremony be too noisy? How about microphones screeching in his ears? Would they be able to get his graduation cap on his sensitive head? These were issues that still plagued us, still needed to be worked with, but suddenly none of it mattered. *We were here!* That was all that mattered. With my heart pumped full of that amazing grace Rex had sung about, the ceremony began.

Music played as all of the Center's student body marched out with their respective teachers. First came the parade of babies, with their teachers and mothers, the Mommy and Me class where we'd begun, then on up through the years. There was a three-year-old using his cane to guide his class, others holding the hand of a teacher. Then came the graduates, wearing caps and gowns of royal blue. I'd never seen graduation gowns on preschoolers before, but somehow it seemed fitting here, and they all looked so proud in them. Rex's class came last, and he brought up the rear, with his head bobbing ever so slightly to the beat of the music, the tassel on his cap jiggling as he moved.

Arranged by class, the students sat down on wooden blocks skirting the parent chairs. Each class had prepared a song for the ceremony, and Rex would be singing a solo during his class presentation. But before the kids took the stage, I was to take it myself. Each graduation the Center chose a parent to say a few words, since they knew it was as much our graduation as our kids'. We had all grown in ways we hadn't thought possible. As I stood on the stage, I looked first at the parents, so full of their own emotions, then at members of the teaching staff, who'd become like family over the years, then finally at the kids themselves. My eyes panned from the babies all the way over to the graduates, but it was my own son I was seeing in each face, the kaleidoscope of his years parading in my mind's eye. I took a deep breath, pulling myself together, and then I spoke.

"I remember the first day I walked through the doors of the

Blind Children's Center as though it were yesterday. And yet, it was over four and a half years ago, a lifetime ago. Rex's lifetime." I looked once more at the babies, so like my son in the beginning, then back at the parents, and continued, "Rex was barely five months old at the time, and the world as I'd known it had been shattered two weeks before in the space of an instant by a doctor's blunt words: 'Your son is blind.'"

I went on to pour out the emotions of the journey of those four and a half years, and to thank the teachers and staff at the Center for helping us make it through. Holding back my tears, I said, "Thank you for helping me see the child Rex, to hear his laughter and to see how the similarities between him and other kids far outweigh the differences." Like a family, they had seen me through sorrow and had shared my joy when things started turning around. I looked around the emotional crowd that seemed to be hanging on each word, and I continued, animated. "Thank you for helping Rex fight the monstrous odds he faces each day."

As I stood there speaking, I knew the future was holding out its hand to us, beckoning. The "real world" outside the safety of the Center, which had once been so scary and chaotic, now seemed to hold promise. And the light of that promise seemed very bright from where we stood today—on the other side of darkness. My voice swelled as I thanked the staff a last time and thanked the other parents. I was just getting ready for my final, very special thank-you, when it suddenly became too much, the feelings too intense. My voice began shaking, my knees buckling. Five years of raw emotion swept over me in a torrent as I fought to keep from breaking down. I paused to steady myself, my eyes sweeping the audience to give me time, and then they came to rest on a little blond graduate. He was flicking the tassel on his cap with the back of his hand. My eyes blurred, seeing those perfectly formed baby hands reaching out for me that first time, almost five years before. Then, with my heart full and my own hand extending out toward him in honor of his being, I spoke my final words. "And thank you to my own little sweetheart, Rex, my hero. I want everyone here to know what I tell you every day: I am *so* proud of you!"

"I am *so* proud of you!" Those six words played over and over in my mind as I waited for him to take the stage. Then I saw Rex trooping onto the graduation stage with his three class-mates and teacher. Of course, it was no surprise to me that his class would be singing a song from the '70s, and for this big event it would be Three Dog Night's "Joy to the World." And my boy would be singing a solo. The crowd was expectant. Then the foot stomping began, with Rex ready to burst from excite-ment, as they sang of a world full of girls and boys and fish and joy!

Rex looked like he'd split his seams from the thrill of it all, clapping his hands to the beat. Then as leader of the band, the child they'd thought would never speak, shouted, "One more time" into the mike. *One more time! Just to show them that you can, show them it's real, is that it? No more crisis of doubt, just give 'em all you've got, Rex!* After another chorus it was his solo, and with his teacher holding the mike up to his mouth, and belted out the lyr-ics like a rock star:

"If I was the king of the world . . ."

Yeah! This time I was the one ready to split my seams with pride as my son finished his verse and the crowd came to their feet, cheering. Then the class hit the final chorus amidst a jumble of Rex jumping up and down, stomping his foot, and clapping his hands, somehow all at the same time. It was his exclamation point to say, "I really made it!" Now he would be moving forward, beyond these walls. By the looks of it, I believed he'd be clapping and stomping his way full-speed ahead into the world of the sighted!

CHAPTER EIGHT

The Real World

You too must not count too much on your reality as you feel it today,
since like yesterday, it may prove an illusion for you tomorrow.

—Luigi Pirandello

That summer, Rex learned to ride a bike, just like other kids, sort of. It was hard to believe how far he'd come, far enough to be pedaling an adaptive bike. It was actually a three-wheeler with a backrest to aid his posture and Velcro straps to keep his feet from sliding off. But it was shiny and red and had a bell, and he loved it just as much as any other five-year-old loves his first bike. It took some work to get his feet and legs to move the pedals at first, because he did not really understand the motion, but he got it. On the other hand, his balance was surprisingly good, and he became very adept at steering, adjusting the handlebars "just a tad to the right" or "a smidgen to the left," as I guided him with my voice. If he made more than just that slight adjustment to keep him in a straight line, he'd throw the bike into a sideways tilt and fall over.

His favorite place to ride his bike was near our house down the roadway that skirted the beach. The "beach road"—that's what we called Latigo Shore Drive. It was a private road with few cars. But it had lots of warped pavement with cracks and odd tilts and slants that made Rex's rides more harrowing, challenging, and, to my surprise, more fun. He loved all the rockin' and rollin' that the aging and weathered road gave him on his little bike. When his legs would tire, he would a rest in the sand, listening to the "small, rippling" waves or the "big, booming" waves, depending on the day. Then it'd be back home for some rockin' and rollin' of a different kind. It was time for more piano and his latest musical passion—the Beatles. The sun had barely set on his pre-school graduation, and the '70s music was out in favor of the Fab Four! Even his classical favorites, Mozart and Beethoven, couldn't compete with such Beatles tunes as "Here Comes the Sun" or "Let It Be." Not that summer. He was just being a five-year-old. It was a summer of bikes, the beach, and the Beatles. Life was sunny, and he was feelin' groovy!

LABOR DAY signaled the end of summer, and the back-to-school bell was about to ring in the first day at Rex's new school. Older kids were rushing to their classrooms, while the younger ones walked more tentatively with their parents. But all were excited to find a new class, meet a new teacher, make new friends. I'd brought Rex in early, not knowing the routines or how long any of it would take, and so we were sitting on the classroom rug waiting. Ten more minutes until the bell was scheduled to ring.

A little girl saw Rex and ran over and plopped down on the floor next to him. She was long, lean, and very pretty, probably a couple of years older. "Can he see?" she asked me. "Is he blind?"

Not what I was expecting. I steadied myself before responding, "Well hello. What's your name?"

"Cindy," she answered.

"Well, Cindy, this is Rex, and no he can't see in the same way you and I can see. And yes, he is blind, which means he uses his hands or his ears to be his eyes."

She peered closely into Rex's face, which was slightly downcast, obviously trying to get a look at his eyes. She had to lower her own head to see them. "But it looks like he can see." I assumed she was referring to his open eyes.

It had been innocent enough, a child's curiosity. Her questions had just caught me off guard; I wasn't expecting it on day one in Rex's new classroom. The teacher must have said something to his new classmate, and she would do the same with the other kids in the class. That was normal.

Cindy had obviously been caught by surprise herself on her first day of school. She seemed stricken by the idea of her new classmate being blind. "I didn't know a kid could be blind," she said quietly.

As Cindy jumped back up to join two other students, having obviously satisfied her curiosity, I realized I didn't know how to educate kids about blindness. We were clearly entering a brand-new world. But this was the first day of kindergarten, and it was an exciting new world. It *should* be exciting! Here we were in the real world outside the walls of the Blind Children's Center, and although the children in Rex's classroom all had some kind of special needs, it was in a regular school with "regular" kids. *It's a new miracle just being here*, I thought to myself. But still, I couldn't quite ward off a sense of foreboding.

I HAD begun the search for a new school for Rex six months before his preschool graduation. Given his significant needs, I was sure it would be a formidable task finding a school that would be able to educate him. The whole process made me nervous and worried, but in the parent support groups at the Blind Children's Center, Miranda had told me the best way to do it was to compile a list of potential school programs and then go visit them. Seeing the classroom would be telling, and hopefully I'd find one to fit.

After some research into what was out there, I came up with three options—three very different types of programs that might be able to educate Rex. I made school visits to each. The first was to another school for the blind, similar to the Blind Children's Center but for elementary-age kids. Like the Center, it had the advantage of a highly qualified staff to work with the students. I definitely liked the idea of specialists working with Rex, but it was very far from our home, which would mean more years of commuting. Not at all what I wanted. As I was walking to visit the kindergarten facility, I passed a classroom of older students. The line of white canes the students had hung next to their classroom door suddenly spoke to me of isolation. This school wasn't in his community, and it would keep him segregated from his sighted peers who made up the rest of the world. This school couldn't allow him to mix or teach him how to socialize in a real-world situation, which was what he would need when he left preschool.

The second option was another specialized school, but this one worked with children who had various disabilities, a generic mix of children with differing mental and physical disabilities, such as cerebral palsy, mental retardation, or autism. Autism! Even though it had never been officially added to his educational diagnosis, which stood as "multiply disabled," Rex exhibited a fair number of autistic behaviors. There were all his repetitive body movements, his echolalia and scripted speech patterns, and, of course, his "raw" sensory system which created hypersensitivity in his hands and ears. So in spite of the fact that he could socially connect to people in a way many others with autism could not, I couldn't deny he was "on the autistic spectrum," as they put it. Autism was a part of those "multiple disabilities," and a pretty substantial part. I had finally come to accept it. Having been in denial for three years, I had finally come to see the truth in his teacher's frightening assessment of then-eighteen-month-old Rex—"I'm afraid Rex is autistic." I wasn't ready to hear that back then; it was too much, too soon. I simply couldn't handle it. But now I accepted the term "autistic," having grown into it because it was part and parcel of the child I loved so much. And now I was determined to use it only as a source of understanding, a springboard to work from, not in any way as a label that would limit my son.

This school had been suggested to me as a way to address Rex's other non-blindness issues in a singular setting, meaning on-site access to speech, occupational, and physical therapists. In a word, this school was supposed to address the autism aspect of my son. I knew that Rex would benefit from the expertise of staff trained to work with all sorts of mental and physical issues, in addition to blindness, so I made the visit. But when I got there and took one look at the massive concrete structure, I felt my head spinning. It looked more like an institution than an elementary school, with its wide hallways filled with wheelchairs and children wearing protective helmets. Did that mean children were here who had aggressive behaviors in addition to everything else? I wanted to flee as fast as I could, but I felt unsteady on my feet. Staggering back to the car, I slumped into the seat, nauseated and scared. It had been a very big strike two, with just a month to go until Rex's graduation from the Blind Children's Center.

Then I made my third visit. Walking into a garden perched atop a Malibu hillside, with rows of carefully tended flowers and greenery, I stared out at a breathtaking sweep of ocean down below. *Had I taken a wrong turn somewhere? Gotten the address wrong?* My feet were floating more than walking; I felt as if I'd arrived in some sort of paradise. But this was the right place. On this scenic road overlooking the vast Pacific, it was the school I was looking for, located only five miles up the coast from our home. From the moment I set foot on the campus, I held my breath, wanting so much for this to be the place, and not a mirage.

Could a place this beautiful really have a program suitable for Rex? It was a public school just a stone's throw from our house where our neighbors' kids went. Could it possibly be the one?

I'd learned everything I knew about the education of the disabled from parent support groups at the Blind Children's Center. They taught us the intricacies of the system in order to empower us to help our children. We the parents would need to protect our kids once they left the protective walls of the Center. We would need to be their advocates. The Center had taught me about the big shift in education since 1975, when the groundbreaking legislation whose acronym is IDEA became law. IDEA stands for Individuals with Disabilities Educational Act, and it assured children with disabilities a "free and appropriate" education in the "least restrictive environment" possible. The statute states that the public school system will pay to provide all support necessary for each child's needs. The "least restrictive environment" clause focused on the importance of socialization for children with disabilities. Simply put, the law was intended to get the disabled out of institutions or specialized schools, like the schools for the blind, and integrate them into typical classrooms in regular schools to the greatest degree possible. Ideally, it would help children with disabilities learn to function in a real-life setting with nondisabled peers in order to help prepare them for the real world. The goal at the Blind Children's Center was to help our blind kids be normal, or at least fit in as best they can—and that's what I dreamed of for my son.

Prior to IDEA, there had not been any educational equality for the disabled, and a child like Rex might not have received an education at all. Or if he were able to attain anything, it would have been in an institutionalized setting; perhaps similar to the school I'd just visited, which was equipped to address his heavy-duty issues. But the law was clear—discrimination on the basis of disability would not be tolerated, and no child would be neglected in government-funded facilities because of a disability, no matter how severe. The burden was on the schools to meet the needs of our children through the provision of an appropriate program and extra supports necessary for each child to function within his school placement. The law was obviously a big social victory for the disabled and for their parents. We the parents were to be included in the whole educational process, from finding a program to helping set priorities and goals for our children. The law itself empowered the parents by making us important members of what would become an educational team. The teacher wouldn't be a lone gun but would be the head of a whole team, where collaboration would be the key to success. Information and expertise would be shared to support the child. Since I had long been aware that it took not only a village to raise Rex but a highly skilled village, I loved the idea of teamwork among specialists. The law was behind me, it was behind Rex, and so maybe . . . just maybe . . .

I'd stopped in the front office and gotten directions to my destination, Room 30. As I walked down the corridor to the classroom, I passed the playground. Kids were rushing to form lines. As I watched a little boy, maybe a first grader, race back up to the top of a winding slide for one last go, just beating his teacher's whistle, I was praying for nothing short of another miracle. My heart was aching for it. I wanted Rex to come to this school, make friends with these kids, be a part of the real world.

I stopped for a moment to watch the kids as they waited in their lines, and I was approached by a woman whose smile preceded her. I felt as though she fit in this place of sunshine and flowers, where the corridors were lined with such neat rose gardens. In fact, she looked to be someone who must love flowers and dogs and children—and who was loved back. Extending her hand, she introduced herself. "I'm Pat Cairns, the principal."

Well I'd been right; she did fit in this school like a hand and glove. "Cathleen Lewis," I said in return, shaking her hand. "I've come to visit your special-ed program for my son Rex." And then, feeling the need to explain, I continued. "He's blind, and . . ." I paused for a second and then voiced what I hoped wouldn't exclude him from her school, "and multidisabled."

I searched her face for a reaction, but there was none. She smiled again and said, "They told me in the office you were here, Mrs. Lewis, and I think you'll find we have a lot to offer Rex." She used his name with such loving ease. She also caught my look of longing as I glanced one more time at the kids on the playground. "And they say, here at Cabrillo, we have the nicest students in Malibu because our kids are used to being around children with disabilities."

As I listened to her, it was obvious this woman loved children of all abilities. It was in her voice and on her face, like she wanted this to work out for Rex as much as I did. She told me that all the children in Malibu with disabilities were grouped in this school, and that there were two different classrooms on the campus solely devoted to special ed, along with a lot of other services they would be able to offer Rex. "Room 30, where you're headed, is a special day class with intensive services."

"What, exactly, does that mean?" I asked hopefully.

"It means that all the students need supports such as speech or occupational therapy, and maybe physical therapy, along with academic help. Of course, the district would also provide your son with vision specialists, who would come here to work with him and consult with his teacher as well."

It all sounded great, with therapists to address feeding and use-of-hands issues as well as communication. Plus, Rex would also have the vision support as he had at the Blind Children's Center. That meant Rex would receive orientation and mobility training to help him learn spatial concepts and how to use a cane to navigate

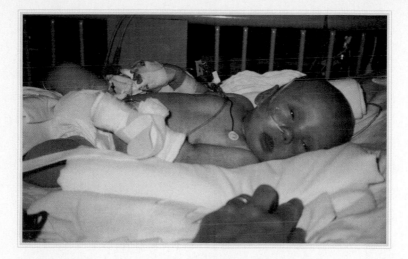

Rex's eyes were frozen, transfixed on me, as though he was just waiting for an explanation . . . but how do you explain invasive brain surgery to an 8-week-old baby?

Here we were at home, right after learning Rex was blind. But "at home," and the safe refuge that implied suddenly seemed to have no meaning. How were we to go on in a world that was suddenly so unsafe?

"It's my party and I can cry if I want to." Rex turning one at the Blind Childrens Center.

We came here to his favorite park almost every day to swing, hopeful he'd take his first step. "You can do it Rex! Just lift your leg and put it forward." Rex, however, remained obstinate in his refusal to budge or be budged without his legs going spaghetti.

Why do they keep tricking me into putting my hands in this stuff? This 2-year old does not like finger-painting!

Saving sensitive hands for the piano? Two-year old Rex testing the limits of the Blind Childrens Center piano, with Barney the Bear standing guard.

"No more spaghetti legs for me, thank you very much"! Three and 1/2 year-old Rex walking proud along his home beach.

Above: Rex has always loved the water, fearless in the pool with mom and inner tube

Below: "Just when I've got this walking thing down, leave it to Mom to put me on wheels"!

Above: Rex gets a winner's hug from mom, after completing the 1 K walk/run at The Long Beach Marathon for team Blind Childrens Center.

Right: A moment unto itself at home for Mom and 4-year old Rex. With love and laughter, all the rest doesn't exist.

Above: Rex demonstrating his "difficulty crossing midline" has no place at the piano as he executes effortless crossovers, and floats up into that world where disability doesn't exist.

Below: Proud Blind Childrens Center preschool graduate Rex, ready to take on the sighted world.

Above: To Rex, my hero. I want everyone here to know what I tell you every day. I am so proud of you!"

Below: "We did it Rex"! Rex with Mom and Uncle Al proudly showing off his preschool graduation diploma.

Below left: Rex taking the lead! He discovered newfound freedom now that his hands will actually hold a cane. Leaving playground swings behind, he is proud to change roles with his faithful friend and aide KD, who is used to guiding Rex around.

Below middle: Leaving hard school days behind, Rex takes refuge in the world where he is at ease. Like a great artist standing before his palette. "He sees all the colors, each subtlety, instantly, while the rest of us see only black and white."

Below right: "Feelin' Groovy! A new big boy bike, the beach, and Rex barreling down the boardwalk to the beat of life!

Above: Rex not only lives piano, but dreams it as well, and at times turns it into his bed. "Mom, I know it's past my bedtime, but I think if I just rest for a second I can play my new Beethoven Sonata one more time!"

Below: Mother and son—an unbreakable bond of love. The one absolute.

Above left: Rex takes to the slopes at Park City, Utah. "I think I've got the hang of it. Now can I bomb down the mountain"?

Above right: Now this is living! Rex bombs down the ski slope, lands in a heap, and begs for more—here with mom and National Ability Center Ski Instructor Don.

Left: Rex gets more skiing, and even puts sunglasses on for the photo op (before asking mom to take them back off his sensitive face)

After playing his piano for a Young Presidents Organization (YPO) Regional Conference in Arizona, Rex goes off-site and shows that the sky's the limit! Not only does he get to touch the clouds in his hot air balloon, but he has fun with Mom making a bouncy desert landing as other YPO Conference-goers touch down behind.

Above: Rex begins to travel—when in Paris . .

Below: In Paris . . .Rex does a happy Louvre pose with Mom, but will forego the master-pieces inside in favor of a jazz afternoon in the cross town Luxembourg gardens.

Above: Tokyo performance by night, visiting the city by day. Rex is intrigued by the sounds of the busy marketplace Asakusa.

Below: Taking it to the limit one more time! Rex is honored by Austin YPOs (Young President's Organization) to play on the famous Austin City Limits stage.

Rex sharing a laugh with older British counterpart Derek during filming break for Discovery Health documentary, "Musical Savants."

Above right: Rex taking on a sophisticated air as his music branches out into a new genre . . . jazz.

Above left: Rex's Time.

his way around his class and campus. It also meant he would have a teacher to teach Braille and skills such as tactile discrimination. Mrs. Cairns went on to explain that Rex's class would be made up of eight to ten kids of various disabilities and ages, ranging from kindergarten to fifth grade. They needed to group different ages together in order to get enough kids to justify the program, but each student would have an individualized curriculum.

I hesitated, almost not daring to hope for even more. "But will he be able to interact with those kids," I said, pointing out to the playground.

This woman was probably a mother herself, and she knew exactly what I was feeling. "Of course he will," she said, placing her hand on my arm in a reassuring gesture. "At recess, lunch, and then he'll most likely 'mainstream' for part of his day." She used the word I knew that meant Rex would spend part of his day in a regular classroom.

It was the perfect situation, a small classroom to provide him with the quiet environment his sensory system still required, while gradually allowing him to acclimate to more noise and "real life." Finally, in addition to all the other supports, if the team felt he needed it, a one-on-one aide would be hired to assist him throughout the day.

This caring principal walked me to Room 30, and as she delivered me to the teacher, her parting smile told me God had hit this one out of the ballpark!

THE TEN minutes were up, and the first bell rang in the day, but it wasn't easy to just leave—leave Rex. Did other parents have an easier time? I couldn't believe any parents of a kindergartner would feel any differently, even if their child didn't have special needs. It was more than normal for me to suffer the separation, with all of Rex's needs. Things had been different in preschool, where I could always go back and sneak a peek into his classroom to see how things were going. But this was a public school, and that meant parents weren't allowed to just drop in. I was really handing Rex over to his teacher, and it was very hard.

I'd met his teacher, Mrs. Spader, on three occasions already: during that first school visit, during the team meeting to plan Rex's goals for the year, and when she had made a home visit before the school year had begun. She had wanted to see Rex in his home environment, and I considered the visit a wonderful gesture on her part, promising a teacher who cared. She had watched in amazement as he played his piano, and when I asked if it would be possible to bring in a keyboard for him to have in the classroom, she said it would be great. All systems were go, and she was excited with the prospect of having a blind child in her classroom. A first!

I gave Rex a last hug, to reassure myself as much as him, then I extended his hand to his teacher. As I steadied myself to go, Mrs. Spader gave me a smile, a reassuring nod, and said, "He'll be just fine." Then she led him to a semicircle of chairs where the class would begin their day, while I backed up to the door, needing to see him up to the very last second before the door closed behind me.

Trusting that he would be okay was all part of the process of being a parent. I knew that. I also knew that all parents go through it to some degree, but with Rex's intense needs the whole thing was multiplied exponentially. However, during those first weeks I allowed myself to trust the system because I was trusting in God to watch over my little boy.

Rex became entrenched with his schedule, with all the specialists who came to teach him so many needed skills, and with his group classroom activities. He had been provided with a one-on-one aide named Khadevis, or KD for short, who helped him during the day. I had Rex's schedule written down and knew his days were full, but I found myself ignorant of what he was actually doing during all the different services and activities. Rex couldn't tell me, because his conversational skills were still extremely limited. When I tried to get specifics from Mrs. Spader at the end of each school day, she always seemed to be in a hurry. Granted, she was still in class with the older kids when Rex's shorter kindergarten day ended, but her manner also said, "You need to trust me to do my job." This wasn't the collaboration I had been hoping for, but I hung on to the small bits I did get. From time to time, she would tell me about some skill she was working on with him, such as learning the days of the week, but generally a "He's doing fine" comment was all I would get before she'd rush back into the classroom. I tried to tell myself that not being able to share my child's school day was normal, but then I would be reminded that other talkative little kindergartners could tell their parents the things Rex couldn't. What they did in school, what they liked or disliked, giving their parents at least the gist of the experience.

So one day, I pushed the matter with Mrs. Spader as she led my son out at pick-up time. "I would really like to know what skills you're working on with Rex, so I can reinforce them at home." Hadn't that been the philosophy behind education for the blind? Skills had to be reinforced around the clock.

Smiling at me, as though indulging a needy parent, she gave in. "We're working on a lot of independence skills with Rex. I'm sure you know how difficult that is for Rex, things like washing his own hands, hanging up his own backpack."

"Yes, of course I know. So how's he doing?"

She shrugged. "It's slow," she said. "But on the other hand, he has a great memory for numbers and rote sequences. He always knows the day of the week and the date. He's doing very well during Calendar. And in P.E. today, he really surprised us. Coach Gary had begun leading warm-ups by counting in different foreign languages. He did it for the first time yesterday, and today Rex was able to count along with him!"

Thinking he had probably counted along in Spanish, I looked at Rex and asked, "What did you do in P.E. today, sweetie?"

"I counted to ten in P.E. today," he answered. He went on to say, "And I counted to ten in German in P.E. today." Then Rex proceeded to list all the languages he had counted in: French, Spanish, Japanese, Hawaiian, Farsi, Russian, and Biepenese (I figured that might be Vietnamese). With the look of a boy with a big secret busting to get out, he said, "I want to count to ten in German."

Then as he began his counting, Mrs. Spader extended her hand toward Rex as if to say, "See for yourself, he's doing fine," and then waved to say, "Gotta go. Kids are waiting." The classroom door banged shut. I was dismissed. We headed to our car with Rex counting first in one language, then another, until he had exhausted his list of eight foreign languages! Order, tonal sequences, that's what he excelled in, but what about all the rest? What about speech? Communication with other kids? His involvement in the class?

Mrs. Spader had given me something to chew on, to keep me in a holding pattern, even though I had a growing sense I wasn't being included in his education at all. I let it go until a morning in late October. I had just gotten Rex out of bed, and he greeted the day in the usual way, with his calendar spiel. He said exactly the same thing every morning, just changing the day and the date. "It's a brand-new day, Mommy. What day is today?" Without taking a breath, he answered himself. "Today is Friday, and the date is October 19."

"That's right, Rex. It's Friday, and it's a brand-new and beautiful day," I said, adding some information. "So what's the weather like today?"

"It's sunny, Mommy! A beautiful day is a sunny day."

"Yes, it is. That's exactly what beautiful means here." I got his shirt ready for him. "Let's put your shirt on, sweetie. Left hand, right hand—over your head and . . ."

"Jump up and down!" Rex had the shirt on and was jumping up and down, loving the dressing game I'd made up to help him sequence his movements.

I continued. "Left sock, right sock, shoes on . . ."

"To beat the clock!" He was beaming and ready for the day.

"All dressed for your last school day of the week. And when I pick you up, before we come home, you have a birthday party to go to. Arthur's birthday. Won't that be fun?"

"That will be very fun!" he answered.

In fact, it was Arthur's mother who had invited us. They were our neighbors in our condo complex, and Arthur was in first grade at Rex's school. So she'd asked us to join some of Arthur's first-grade friends for a small celebration at the school.

I accepted gratefully, wanting so much for Rex to be included with other kids. That was the whole point of his going to the school he's in. Rex never talked about any kids at the school unless I asked him about a specific child. He could recite the names of all his classmates when asked, almost like they were numbers and not kids. Like the rest of his school day, I wanted to know. "Rex, can you tell me who your friends are at school?"

He was still revved up from the dressing game, but he didn't respond. I made the question more specific. "Rex, can you give me the name of one friend you have at school?"

"KD is your friend," he said, confusing pronouns as usual.

"Yes, of course KD is your friend, sweetie, but he's your aide. What kids are your friends? Can you give me the name of one kid who is your friend?" Rex grew silent, with a perplexed look on his face. "Who do you play with at recess?" I asked, trying to help him.

"You play with KD at recess," he said, again exchanging "you" for "I." The look on his face said he was hoping this was the right answer, the one his mother was looking for. Even though I felt my heart aching, I couldn't let it go.

"Okay, sweetheart, that's fine. I'm sure KD helps you swing

and play with the other kids. So what kids do you have lunch with?" When he didn't answer, I changed the question, making it unmistakably specific. "Who do you sit next to at lunch?" The tone of my voice had a slight tinge of frustration, in spite of myself.

"KD," he said quietly, sensing his mother wasn't happy about something.

Rex was so sensitive to my tone of voice; I didn't want him to feel anything other than excitement for his school day. As I drove him to school, I told him how much fun I knew school was going to be, all capped off by a birthday party! But the instant I handed him over to KD, I acknowledged my own thoughts, my concern about his reticence (or was it inability?) to talk about the kids in his school. I would have asked KD myself that morning, but I had been informed about the district policy that aides were not allowed to discuss their students with the parents. Only the teacher could do that. All of a sudden, that policy seemed absurd, even troubling, and I decided it was time I took a look myself at what was going on at school. Today was Friday, which was a minimum day, meaning the students would be dismissed right after lunch and the final recess. I would go in a little early and observe. Although I couldn't go into the classroom without a scheduled observation, no one could keep me from observing lunch and playground activities, visible as they were from the parking lot at the back of the school where the disabled parking spaces and school buses were located.

So there I was, parked and watching, waiting for the kids to come out for lunch. I felt excited and a little covert, but also anxious. Then I saw the door to Room 30 burst open, and just as a third grader named Justin was about to run off, a classroom aide slowed his movement. There were the other students and classroom aides, and they were all moving down the corridor toward the lunch area. But where was Rex? And where was KD? The other students had reached the picnic table, and Rex still hadn't appeared.

Just as I was about to go marching down to his classroom to find him, I saw the red ball on the end of his new white cane appear in the doorway, assuring the opening was obstacle-free. I had a proud catch in my throat as I watched him grip the cane his sensitive hands had refused to hold for so long. He stopped in the doorway, and KD handed him his baseball cap to protect his sensitive eyes. I watched as Rex put it on crooked with the backside smashed underneath. KD took the hat off and handed it to him again. He made another attempt, and this was better, a bit crooked but not scrunched up. KD helped him straighten it and gave him a high five. It made me smile, and Rex was smiling too, as his aide walked with him to the picnic table. It was obvious his aide knew well how to work with him, and they did look like pals walking along that corridor, just like Rex had said.

KD was pushing independence, I could see that as Rex led with his cane. This was good, but it seemed to take forever to get to the table to join the others. And then, when they finally got there, came an endlessly long process of getting him seated at the table, reminding me of his physical therapy sessions. Find the table, then the bench, sit down, swivel right leg, then left leg over to face the table. There it was, another sequence, but here it seemed interminable. KD gave him minimal assistance, and he finally made it. His aide then placed his lunch container on the table, and just as I was thinking how grateful I was he wasn't refusing to eat these days, Justin and another boy finished their lunches, having obviously gobbled them down, and ran off to recess. By the time KD unscrewed the top on Rex's container, two girls had left the table. I wanted to hold the kids there, or hurry Rex up; the whole thing was beginning to make me uncomfortable. By the time he had finally scooped his lunch onto his plate, the others had gone off to play. Off to play, while Rex's work was just beginning. There he sat, my little son, scooping and spilling and scooping again, eating his lunch all alone with his aide.

Finally he made it to the playground, where I hoped he would join some of the others to play. But each time he managed to catch up to a couple of classmates, they would be at the end of their activity and running off. I saw it on the climbing structure and the teeter-totter boat, as if he was out of sync and just couldn't quite get there in time. A student who wasn't in his class came up to him as he walked toward the swings, maybe to greet him. KD looked to be trying to facilitate interaction, to hold the boy there with Rex, but could keep him only a second before he ran off again. With only minutes to the bell, Rex climbed on the swing. As the other kids were now moving in the opposite direction, heading back toward the classroom, there he sat at the far extremity of the playground, swinging back and forth with the faithful KD. He seemed content in his own little world, with KD clearly filling in a lot of gaps. And once again, it was clear, his aide *was* his friend, but what about other kids? Was there not even one playmate? And as I watched my little boy being pushed by his tall companion, seemingly his only school friend, my heart ached for him, flooding me with an intense feeling of loneliness.

The bell rang, and Rex's classmates headed either for parent pick-up in the front of the school or to catch a bus at the back. I'd come from my observation point in the parking lot to walk Rex over to the birthday party. As we approached the picnic table, I was determined to help my son get to know some of the kids at Arthur's party. I was determined now to get him to be included with the others. The table was full of kids I didn't recognize, except for Arthur and his older sister. Arthur's mother was getting the cake out and passing around paper plates. It would be a simple gathering, and the good news was that the kids would obviously be captive here at the table, eating cake, and couldn't leave Rex in the dust. He would have a chance!

Rex and I sat at the end of the long table, across from a girl and two boys. My son looked small next to this table full of first graders, and Arthur was down at the far end. I asked the girl next to him her name. She looked shy and said, "Susie."

"Susie, this is Rex. Rex, can you say hello to Susie?"

He said, "Hi, Susie. It's nice to meet you. How are you today?"

"I'm fine," she said, giggling like a shy first grader meeting someone new.

Then I asked the girl across the table her name. She said it was Maria. Rex said, "Hi, Maria. It's nice to meet you. How are you today?"

"I'm fine," she said, giggling as well, but this time it was more amusement than shyness. I thought it was because Rex's voice still tended to be singsongy, especially when he spoke lines that were rote to him, like greetings. It sounded a bit robotic, I suppose, with the same tonal cadence repeating exactly the same words, like he was repeating lines from a script.

What happened next had a sort of surreal quality about it, it happened so quickly. Indeed, far too quickly. I turned to the boy across the table. His name was Drew, but this time when Rex repeated his scripted greeting, Drew didn't say he was fine. Instead, he began mimicking my son to his buddy on the bench next to him: "It's nice to meet you. How are you today?" This incited his friend to pick up the beat, and he began parroting Rex as well: "How are you today? How are you today?" Then they began laughing, making themselves hoot. Maria looked uneasy, having caught the outrage in my eyes. Before I could say anything, Rex had plunged his fingers into his ears, hiding from their taunting voices. But the boys were caught up in their own meanness. They'd found their mark, and they were going to drive it home now. Before I knew it, the boys had stopped the mimicking and had now begun whispering to each other while pointing at Rex, who was just now daring to pull his fingers out of his ears. Suddenly, Drew flung his hand out and began waving it right in front of my son's face. When there was no response from Rex, who obviously hadn't seen the hand, his friend did the same thing. And that really made them hoot!

I had felt hurt rising in me when they had first parroted my child's voice. But now, as Drew flung his hand out once again, a real bully on a roll, the hurt changed to rage. Standing up, I grabbed the waving arm as it approached Rex's face. "Stop it!" I shouted, his arm still in my grip. "What do you think you're doing? Do you think it's funny to be blind? To not be able to see?" I was looming over Drew now, having released his hand. "How dare you bully a blind child! How would you like to have to try so hard all the time? Yeah, you don't know anything about *trying*, do you?"

> "Stop it!" I shouted, his arm still in my grip. "What do you think you're doing? Do you think it's funny to be blind? To not be able to see?" I was looming over Drew now, having released his hand. "How dare you bully a blind child!"

The anger in my voice as I shouted made the boy shrink down and back into his friend's shoulder. No longer a bully caught up in automatic meanness, knifing until he drew blood, he was changing back into what he was, a six-year-old who had obviously not intended to take on an adult. He was a kid again, and I was an adult, and he got what that meant, murmuring, "I'm sorry."

With my eyes locked on the boy, who didn't dare look away, and barely controlling myself, I said, "How would you like it if your eyes were broken?" In one hurried movement, I whisked Rex off the bench and then, putting my arm around his shoulder, I hustled him away from that table. I needed to get him away, to get him home to safety.

CHAPTER NINE

Savant

The human mind—so mystifying in its capacity to accommodate
both disability and genius in the same person.

—Lesley Stahl, *60 Minutes* correspondent

Who was I kidding? Rex wasn't even safe in his own home. As I watched my son struggling to find his rocking chair in the living room, I wondered how many times I had walked him through the route—twenty-five, thirty times? Giving him the essential spatial indicators: pass the big fluffy chair (feel the wrought-iron frame), the coffee table (feel the stone edge), then turn left to the chair. Yet he did the same thing all the time—he got lost in this small room. He had made it past the coffee table, but then he had turned right instead of left, bumping into a plant. The leaves brushing his face made him stop, then take a step backward. But then, as though the plant would just go away on a second try and the rocking chair would magically appear, he stepped right back into the plant. Touching leaves again, he looked confused. *Where did the rocking chair go?* "The rocking chair is to your left, Rex," I said, trying to keep my voice level. "It's where it always is." Finally, he turned left, but he might have walked right in front of the chair if his right hand hadn't mercifully grazed the armrest.

On other days, without my help he might have circled the coffee table endlessly. It was like his brain was filled with spatial confusion. The routes I had worked on with him, again and again, came back randomly when he tried them on his own. Today, once he found the rocking chair, I watched him place his right hand on the first armrest, like I had shown him numerous times. A reference point. But instead of locating the seat and turning his body around in front of the chair so he could sit down, he swiveled his body in the wrong direction. That put him to the side of the chair, causing him to try to plant his bottom in open space! He just didn't get it! I couldn't just sit back anymore, not today, when I was still reeling from school bullies, and so I rushed to assist, to provide safety once again.

The only thing Rex could find easily in the room was his piano. It was uncanny, almost like that little keyboard was emitting an electronic pulse my son couldn't miss, and he would walk straight to it every time, sitting on his piano chair with ease. No randomness there! And there was certainly nothing random about his sense of space when he was seated at the keyboard. Each interval seemed to make sense to him, his fingers knowing how to jump to the notes he wanted, and his brain could relax and just "be." And he was safe. There at his piano he was safe.

It was the safety of that piano that I needed on what I considered my least favorite holiday, at least since Rex's birth. For the last five years I had considered Halloween a chore, an obligated ritual, unchosen and unwanted. Ghosts and goblins had been such fun for me as a child, but now they were just unseen costumes that meant nothing to my son. And what was trick-or-treating? Getting a bag full of candy he couldn't eat? But this year I had wanted to get him connected somehow to the holiday, at least to the social side. In the aftermath of those boys making Rex a target for ridicule, I accepted a mother's need to keep her son safe, to protect him, but I knew that withdrawal wasn't the answer. Somehow I needed to bring safety to the real world for Rex and for me.

Although ninjas and pirates had been popular the morning of his school Halloween parade, on this holiday of childhood dreams and fantasies, Rex had to go as what he was—a musician. Not just any old musician, but one he would really relate to. Who else but one of the Beatles? However, it wasn't the black suit or white shirt or even the Beatles bob hairdo that meant anything to him. It was only the mini-accessory guitar slung over his shoulder and the songs "Hey Jude" and "Yesterday" he got to play on his keyboard during his class party that allowed him to understand why he was supposed to say, "I'm dressed as Paul McCartney" whenever someone asked. Safe and yet connected.

Rex's school activities were followed by a Halloween party in our condominium clubhouse. It was a first for us, since I'd never dared come to such a party with Rex's ears still so sensitive. But this year, in the form of his keyboard, I'd found an entry point for us into that noisy environment. With swirls of ghostly white cobwebs hanging from the ceiling and jack-o'-lanterns flickering by the entrance door, I stood by Rex in the far corner of the clubhouse. With his costume accessory of McCartney's bass guitar lying next to him, he was filtering out the party din by playing "Let It Be" on the piano. As I took in the room—mostly adults, with a few kids—I had hopes of actually getting to know some of my neighbors tonight.

A couple who lived a few doors down from us meandered over, catching the last half of Rex's song. When he finished, the man said, "You've given 'in costume' new meaning. That was amazing." Rex seemed to be enjoying himself, proceeding through his Beatles repertoire, playing song after song, so I took the opportunity to leave him "safely independent" as I crossed the room to have a rare moment of adult conversation. After a couple of minutes of conversation, I was about to rejoin my son when I became aware of a tall gentleman a few yards from him. The man was dressed casually, slightly rumpled, with the look of an intellectual. His head was closely shaven, to within a mere quarter of an inch, with a balding half moon in the front. But what was more striking than his appearance was the intensity of his gaze. He was watching my son, transfixed. A neighbor named Rick said something to the man, but he didn't respond, so intent was he on studying a little blind boy playing a keyboard. Rex was oblivious to the rest of the party, but so was this man as he stood there, his eyes not wavering. I was just about to go introduce myself when a woman grabbed the man's arm and pulled him into her group.

The party was still in full swing, but it was after Rex's bedtime, so I unplugged his keyboard, getting ready to head home, when the man approached us. After a brief introduction that told us his name was Richard Morton and that he lived in the very front of the condo complex, he asked simply, "Has your son ever played a full-sized piano?" Without waiting for an answer, he said, "Because I have one in my apartment, and I think he might like it."

I asked this Richard if he was a pianist, to which he responded, "It's a passionate hobby, not my profession, but I'd love to have your son play my piano."

So I put the question to him. "Rex, would you like to play a real piano?" Using "real" as the word he would associate with an eighty-eight-key instrument.

"You would like to play a real piano," he answered. *You would like to play a real piano!* Even with pronoun confusion and echolalia combined to form a response, those words came straight from my son's heart. I would take him to play our neighbor's piano, but little did I know the dramatic events that would come into our lives as a result of this chance meeting at a party we almost didn't attend.

Two days later we were knocking on Richard Morton's door. His six-foot-three heavyset frame towered over my diminutive five-year-old, providing a striking visual contrast as we walked into the room where the piano was located. "I'm so glad you could come, Rex," he said, smiling broadly. Richard was dressed in baggy shorts and a T-shirt, standard beachwear, and in spite of the intellectual air about him, the excited twinkle in his eye gave him a childlike quality.

Rex laid his tiny fingers on the piano, and he became instantly captivated. This instrument had the rich tonal quality of a real piano, but because it was digital, he didn't have to fight with the keys to get sound out, and my son's usual light touch was sufficient. Absorbed into the rich resonance of the notes, his improvisations took flight.

Richard watched with a look almost as faraway and absorbed as the one on my son's face. "No one taught him how to do that?" he asked in disbelief.

"No. He's taught himself everything," I said. I also knew that Rex's home instrument would now need to be seriously upgraded.

"Unbelievable!" he said, shaking his head in amazement at Rex's mastery of the keyboard, the quality of the harmonies he was creating. After watching in silence for many minutes, Richard asked, "Rex, can I play something for you now?" I helped my son off the bench and onto my lap; then our host took his place.

He turned to us and said, "How about a little Bach?"

I repeated the question to my son. "Rex, how about a little Bach?"

Rex's answer was complete echolalia. "How about a little Bach?" he asked.

I nodded to Richard, and he said, "This is called the Goldberg Variation Aria: in the key of G." The Bach notes were light and ephemeral, hanging suspended in the air at moments, and the look on Rex's face said he wanted to rise up and grab them, make them his own, or maybe flit off with them. My son looked to be leaving his body there on his mother's lap, while his spirit flew free and weightless on the melody.

"Did you like that one, Rex?" Richard asked as the final notes came to rest.

"Yes," my son responded, in a trance.

Richard tried a couple of other pieces, but Rex started objecting very loudly, whining. So our host relinquished the bench back to his guest, otherwise known as my tyrant son. It was hard for Rex to be near a piano for long and not be the one doing the playing. I acknowledged he was a bit rigid in that regard, but it seemed to affect him so physically that I never went against his will. At home, nobody could even touch his piano in his presence. Now he was happily back in possession of those keys that were so essential to his being. But this time he didn't begin more improvising. Instead, the melody that came forth, rising up from the keys, surging from the depths of Rex's musical being, was what Richard had just played! He didn't have to trouble it out or listen to it a few times, as he'd done with far simpler songs in the past, but he played the Goldberg Variation Aria melody back almost verbatim! My son's tiny right hand had instantly replicated hundreds of notes, complete with intricate trills, while his left hand provided musically sound harmonies.

"How many times has he heard that piece?" Richard asked as soon as Rex had finished. It was a normal question, but the answer he got back was anything but, and left him dumbstruck!

Solemnly, I said, "That was the first time," feeling reverence was required. Tears were rising up at the feeling of being blessed to bear witness to something so phenomenal and holy. No one spoke then, as though words simply could not express what had just occurred.

I began taking Rex to Richard's house almost every day so he could play that piano he loved so. And the man who had studied music and musical theory in depth watched and assessed. He wasn't a piano teacher; he was a writer and the intellectual I had taken him to be, a Rhodes scholar. Richard's fascination in my son grew daily. After a couple of weeks he began explaining parts of my little boy's gift to me in musical terms.

"Not only does he have absolutely perfect pitch, but he has exceptional memory, and he can transpose a song instantly from one key into another."

"I get the memory," I said, "and perfect pitch is hearing a note and being able to replicate it exactly. But what does transpose mean?" I asked. I hurried to add, "In simpleton's terms, please," before Richard could hit me with an intellectualized explanation that would confuse me even further.

He thought for a moment, struggling to translate concepts that were second nature to him into terms a nonmusician would understand. His brow furrowed, perplexed by the challenge, but then his eyes lit up. "Imagine taking a word, say 'tambourine,' and spelling it. To transpose to a different key, you would replace each letter in the word with a letter of the alphabet that follows or precedes it by a given value. For example, shift up one value, and the *t* of tambourine becomes *u*, or up two place values and it becomes *v*. The *a* becomes *b* or *c* and so on."

I was beginning to get it, likening transposing to encoding.

Richard went on. "Then imagine being asked to shift every letter on an entire written page up or down three or five places in the alphabet and trying to spell without pause or time to calculate! That's exactly what Rex can do with the notes of a musical composition!" He was excited now by his own analogy.

For my part, I was dumbfounded as the complexity of it all was beginning to dawn on me. To do that, automatically and without reflection, would have to mean my son's brain was like a musical computer. All I could muster was, "But what does that mean?"

"It means Rex's musical brain is light years ahead of his motor, his technical ability to produce it." He looked at me intently. "His hands need some serious work to catch up. He needs a teacher."

Over the days that followed I was torn between wanting Rex's piano to remain "his," without outside interference and instruction, and a desire to help my son develop his obvious gift. The piano was his inspiration, and I didn't want it to become a chore. As with all the important things in our lives, I presented the situation to God through prayer. The answer that came to me was in the image of a little boy playing hundreds of Bach notes he'd just heard, pushing three fingers of his right hand into overdrive to stay true to the music, merely because he didn't know how to use his thumbs or pinkies.

Richard had been teaching little tidbits to Rex for weeks now, and I would have asked him if he would consider giving some more formal lessons, but he had to move from our condo to a location forty minutes away. He would definitely continue to work with Rex as time permitted, but I knew we needed a formal, local commitment as well.

Our search was over before it began. One Sunday at our church I asked the musical director, Lynn Marzulli, if he knew of someone who could teach piano to Rex. This devout man of God looked down at my little blond boy whom he'd seen around the church only from afar, reached into his pocket, pulled out a card, and handed it to me, saying, "Give me a call."

A few days later, after Lynn and I had both apparently prayed about it, we went for an "assessment visit." After driving up a long and winding road, through a rather precipitous canyon, we arrived at the musical director's house, rustically tucked away in the hills of Malibu. The house was perched on a hill, with the lushly green property more vertical than horizontal, plunging down a steep slope into a dry creek bed. Lynn greeted us at the front gate and led us through vines and thorny rosebushes and down some rather jagged and uneven stone steps to the "music studio," which was a small, windowed gazebo jutting out in space overlooking the stony creek. This man had the benevolence befitting the man of God he was, and I got the feeling he had accepted the challenge of potentially teaching my little blind son out of a sense of service. However, benevolence was quickly transformed to astonishment when he saw Rex demonstrate his piano skills. I realized it hadn't been what he was expecting, as I watched him rubbing his chin, pondering the unlikely pianist in his midst. He summed up the visit with, "He clearly has incredible talent. We just have to see where we can take it." And so we were on.

It was a magical setting, a musical gazebo in nature's palm, and Rex would come to call our twice-weekly drives to Lynn's house our ascents up "the magical, musical mountain." And so his formalized musical education began three months before his sixth birthday. The greatest challenges the piano teacher faced were more logistical than musical. It was a weekly battle between teacher and student—Rex would swat and tug at Lynn's arm, while the teacher would try to dodge the student's grabbing hands in order to demonstrate. To my amazement, Lynn took it all in stride, treating the grabbing, piano-possessive hands of this five-year-old as an integral part of a strange and fascinating package.

During the first lesson, Lynn played a C-major scale while Rex sat on the bench next to him, with me neutralizing my son's grabbing arm from behind. "Listen, Rex, to the notes," Lynn said. Then, as he played the notes, he named them, "C–D–E–F–G–A–B, and back to C. That's a C-major scale." By that time, Rex had managed to snake and squirm out of my grasp. Which meant as soon as Lynn said, "I will play the C-major scale one more time," the student grabbed the teacher's hand, blocking him. Without preamble, and with lightning speed, Rex's right hand hit the piano keys. And there they were, all the C-major scale notes, as if my son wanted to say, "That's easy."

Lynn raised his eyebrows, perhaps believing Rex had already been shown a C scale, and said, "That was perfect. Okay. Let me show you another scale then." His piano teacher hit a G note. "And this is a G-major scale," he announced. But before he could demonstrate, Rex's piano-hungry hand jumped the gun straight to the G note and he zipped through his own perfect G scale. "He knows his scales?" Lynn asked me.

"No," I said. "You just showed him his first one." I confess, musician that I'm not, I didn't even know what a musical scale was myself until that day. After that, I just sat back, letting the session flow, with the teacher's eyes growing wider with each passing minute, as my son proceeded through each of the twelve major scales in turn, after having heard that one single scale played that sole time.

Two weeks later, it was a lesson on the minor scales, but this time Lynn didn't even play a scale in demonstration, just a single C-minor chord. Rex's fingers again aborted any further demonstration by intuiting the accompanying scale himself. "Who showed him that?" Lynn asked this time, as though it was impossible that Rex could just play it from the chord. Again, the answer came back, "No one taught him that."

Because of the difficulty Lynn had playing his own piano for Rex during the lessons, he had devised a noninvasive way to teach him songs. He would record a "homework" piece onto a CD, recording a track with both hands together, and then tracks with the left and right hands separated out. That way Rex could listen to the piano on CD at home. Because of his exceptional memory and instant note recognition, he began "eating" musical compositions at a rapid rate—the very first week it was a Handel minuet in F; a week later it was a Bach minuet in G.

Lynn faced a major task in the beginning getting Rex to use his fingers properly. My son had come to his first lesson with only self-taught use (or non-use) of his fingers, having obviously never even had a visual example to emulate. That meant his hands were flat as pancakes, with thumbs tucked into his palms, and pinkies only dragging along as part of a three-group to play a note. In sum, he used three fingers on his right hand and two on his left to somehow play everything. So Lynn gave him numerous exercises to allow his fingers to gain speed and precision, and surprisingly, he loved all those finger drills. Or maybe not surprisingly, since that was what allowed him to play classical pieces that were becoming more and more complex each week, even though it would be almost six months before he would use his thumbs with any consistency.

During the same months we made our ascents faithfully up the mountain to study music with a man of God, there was a man of the intellect who was just as faithful in his weekly Saturday commutes to our home. Richard Morton's fascination with Rex had continued to grow, and he came to complement the lessons with Lynn by exposing my exceptional child to different kinds of musical harmonies and rhythms in order to challenge his brain. Not only classical, but jazz, blues, and the wide-open country rhythms of Aaron Copeland. Unlike Lynn, Richard would intellectualize about Rex's extraordinary piano skills, trying to grasp, to quantify and explain what seemed beyond explanation. As the weeks passed, it became apparent that the Rhodes scholar in Richard was hooked—like a mathematician on a complexly integrated equation, hooked at once on the potential of the child and on the intrigue he had stumbled upon. He saw it as destiny—albeit destiny with a double edge. He would say, "Part of me feels like I've won the lottery, and part of me feels like I've been drafted." Huge potential required huge responsibility. He saw Rex as an intellectual conundrum he wanted to understand.

With the precision of a mathematician, Richard would carefully and painstakingly plan out lessons, working out chord progressions and advanced musical theory, spending hours on concepts Rex would grasp instantly. Although Richard attacked the lesson planning with a scholar's vigor, trying to rise to the challenge of his student's musical intellect, it didn't take long before he realized that the success of his work was ultimately in its delivery! I clued him in pretty quickly that if he wanted to pass the lesson onto the child, he needed to become a child himself. Although it couldn't have been easy to park that massive intellect at the door, in order to enter into a child's world, that's what he did.

So each Saturday, I got to witness the astonishing transformation of a Rhodes scholar into a lumbering child there to play musical games with a five-year-old. The heart of the communication between teacher and student was in the music itself, speaking through a melody, a chord progression, or a chosen key. They would play back and forth, the equivalent of a musical conversation; Richard would play a line, which Rex would answer. Then Richard would lead somewhere musically, and Rex would pick it up and run with it. Almost like a chess game, Rex would strive to back his opponent into a musical corner, which would stump the teacher, leaving his fingers mute and frozen. Unable to make a move, the teacher would have to acknowledge, "I've got nowhere to go," causing the student to squeal and laugh, shaking his head back and forth with excitement, knowing he'd just made a "musical checkmate."

> *Music was like colors to him, and he could distinguish any nuance, any shade without hesitation, in the manner of a great artist standing before his palette.*

As the months went by, Rex's musical brain seemed to know no bounds. He easily learned the names for the notes and chords, the keys and chord progressions he heard so distinctly in his mind. Music was like colors to him, and he could distinguish any nuance, any shade without hesitation, in the manner of a great artist standing before his palette. That's the way Lynn Marzulli described my son's perfect pitch: "Rex sees all the colors, each subtlety, instantly, while the rest of us see only black and white." Like Lynn, Richard pushed Rex to develop his technique, in the hopes his fingers could catch up to the warp-speed growth of his musical brain. He moved Rex into exercises to facilitate playing more sophisticated pieces, not at all an easy task since he only had a finger span of a six-year-old to work with. By the time Rex turned seven, he was diligently working on left-hand leaps that would open the door to a world of waltzes and even the rhythmically more complex Chopin mazurkas. The "jump bass," up and down the keyboard, was the foundation for any such waltz or mazurka.

That's when the growing paradox of my son hit me full force. It was the vision of Rex's tiny left hand mastering precise two-octave jumps up and down the keyboard to a "1, 2, 3" waltz count that left

> *How could he have such a flawless sense of space when seated there in front of the keys and yet get lost in his own living room?*

me stupefied. Absolute spatial precision! How could he have such a flawless sense of space when seated there in front of the keys and yet get lost in his own living room? For an even more glaring comparison, I could visualize my son's hands getting lost on a single page of a tactual book—top, bottom, left corner, right corner, it was all a jumble in his brain. It was the same thing at a table; he was incapable of locating anything in a methodic manner—meaning sweeping his hand left to right, back and forth, beginning at the top of the desk and proceeding down to the bottom. Despite repeated instruction in just that, there was no methodology in Rex's search pattern, and each time he'd be asked to locate something, his pattern would morph into some sort of random jabbing with his hand, combined with partial sweeping of a minute fraction of the required surface. And yet, wasn't it the same discipline—spatial awareness? A single discipline meant a single area of the brain would be used; at least, that was the theory. How then could you have one specific part of the brain functioning so differently in "space-related" tasks at the piano and in "space-related" tasks elsewhere—running the gamut from hyperperformance to complete breakdown? I asked myself the question, *Could it be possible that when Rex played music, he was interpreting spatial distance in terms of tones instead of physical space, and as such, was operating from another part of the brain altogether?* A part that not only wasn't damaged, but that was hyperdeveloped?

The same question applied to finger dexterity and fine motor coordination. Why didn't Rex's coordination at the piano translate into other areas? He couldn't even unsnap his own pants, having neither the strength nor coordination in his fingers to do so. What was it in music that created such spatial order out of chaos in his brain and changed weak and fumbling fingers into vibrant strength? More important, how could music be used to accelerate my son's development in other areas?

Rex had just begun second grade, and Richard called me with a request. "Would it be okay to test some of Rex's musical skills, as a sort of assessment, during the lesson this week?"

It seemed like a normal request at the time. I didn't hesitate in responding, "As long as it doesn't tax Rex." I was jealously guarding the fun I knew my son had during those times with Richard, all the while secretly wanting to understand the extent of his gift myself.

"Don't worry," he assured me. "He'll have as much fun as usual with it."

Saturday came, and Rex was already seated at the piano,

playing, as he awaited his teacher's arrival. The usual knock came at the door. "Richard!" my son said, his voice brimming with anticipation.

I opened the door to allow Richard's large body and presence to enter. Normally he made a beeline for Rex and the piano, jumping right into the music. But today, he had a preoccupied look on his face. "I've begun doing research into perfect pitch," he threw out as a greeting. Then without so much as a hello, he went on. "And Rex's prodigious memory when coupled with his sophisticated harmonic sense and intervallic awareness . . ."

That's when he caught my "park it at the door" look, and it stopped him in mid-sentence.

"Oh, sorry," he said, flashing the boyish smile that was so endearing once he took off his intellectual hat. He had known for some time how he needed to shift gears in Rex's presence, and in my presence as well, for that matter.

Like an actor walking on stage, Richard went through an instant character transformation as he stepped over to Rex and gave him a big "squeeze" hug that lifted my son straight off the piano bench and into his bearlike arms. Richard was now like a big, oversized kid himself. Rex laughed a boisterous laugh as the big man set him back down.

Then as he often did, Richard began the lesson making up a tune and singing his sentences. Today it was:

> Rex, you're laughing!
> Oh yes, you're laughing!
> What a wonderful sound, that laughing!
> Ha, ha, ha, ha, ha!
> That means you're happy,
> You're ha, ha, ha, ha, happy!
> Let's play something happy!

Then Rex jumped in to the same tune:

> Let's play something happy!
> Major keys are happy;
> They make me want to laugh!
> Ha, ha, ha, ha ha!

He was playing a joyous melody as he sang the words, and Richard said, "That is very happy. Your G major is happy. But now let's play something sad!"

Rex instantly changed to a melancholic tune and said, loving the game, "Minor keys are sad keys; they make me want to cry." Then making a sad face, without stopping the melody, he exaggerated, "Boo, hoo, B minor makes me very sad."

"That's great Rex, now back to a happy D, please!" And the child was instantly playing in D major. The teacher was clearly assessing, even as the game progressed through different keys, the student never missing a beat. Richard had explained to me how he wanted Rex to associate emotion with music and had created the sad/happy game as it related to types of sounds and different musical keys.

Richard then led Rex through a music building game, showing Rex's ability to construct music from individual chords and notes, in the same way another child might snap legos together into a building. Richard clapped for his student's success as Rex finished with a chord progression. "Good, Rex. Now, if Beethoven had written that same thing as a waltz—one . . . two, three, one . . . two, three—what would it sound like?"

Rex struck the same chord progression his teacher had requested, but in waltz tempo now, instantly recognizing the song he was building. "It would sound like the 'Moonlight Sonata,'" he said as he played the famous notes.

"*Molto bene!*" said Richard, in the Italian my son loved so. "Now let's turn it into a song and sing along."

"*Adagio cantabile,*" said my son, caught up in this magical musical world. "That means 'slowly singing' in Italian."

Then as Rex began playing the waltz chords of "Moonlight Sonata," Richard began singing, "We're writing a song in the style of Beethoven."

Rex joined his teacher's singing. "Writing a song, and it sounds like the 'Moonlight Sonata.'"

As he joined his own pure soprano voice to his teacher's tenor, "We're writing a song, in the style of Beethoven, in the style of Beethoven," I wondered how it could possibly get any better.

I didn't have to wait for an answer. Richard said, "*Bravo, Signore.* Now let's finish *pianissimo.* Softly, Rex, softly."

And Rex countered with plans of his own, "*Non—forte!* Loudly! I want to play *forte!*" And he threw his whole body into the keys as he sang out, punctuating each one-beat syllable, as though it came straight from a waltz lover's soul—one . . . two, three, one . . . two, three. "WRITING a SONG! And it SOUNDS like the MOON light Son AAAA ta!"

There they were, the two of them, the oversized teacher with his balding head and the giggling, wiggling little boy at his side. It was like they were in an insulated capsule, a bubble world of their own. Childlike in their interaction, they seemed able to tap into something higher than intellect. With my son trailing out his last victorious "and Forte Son AAAA ta," I felt at peace, like I was in my own insulated capsule, untouched by the rest of our existence.

> *It was like they were in an insulated capsule, a bubble world of their own. Childlike in their interaction, they seemed able to tap into something higher than intellect.*

Then the bubble burst. Richard said, "Rex, you can play whatever you want now, while I talk with your mother. You did a great job." In the space of the four meters it had taken him to join me on the couch, he had snapped back into his intellectual garb, the magic gone. I couldn't help resenting it when he said, "Well that proves it." He seemed deep in his own thoughts, talking to himself more than to me.

"Proves what?" I asked, somewhat annoyed.

"I've been trying to figure out the significance of his musical talent and have begun networking. The science of it is almost overwhelming," he assured me, as if he was making mental calculations rather than communicating personal information to me.

Then, like a treasure hunter who had stumbled onto a priceless find and was staking a claim, he blurted out, "He's a savant! A prodigious musical savant." I sat there, mute, not knowing what that meant and not knowing what to say. He went on without me. "And there aren't more than twenty alive in the world today!"

Richard explained what it meant—a scientific anomaly, causing an extremely rare island of pure genius to exist in a sea of disability. It was simply too much for me to view my child in such terms. Like an oddity? An extremely rare and precious oddity? When all I had ever wanted for my child was normalcy?

IT WAS with my head still reeling and confused from Richard's announcement that I began the ascent up the mountain for a lesson with Lynn two days later. Maneuvering around hairpin turns, I was driving slower than normal because there was little visibility. September was typically a month of pristine days, but today the weather seemed to mirror my mind. It was the kind of day we normally got only in the springtime, with the coast submerged in dense fog. We called it "June gloom," and there were days when it never burned off. With my own mind so full of murk and confusion, I felt surely today would be one of those no-burn-off, depressing kind of days.

Rex was often exhausted from his days when I picked him up at school, and today his own fatigue seemed in keeping with my own. In an attempt to lift both my son and myself from the fog of our spirits, I began to sing our favorite driving-up-the-mountain song. "The long and winding road . . . to Lynn's house." Our car hugged the mountain on a sweeping right curve, slowed into a hairpin left that took us up a steep slope, and as we climbed, the thick soupy haze suddenly, and surprisingly, began thinning, the coast receding behind us. Just as we were readying for another mountain-hugging pull to the right, the sun burst through the haze, its luminescence staking a victorious claim on the mountaintop.

By the time we pulled into Lynn's driveway, the sunlight was practically blinding us with its intensity. No more room for stodgy spirits here. In much the same way, our drive today had taken us from dense murk to lightness and air, so the weight of my thoughts was all but gone by the time we arrived.

On this day, with Rex playing an arabesque far beyond his years and the sun's brilliant rays streaming through the trees, science was now only hanging on to the periphery of my consciousness. That's when Lynn turned to me, and for the first time in a year and a half, voiced his innermost thoughts about my son like a sacred confidence. "When I watch Rex playing the piano, it's as close as I feel I've ever come to God. It's like he has a direct connection to the Creator." There it was, absolute, without measuring stick or qualifying criteria, a direct counter to the science of it all. Hadn't I felt it too so many times, during lessons or at home, with heaven-sent notes cascading up and down the keyboard? Lynn continued speaking. "His brain is already wired with things it takes normal musicians years to acquire—he just hits a button and has immediate access to knowledge." I was hanging on his words. Then, with mock exasperation, he said, "It's depressing how easy it is for him! Look at me; I'm fifty. I've been a musician all my life, and I can't do some of the things Rex does automatically. That's depressing!" But he wore a smile that said Rex had wowed him once again, a smile that said the teacher stood in awe of the student, humbled in the presence of something higher than human comprehension. He nodded his head in acknowledgement, in reverence, and said, "Rex has a touch of the Divine."

CHAPTER TEN

A System Out of Touch

We find comfort among those who agree
with us—growth among those who don't.

—Frank A. Clark, author

Rex had the appearance of neither a musical genius nor a child touched by God as he stood outside his classroom door tapping his chin with his hand, repeatedly, mindlessly. It was one of his many stereotypical behaviors. I could see him from the parking lot, and I had no idea what he was doing out there since classes were in session. He was alone except for his new aide, who was perched on a nearby bench, ignoring my son, like she was waiting for something. I'd gone to school mid-morning, after discovering I'd forgotten to put Rex's hat in his backpack. His eyes would be too sun-sensitive without it, and so I'd come to deliver it. I watched for a couple of minutes, confused. What was he doing? Or not doing? I walked over to see what was going on, but his aide stopped me. "You can't talk to Rex. He's in time-out."

"He's in time-out?" I asked, surprised, thinking that for Rex "time-out" was probably about giving him a brain break. "What's he in time-out for?"

Before she could respond, the bell rang, and Rex's classmates filed out of the classroom. It was time for adaptive P.E., the reason for my rush to get my son's hat to him. I saw Coach Gary on the playground, waiting as the kids joined him. Just then, Rex's teacher stuck her head out of the door. If she was surprised to see me, she didn't show it. "Rex can come out of time-out now," she told the aide.

I stepped over to his teacher, who I knew hated being questioned, and repeated my question nonetheless. "Why is Rex in time-out?"

Still convinced "time-outs" for Rex would be used more as a break than punishment, I was taken aback by her answer. "He needs to learn how to take turns. He answers for other students during morning calendar, and he does the same thing during phonics."

"So you bring him outside and let him stand by himself, hitting his chin"? I asked, incredulous.

"We tried to keep him inside, turning him around in a corner for time-outs as we do with the other kids, but it doesn't work. The other students understand what facing a wall means, but Rex can't see the wall, and he can hear just as well from there. So he still interrupts. He needs to learn to work in a classroom setting," she said.

I was afraid to question any further because I always felt my parental input was resented more than anything else, with his teacher alternately snapping at me or indulging me as though I were a child myself, as she just had. She'd been doing the same thing since Rex entered her classroom in kindergarten, running the class with an iron grip without much room for outside input. It was far from the collaboration I'd been promised in the public school system, but I had to acknowledge Mrs. Spader had made gains in many areas with Rex. In spite of her strong-arm teaching style, my son had learned to feed himself, was learning to write in Braille (although he couldn't read back what he wrote, with fingers still too sensitive), and was learning phonics skills.

Stifling my desire to know more, having accepted the parent-teacher disconnect as the price I had to pay for my son to be in this school, I handed his hat to Mrs. Spader, saying, "Rex will need this for P.E."

She looked me in the eye and said, "Rex won't be going to P.E. today. He has to finish the work he missed during his time-out."

I glanced at my son, still mindlessly tapping his chin in the corner. Then I looked out onto the play field, where Coach Gary was just getting the kids ready to play kickball—Rex's favorite. I saw two of the older kids kicking the ball back and forth, like a soccer ball, as the coach set out the bases, and I snapped.

"Rex can't miss P.E.," I said coldly. "It's in his I.E.P.," I said, referring to the yearly special-ed plan which guaranteed my son his educational supports. The plan stated Rex would have twenty-five minutes of adaptive P.E., four times every week, or this teacher was in effect not observing the regulation. *I* knew it . . . and *she* knew it!

She stared at me, her eyes not flinching . . . but neither did mine. Then, suddenly, her face relaxed, knowing too well she couldn't win this one, not when a parent played the "I.E.P." card. It was definitely the trump, but it had to be used judiciously so that the educational process didn't turn into a battle of wills. "Of course, Rex will go to P.E.," she said wisely. Then, "He'll make up his work during recess." If I knew the system, she obviously knew it too, and my son's weekly recess time wasn't carefully delineated like P.E.

I felt my stomach clutch, realizing how dependent I was on this teacher's goodwill. She had my son seven hours a day, and, law or no law, nobody really controlled what went on in the classroom. "Do you know how important it is for Rex to get exercise?" I said, my voice tinged with anger, in spite of myself. "If he doesn't get outside and move around, his body and his brain just shut down. He needs fresh air and movement."

"He also needs to learn consequences of his behavior," she countered, not one to be trifled with. "And if there's no loss of privilege when he doesn't stay on task or do what he's told, then he'll never learn. Rex has behavior issues I'm addressing through a behavior plan I have him on. I know very well the only thing he really loves is being outside, so losing that privilege has to be his consequence."

Behavior plan? Why was this the first I was hearing of it? With that, she had thrown down the gauntlet, and the battle lines would be drawn. I couldn't trust the system anymore, and as a mother I needed to know what was going on behind the closed doors of the classroom. "Okay, I understand," I said, hiding my outrage, not wanting to risk making an enemy of my son's teacher but knowing at the same time there was a greater risk in doing nothing. "But I'd like to schedule a classroom observation, so I can see what you mean." I hoped by my tone she would consider me an ally, there to support Rex's well-being, someone she could collaborate with and not attack.

She immediately agreed I could come observe the classroom, knowing I had the right, but wanted to limit the time to the very minimum guaranteed by the regulation, twenty minutes. I couldn't believe the gall of this teacher I had tried so hard to trust. "I won't be able to observe anything in twenty minutes," I said, the color rising in my face.

"I can't have parents disrupting the class," she retorted. "It will distract Rex, having you in the classroom, not to mention the other students."

How astute she was at playing that "student card"! But I wasn't about to back down on this one. With my adrenaline really pumping now, I was committed to my course. "First of all, Rex won't even know I'm there because I won't speak. And I'll need to observe for a couple of hours . . . or there is no way I'll be able to give you my permission to have Rex on any behavior program." I once again played the trump she didn't seem to think she had to consider. She hadn't advised me even of her intent to put my son on a behavior program, let alone gone about obtaining my consent to do it.

She raised her eyebrows, surprised. That I knew the regulation? Or that I was calling her hand? She conceded immediately. "You can sit in the classroom from the morning bell up to recess. You'll see for yourself what I'm talking about. But you understand that it's observation," she said, treating me to her "teacher" voice. "I can't have you interrupting."

"Of course not. I wouldn't think of it," I said, mimicking her patronizing tone.

The observation was scheduled for the following Tuesday, none too soon as far as I was concerned. Thankfully, in the interim, Rex didn't miss any P.E. or recess. That was one thing he would always tell me after school. I assumed Mrs. Spader knew she had been overstepping her authority and had diplomatically pulled back on the "behavior plan" until she had parental consent. Although I suspect the decision had come from higher up, as in the principal. Walking back to the car that morning, I had bumped into Principal Pat. She must have seen a mother's distress plastered across my face, so she had asked me what was wrong. I had confided to her my concerns about Rex and his current schooling. I knew this principal would go to the mat for her teachers, supporting and believing in them, but I also knew how innately good she was. She had a heart for us parents to be sure, but most of all, she was guardian and protector of the kids. I believed she was doing what she was doing because she loved her students and knew how vital their education would be for their lives. So ultimately, like any good principal or teacher for that matter, she was in Rex's corner.

My observation day in the classroom started off with fifteen minutes of free time. Each student was asked to pick an activity to carry out, independent of instruction. Five students had formed a circle on the rug and were playing some sort of board game, two others sat at a table with a puzzle, while a younger boy was staring into the aquarium. "Tony, would you help Rex get to his keyboard?" I was happy to see the third grader walking with my son, guiding him with proper technique, to his piano. I had brought the piano there as a social bridge, to create interaction and a subject of conversation, as well as a tool to enhance Rex's self-concept. But when he sat down at the keyboard, instead of playing some music for the other students, his teacher said, "Your headphones are right in front of you, Rex, as they always are—you know how to put them on." And that's what he did—began his school day, as apparently was his usual routine, cut off from his classmates at play, isolated by the headphone barrier.

During language arts instruction, the classroom was divided by ability level, which meant sometimes by age and sometimes by cognitive level. While the "youngest" group began doing more visual work with a classroom aide, Mrs. Spader took four students between first and third grade to desks right in front of the blackboard. Just as I was beginning to wonder what Rex was going to do alone at his desk, his teacher of the visually impaired arrived.

Walking to my son's desk, the vision specialist saw me in my distant, silent corner and nodded. She sat down beside my son and greeted him. "Hi, Rex."

"Hi, Karen," came the return greeting. "It's Braille time," he said, obviously knowing what Karen's presence meant.

"That's right, Rex; we're going to do some reading and writing in Braille today." Karen spoke in a low, rather flat voice, which made me crane my head forward so I could hear. I watched her hand my son a piece of Braille paper. With teacher assistance, the student struggled through the process of putting the paper in the Braillewriter, which resembled a very heavy old-fashioned typewriter. But he managed to get it in and was happy with his accomplishment.

Looking at a list of words, Karen asked, "Can you Braille the word *sled* for me?" Rex said yes, but his hands remained in the air. I wasn't surprised, since Karen lacked the energy of voice my son needed to motivate him into movement. "You need to put your hands on the Brailler, Rex," she continued in the same monotone. I knew too well how dependent my son was on the energy of those who worked with him, energy that was conveyed through tone of voice. So, listening to this woman, I had a sense of foreboding.

At the same time, in the front of the classroom, Mrs. Spader was busy with her group. She had a pile of phonics cards in front of her as she faced her students. "We will be working on the short *e* sound today, pronounced 'eh.' Who can spell *sled*?"

Three of the four hands shot up, but before the teacher could call on a student, Rex had become very excited and called out, "S-L-E-D—SLED!"

Mrs. Spader sighed and said, "Thank you, Rex. That's right. But you need to focus on your own work." She cast a glance in my direction as if to say, "You see?"

Karen put slight pressure on Rex's hands to prompt them down onto the Braillewriter. My son depressed a single key and then his hands shot straight back up again, distracted, and not liking what he was doing. It was obvious he was listening to Mrs. Spader as she held up another phonics card, and said, "*Bed*. Who can tell me the sounds in the word *bed*"?

Again, hands shot up, and again Rex called out from across the room. With precise enunciation, he said, "Three sounds. 'B-ehh-d.'" Then proudly, "Bed."

Rex's hands were flapping excitedly, knowing he was right

again. The teacher looked across at him, her exasperation rising. Karen leaned forward to my son and sighed, as if to say 'same old, same old,' and said, "Rex, Mrs. Spader just asked you to do your own work and let your classmates do theirs. You have your own *sled* and *bed* right here." She placed a page of Braille words on the table next to the Braillewriter and put Rex's hands on the page. My son's hand shot back up. And why not? He couldn't read Braille. He'd been trying for two years now and couldn't even distinguish one letter from another, let alone read words. His hands were still too hypersensitive.

"I don't want to touch the bumps," he said, getting agitated. And yet that was my son's sorry task, touching bumps that had no meaning; all the while he wanted to be in the group spelling and doing phonics out loud. It was as plain as day . . . painfully plain. And that's what he was good at—spelling and decoding with his voice and ears, not his hands. I shifted uncomfortably in my chair, living my son's frustration, as Karen once more guided his hand onto the Braille page. Rex sat there listlessly, like a child condemned to prison, bored and apathetic. He actually almost toppled out of his chair from pure apathy. Just when I thought I'd seen enough, a girl student stepped over to the electric pencil sharpener near the door. I wanted to jump up and scream, "No!" at her as she stuck her pencil in. Terrified, I looked over at Rex as the high-pitched sound of the pencil grinding down hit the airwaves and his nervous system, so overly sensitized by blindness mixed with autism. His response was instantaneous. Like he'd

> *"I don't want to touch the bumps," he said, getting agitated. And yet that was my son's sorry task, touching bumps that had no meaning; all the while he wanted to be in the group spelling and doing phonics out loud. It was as plain as day.*

been struck by a massive electric current, his limp, listless body went rigid, his jaws clenching and trembling, as he pulled his hands away from the book to ram his fingers into his ears, crying, "Turn the pencil sharpener off!"

Mrs. Spader looked at Rex, whose face was beet red with the impact of the shock, then said, with unseemly, almost eerie calm, "Trisha, you know you're supposed to let Rex know every time you sharpen your pencil."

Acknowledging her oversight, the girl mumbled, "I'm sorry," as she returned to her seat. Slowly, Rex pulled his fingers out of his ears, although his face was still flushed. He had a wary, defensive look, lest there be a new assault on his sensitive system. I was beginning to see why my son was always so tired after school, as Karen said, "Come on, Rex. You need to calm your body down and do your work." Calm his body? Didn't they understand what that did to him, the extent of what had just happened?

I took a deep breath to calm my own body down, while Rex's hands finally came to rest on the Braille page, not calmed but numbed. He ran them mindlessly back and forth across the page, clearly not feeling anything he was touching, accomplishing nothing. He sat there in a numbed state for a couple of minutes, emotionless, practically comatose, ignoring the specialist who had come to work with him. I wanted to walk over to his teacher and ask why Rex wasn't in her group, participating, but bit down on the temptation. I was there to observe, not interrupt or advise.

All of a sudden, the school bell rang, another jolt that shocked Rex out of apathy back to hypertension. His fingers shot back to his ears as Karen pulled the almost-empty page Rex had Brailled from the Braillewriter. Mrs. Spader said, "Time for recess, everyone. But remember, we all must wash our hands before we can have our snack and go out to the playground."

Her students pushed back from their desks and scrambled

toward the sink, just behind Rex. The younger students jumped up as well, and the resultant hubbub all around my son caused him to push his fingers even deeper into his ears. As I watched the kids taking turns to wash their hands, I cringed, fearing the running water sound that had always been so hard for Rex. Then I became aware of a sustained pitch emanating from his mouth. "AAAAHHHH." It was his own personal white noise. Like a pacifier, the sound soothed him, somehow holding the cacophony around him at bay. But for how long?

One of the older boys was just heading for the door when Mrs. Spader stopped him with a request. "Thomas, I'd like you to help Rex today."

Thomas turned around. "Okay," he said, walking over to my son's seat, obviously knowing what his task was. Rex still had his fingers in his ears as Thomas told him, "Rex, I'm going to help you walk to the playground."

Rex didn't respond, and so the teacher said, "Stand up, Rex. You need to wash your hands." When there was still no response, she placed her hands under his arms to prompt him into movement. Slowly he stood up, and she turned him around so he was facing the sink. "Come on, Rex. The sink is right in front of you."

Just then, a girl who had just finished at the sink turned quickly and bumped into Rex, knocking his fingers from his ears. He stumbled, and as he shifted his weight to avoid falling, his sustained "AAAHHH" sound grew louder, a protective, almost desperate crescendo, struggling to filter out the chatter and chaotic crush around him, struggling against autism and the distortion it caused in his brain. Thomas, impatient to get outside, took Rex by the hand, saying, "Come on, Rex. We've gotta go." He tried to pull him forward to the sink, but Rex couldn't take any more jostling and jerked his hand free as two more classmates moved past to go outside.

Mrs. Spader instructed, "Try again, Thomas."

The boy tried again and was resisted again. Rex yanked his hand once again from the older boy's grasp, saying, "Bye, Thomas. Bye, Thomas. Bye, Thomas"—a desperate try at dismissal.

Mrs. Spader said, "Thomas, you can go ahead. I'll take care of Rex." And the boy ran off, relieved. As the last student turned on the faucet, Rex backed up to remove himself from the scene and bumped into his desk. That was the final straw, and it snapped his brain wires, plummeting him deep into the vortex of his autism. He began spinning his body in space, like a whirling top, his brain having been turned to chaos. I watched my child with a searing pain in my gut, as if I was bleeding internally.

I jumped up to intervene, but the teacher stopped me with a look that said, "I will handle it. This is my classroom."

But this is my son! I thought, clutching my stomach. She spoke firmly, right at him. "If you want to go outside with the others, you need to stop spinning and wash your hands. The sink is right in front of you, Rex."

I watched in disbelief. Teacher and student were on separate planets, with no lines of communication between the two. As if I were seeing some tragic, distorted theater of the absurd, I was frozen, watching my beautiful son, blind and tragically imprisoned by autism, silently spinning in place, trying to spin his brain back into order. Losing patience, Mrs. Spader demanded, "Do you hear me, Rex?"

That's when I snapped. It was more than I could take. Rushing across the room, I cut in, breaking my promise not to intervene. Staring straight at the teacher, I was livid. "Don't you understand? This is a spatial and sensory issue. Can't you see how hard he was trying to sort out all the confusion and noise? Don't you think he wants to be outside with the other kids?"

"Trying so hard?" she countered, in a tone of disbelief. "He washes his own hands all the time. So I know he can do it if he wants to, and yet today he chose not to. That's behavior!"

How could this special-education teacher just not get it? I wanted to shake some sense into her, some understanding. But here, today, all I could do was put my arms around my boy to stop his spinning, applying firm pressure to reassure him, reaffirming my maternal role of comforter. Then, staring at his teacher with protective outrage, bordering on hate, I reaffirmed my maternal authority as well . . . and with that, a mother's duty to defend her son. And so it was in a voice verging on explosion that I said, "We have to have an intervention! I want everybody who works with Rex to come to an emergency I.E.P.!"

CHAPTER ELEVEN

I. E. P.

For God did not give us a spirit of timidity,
but a spirit of power, of love and of self-discipline.

—2 Timothy 1:7

I hated confrontation. But I knew there was no choice. It was imminent, just moments away. So I called up the spirit of power, love, and self-discipline through prayer, as I had done before so many times during Rex's life. In times of confusion, in times when I'd been paralyzed by fear or doubt or anger, when I'd had to "buck myself up" to fight the good fight.

In the days since my classroom observation, I'd been consumed with such intense anger and indignation that it had left me feeling sick and crazy half the time. Internal dialogues would run rampant in my head, back-and-forth discussions attempting to reach ground where mediation and remedy would be possible, but always ending up with a furious indictment: "How could they?" or, "Doesn't she get it?" Fortunately, the other half the time, I somehow managed to get past the emotion in order to deal with the reality of the situation. That meant doing my homework. What was the reality of the law? And how could theory be made applicable in Rex's case? I.E.P. stood for Individualized Education Plan, and it had become glaringly obvious I needed a plan of my own. A plan to present at this meeting I had demanded. The I.E.P. was an actual document, the result of team planning at the normally annual meeting. It contained all the vitals for a child's "appropriate and least restrictive" educational year. Delineated, in black and white. But what they currently had down on paper for Rex, and in their minds, was not only failing my son educationally but undermining his being.

I had delivered Rex to his classroom, and now I sat in our parked car. My senses seemed muted. I couldn't see blue in the sky or pink in the roses today. The colors faded before my eyes, and textures went flat in this world that was suddenly two-dimensional—black and white, darkness and light. In fact, all I really saw was the door to the meeting room off in the distance, and it was formidable, as the assemblage inside was sure to be. Behind the solid door would be a long table, long enough to seat all the specialists involved in my son's school education. Everybody would be there today—I had demanded it. I was determined the "team" the law promised would act as such and would include me in the process. But to accomplish that goal, I had to calm my nervous stomach. I also had to transmute rage to righteous outrage and controlled power here and now. Other parents took advocates with them to these meetings in order to stand up to a room full of district specialists and fight for their children. But I didn't have an advocate, and so, taking a deep breath, I opened the car door to do the job myself.

I strode across the parking lot, head up, shoulders back, using each step to buck myself up a little more. Walking through the door, my eyes swept the room, making a silent head count of the impressive group. All present and accounted for. The principal sat at the head of the table, even though Mrs. Spader, as Rex's teacher, would be conducting the meeting. Otherwise, the team included the school psychologist, Karen, the vision specialist, the orientation and mobility specialist, the occupational therapist, Coach Gary for adaptive P.E., the speech pathologist, and, upon my expressed request, Rex's aide.

The door closed decisively, as though a court was now in session. As I sat down, all eyes were on me, and I felt the intensity of that moment in the depths of my soul. I knew just how much was at stake right here, with each word having the power to either mend and empower or aggravate and undermine. And my son's future in this school hung in the balance.

Rex's teacher called the meeting to order, looking first at me, directly across the table from her, and then in turn at the other participants at the table. "We are meeting today to discuss some concerns Rex's mother has regarding his education." Then facing me, she said, "So go ahead and begin, Cathleen."

Taking a last silent breath to steady myself, I looked at each person in turn, each member of my son's team I hoped to draw into a greater spirit of collaboration. I had planned out each issue and would be careful to blend any suggestion and concern with suitable appreciation for the positives. And I knew some parts of his school worked well, like his orientation and mobility instruction that had led to breakthroughs in allowing his sensitive hands to use a white cane effectively to guide his walking, or the efforts of his instructional aides to assist him throughout the day. But then, looking across the table at Mrs. Spader, something in her look (was she just humoring me?) made me lose my composure, and suddenly anything positive I might have mentioned as a warm-up gave way to a whole slew of negatives. "Every day when I pick Rex up from school, he's just exhausted, and he's becoming more and more apathetic and nonresponsive when I ask him about his school days. After observing him in the classroom, I

> *His teacher cut in, defensive. "That's the same thing we're trying to address in the classroom: his apathy. It's so difficult to motivate Rex and keep him on task. You saw that."*

understand why that is." I hadn't meant to just lay it all out, but there it was.

His teacher cut in, defensive. "That's the same thing we're trying to address in the classroom: his apathy. It's so difficult to motivate Rex and keep him on task. You saw that."

I leaned forward in my chair, pressing my hands into the table, hoping the pressure would help me refrain from jumping on her statement. Not wanting to play a role of prosecutor, I spoke commands to myself. *Pause. Take a breath. Okay, go.* "But why is he apathetic? The other day, Rex couldn't focus on his Braille. Yes, that I saw. But he wasn't apathetic about phonics—in fact, he jumped on every answer. It seems like a natural thing to want to be part of the group phonics lesson."

"Rex has special needs that have to be addressed," the teacher retorted brusquely. "Karen comes to teach Rex Braille three times a week so he'll be able to read and write. That seems like it should be a priority." Mrs. Spader then gave me that patronizing look I'd come to hate.

I didn't want to answer her directly, not when she spoke in that tone. So I addressed his Braille teacher. "I'd like to talk about Braille in a minute, but first I'd like to know, Karen, if you can schedule Rex's service time outside of the group's time? Rex also needs phonics skills, and he needs to work with other kids."

Karen looked uncomfortable, shifted slightly in her seat, and said, "No. It's the only time that works into my schedule. I have kids with visual impairments in three different districts to provide services for."

That works into *her* schedule? I couldn't just let that pass by me. "Isn't special education supposed to put the child first and work around his needs, not the needs of the teachers?"

Karen didn't answer, but Mrs. Spader did. "We try the best we can to work within the constraints of the system."

I felt as though I was banging my head against a double-enforced iron wall of budgeting and scheduling issues. To pursue that at this point seemed futile and would probably take the steam out of the many other concerns I had. I squeezed my hands together, trying hard to suppress frustration, and took aim at a very critical issue. "I can appreciate how excessive your workload might be, but that only leads back to what your time is really accomplishing. I watched Rex with you for fifty minutes, and he was inattentive to the point he almost fell out of his seat! And his Braille page was all but empty at the end." I wondered what these other specialists here thought about that. Did they think that type of a session was normal? Or acceptable? I felt a nervous sweat building from this emotional issue. Karen was staring down at her hands on the table as though breaking eye contact would somehow stop me from saying what I was saying. But I couldn't stop, because I was a mother fighting for her son. "I think you'd have better luck getting Rex's attention by making his work more engaging, by having more life in your voice."

When Karen didn't reply immediately, Mrs. Spader jumped on it. "What do you want us to do? Make school a game for Rex?"

"No, but it does need to be more stimulating," I countered.

"Stimulating how?" she asked. "By making him dependent on overly exaggerated speech? He won't find that in the real world." She paused, then added with a touch of impatience, "And I think we've had this discussion before."

Why does she insist on baiting me? I thought as I tapped my fingers on the table to calm my nerves. Ever since kindergarten, I had voiced the necessity of speaking to Rex with an animated voice in order to gain his attention. It seemed an obvious necessity, given his blindness and overdependence on auditory input. We seemed to be at a standoff on the issue, and my frustration was mounting as well, having to return to this old issue. "But we're not talking about the real world. We're talking about school, and motivating a child with special needs to accomplish a boring, academic *school* task. What is on every wall of every classroom here? Brightly colored artwork, pictures. Numbers and letters. Why is that?"

The principal was smiling, presumably acknowledging the learning environment in her classrooms. "To stimulate and encourage learning," she said, then added reflectively, "for the sighted students." She nodded, as if to say, *Makes sense a blind child would need some stimulation of a different sort.*

Grateful I'd scored a point, I didn't want to let the momentum slide. "Do the sighted kids expect to find purple elephants or giant numbers hanging from the sky when they go outside the classroom?" I let the words hang for the briefest second, glaring and obvious, then added, "So why isn't my child receiving equal treatment to stimulate him?" Couldn't they see what he needed? Didn't they know by now? My stomach tightened at the thought that they really didn't. "Is that fair to Rex?"

There was a moment of silence in the room, no one daring to touch that one. Instead, his teacher chose a different track. "Cathleen, even when I speak loudly to Rex he doesn't stay on task. He has behavioral issues we need to address before any other teaching technique will have a chance of keeping him on task."

I felt the color rising to my cheeks, knowing how much my son had to contend with on a daily basis. I thanked God that behavior wasn't one of them. "You keep saying that—behavior, behavior plan—but I can't for the life of me figure out what you're referring to."

"Refusal to do simple tasks," she said matter-of-factly. "You saw it yourself in the classroom. We all know Rex can walk to the sink. But that day, he refused—and a simple situation became complicated."

"Refused?" I blinked in amazement, feeling a disconnect

between her words and what I knew to be reality. "Rex wasn't refusing to go to the sink that day. He was unable to. There's a big difference."

"Unable to?" she said, incredulous. "All he had to do was take a couple of steps—"

"A couple of steps that he couldn't take!" I blurted out as the tension in the room escalated. How could it be that they just didn't understand the complexity of what Rex was dealing with? That they thought he was being lazy or contrary? That they could apply some quick-fix behavior plan to something neurological in origin? Reliving that traumatic scene at the sink, I had no choice but to walk them through it. I took a moment, willing myself to convert anger and frustration into an emotional plea to help my son. "I don't think you truly understand what Rex goes through. My son was trying with everything he had to get to that sink so he could go outside and be with his classmates. But his senses became overloaded. First he gets pulled by one kid—then bumped by another—turned this way and that. When a blind child can't get his bearings, he experiences spatial chaos. Then add to that the faucet turning off and on, grating on his nerves, with kids rushing around him and all their chatter setting off his autistic sensitivities, and he was completely disoriented." His teacher seemed noncommittal. "It was as if his brain just couldn't take it anymore and short-circuited. I looked around the room, hoping beyond hope that some comprehension might dawn. Then, pleading, "Couldn't you see that? Don't you know what blindness together with autism can do to a child?"

Mrs. Spader just stared back, not giving an inch. Either she didn't believe me or she didn't want to believe me, because that would mean her student was a far more complex puzzle than she had realized. "I think I know Rex pretty well. I've had him every day in my class for some time now."

Why did she think I was her enemy? Weren't we on the same side—working for Rex? I caught her testy tone but refused to match it, continuing my emotional plea instead. "And *I* think there's a lot about my son that none of us really understands. He has a fragile and variable neurological system that doesn't produce the same thing day to day. I know how hard that is to work with. Believe me, I know." I thought back to so many challenges I'd faced day in and day out to address that very issue. "But that's *our job*," I said, throwing myself into the team basket, desperate to be heard. "Yours and mine, to work from Rex outward, not from what we hope he is or what he would be in a perfect world."

I looked at each face in turn, and everyone was tuned into every word now. "And I believe there are some critical parts of Rex's education that are failing him. It's obvious that his needs are enormous, so I think it's crucial that the areas the team targets are relevant for his life and not just wasting his time—and the time of the people who work with him," I said, looking first at Karen then at each member of the team in turn, trying to get the idea of collaboration and teamwork across.

Still sure of herself and her decisions, his teacher said, "Believe me, we are targeting areas that are very relevant to Rex's life, such as making him more independent."

"And you've achieved some good results on that, I agree," I replied, acknowledging the point. "But let's talk about an area where he's not getting results. Did you know that only 10 percent of the blind population reads Braille?" I asked, having just learned the shocking statistic myself. Mrs. Spader looked as surprised as I had been by the statistic, but she remained silent. "So, why, after two years of failing to discriminate even between two Braille letters, is Rex still being force-fed Braille? He can write it. But he can't read back a word of what he has written. So what's the point? I'd be bored to death too. And I probably would have just as hard a time staying on task if I had to spend hours at a desk making bumps on paper that had no meaning for me." *Whoops! I didn't mean to say "bored to death." That was a bit strong. But the subject is just too emotional for me.* In spite of my emotions, I managed to level my voice and in a follow-the-logic kind of way said, "So isn't that also a waste of Karen's time . . . and the district's?"

"So you want to give up on Rex being literate?" his teacher asked, a bit huffy.

"Of course not," I said. "But obviously, with a 10 percent statistic for Braille, it's not the only option." I had done my due diligence, some eye-opening due diligence, and had come to this meeting prepared—not just with concerns but with solutions. After doing some research, it seemed hard to believe that this educational "team" had never discussed alternative means for Rex, a blind and very tactile-defensive child, to achieve the important goal of attaining maximum literacy. It hadn't taken much on my part to discover the pervasive use of computers and voice actualization for that very purpose. Given Rex's impressive auditory skills, it seemed a no-brainer, but clearly this team needed to be further educated in literacy options for the visually impaired. "Rex is a good speller and does well in phonics, so let him use those strengths in a way that gets him positive reinforcement. I'm talking about computers. I'm sure his piano keyboard skills would translate to an awareness of a computer keyboard."

Then I walked them through my vision. "He will learn to type, and with the screen-reading technology available for the blind, the computer will read back his finished product. And he'll love it!" I said, absolutely convinced. I could even picture Rex getting all excited by a somewhat-robotic computer reading back his work, wanting to type faster just to get that "fun voice." Then, staring his teacher straight in the eye, I added what I hoped would be the clincher. "And that will give him the motivation to 'stay on task.'" I emphasized the words that seemed to be the class mantra, a mantra they claimed was impossible for my son.

There was silence in the room for a moment, while the team digested the import of my words. It was clear that a computer for Rex was a completely novel idea to this team, although as a teacher of the visually impaired, Karen certainly knew the option existed. Was it another budgeting issue that had made her keep silent? I'd heard that school districts advised teachers not to inform parents about potentially costly programs or technology options for their children. Meaning we parents needed to find out for ourselves what's out there for our kids. Mrs. Spader looked at the vision specialist. "Do you think Rex will ever learn to read Braille?"

Karen looked uncomfortable with the attention drawn to her. "He might," she said, mumbling, clearly not wanting to commit.

"Might?" I almost screamed, having run out of patience on the issue. "And you've been working with him three times a week for two years, and he still can't distinguish an *a* from an *l*? And then when he finishes the effort, he's so drained the rest of his day is a struggle. Is that the 'appropriate' education the law guarantees Rex will have?" The words had just come out, but they didn't say enough. So, with clenched fists and fiercely maternal determination, I let out what I was really thinking. "You're not just wasting his time, you're killing him in the process!"

His aide was nodding, looking at me, encouraging me to stay the course. She didn't dare add her input, but she was the one who had to battle with an exhausted boy all the time, so I imagine she hoped I wouldn't back down. At the same time, comprehension appeared to be gradually dawning on Mrs. Spader, both in terms of my own determination and in terms of an alternative literacy option to Braille. And, interestingly, she almost looked relieved, as if she'd found an out. She turned to Karen again, avoiding any acknowledgement that she'd been unaware the option even existed. "Can we get what we need for Rex—computer, software?"

"I'll look into it," she said, in what I took to be a partial affirmation.

"I will need to be informed on your progress in getting it for Rex," I said, with what was meant to leave no doubt as to my determination to follow through.

"You will be," said Mrs. Spader as though she wanted this meeting to be over. She wasn't comfortable with a parent standing up and challenging her. She was used to running the show. But I wasn't comfortable with a teacher's ego when my son's well-being was at stake. So today, whether she liked it or not, I was the one running the show.

"Okay. Then we can talk about the other serious concern I have. And that's Rex's socialization in the class and in the school. He needs to be working and playing with the other kids, not off in corners or working with adults all the time. That's why he's here. That's why I brought in the keyboard. It wasn't meant to be a pacifier. It was supposed to be a creative bridge to his classmates. But you only let him play with his headphones on—so he won't bother anyone—instead of using it to foster interaction with his peers. Do you realize what an amazing gift my son has? I've even been told recently that he's a musical savant—a genius. But you use his gift in a way that further isolates him. My son is here because I want to do whatever I can to integrate him into the world. But if your view of him is so . . . distorted . . . you've already doomed him to failure."

I hadn't planned on making speeches today, but I suddenly realized what an opportunity this forum had given me. This was supposed to be "special" education, and I had to believe that every person in this room had chosen the profession in order to help kids with unique needs. I was crying for them to shelve egos and get back to the heart of their profession. That was the only way for my son to succeed. I wanted to believe it could happen, to believe it wasn't their intent that was distorted, just their perception. For me, that meant their ability not just to think outside of the box, but in Rex's case, to get rid of the box altogether.

I spoke calmly but with quiet determination. "There's no denying my son has some challenging weaknesses. But he also has some amazing strengths. Surely there is a way, between us, to take those strengths and use them creatively to make him part of the world. To help him overcome his weaknesses. Isn't that the point of education? For all children?"

CHAPTER TWELVE

Aftermath

There will always be challenges, obstacles and
less than perfect conditions. So what. Get started now.

—**Mark Victor Hansen, author**

Everyone left the I.E.P. room quickly—hurrying back to duties, perhaps already mentally trying to reschedule missed service time with other students—but not me. I walked out slowly. Did their hurried departure mean they had already shifted gears, pushing plans for Rex somewhere into the back of their minds . . . and priority lists? Were they embarrassed? Had I gone too far? The questions were suddenly too many, the doubts overwhelming. Crossing the parking lot back to the car, gone was the stride of confidence I'd had going into the meeting. Now my steps were careful, poised, so my legs wouldn't go spaghetti like Rex's used to. My arms were limp, hanging at my side like deadweights, and my body felt heavy, drained. I'd given it all I had and could only pray my voice had been heard.

Leaving that room, the truth hit me square in the face, and it was ominous—the law could provide services for a child on paper, but it couldn't guarantee the quality of those services. That meant the law was only as effective as the people carrying it out—the teachers, the specialists, and the way they collaborated and shared ideas. Effective teamwork was a must with a child as complex as Rex, and as such, appeared to be the joker in his educational deck of cards. Would this group truly get behind my son and use his gifts to help him gain access not only to a more suitable curriculum but to his peers? Or would they be too overextended to give the necessary time and creative effort it might take to do that? In spite of my emotional pitch, sadly I felt the jury was still out. Reaching my car, I placed my hands on the hood to brace myself as my shoulders slumped forward, my head drooping. I was sapped, snapped, worn.

But then, cutting in on my thoughts, I became aware of some footsteps behind me, rushing to catch up. I turned to see the principal. *What now?* I thought. But she was smiling.

"Cathleen," she said, a bit out of breath. "I'm glad I caught you. I just had to say a word to Mrs. Spader on her way back to class, but I wanted to let you know how much we love Rex and how committed we are to trying to get it right for him."

"Thank you," I said, allowing some of the tenseness in my shoulders to seep away. "I really appreciate that." Suddenly I felt like a child needing reassurance.

Pat gave it to me in the form of a big maternal hug that made all the difference in the world and said, "What *I* appreciate is parents who stand behind their children." Pointing back to the door, she went on. "And I appreciated your words in there. We do get busy, and there's a lot about the system that's far from perfect, but I hope you believe we want to get it right. We want to help Rex succeed. And I believe we can do it," she said with determination in her voice. And then she added just the guarantee I was hoping for: "If we work together."

THE PRINCIPAL and I had barely finished the expression of belief in Rex's future, when, once again, he was the one who began to stir up his own kettle of hope.

Two of the biggest questions any of us had about Rex's cognitive, emotional development were soon to be answered. Would he ever be able to move past concrete experience into abstract reasoning? To date, he couldn't. And would he ever understand and express complex emotions, or would autism keep them locked up? Like his communication, which tended to be rote and scripted, his understanding of the world was limited to the very concrete. With the flagrant exception of music, where improvisation was his preferred genre and creativity the name of the game, everything else was very literal in his mind, and he showed no evidence of imagination. Whereas Rex's musical world was a kaleidoscope of myriad colors and shapes and forms, the rest of his world was pretty much black and white. Or was it?

Shortly after the I.E.P. meeting, Rex came home from school with a library book in his backpack. Since he went to the school library once a week, I wasn't surprised by the presence of a book, just the particular subject of the one he'd chosen: *Energy Makes Things Happen.* Energy! Now there was an abstract concept.

Tucking Rex in bed that evening, I knew he would ask for his library book. He didn't disappoint me, and as soon as he had the covers snuggly up to his neck, he said, "I want to read *Energy Makes Things Happen.*"

Heeding my son's call for a bedtime story, I opened the book. His face was calm and attentive, like it always was when he listened to stories. However, I wasn't sure exactly what he got out of all that intense listening, since he struggled to answer even basic comprehension questions linked to a story passage. Tonight I would be reading him a science selection, even more complex than usual.

"'Did you know that energy comes from the food you eat? From the sun and wind?'" The language in the book was simple, but the concept was not. "'You need energy to play baseball, or to run, or . . .'" hoping to stretch my son's comprehension, "to play the piano. 'A car gets energy from fuel.' Rex, you get your energy from eating oatmeal in the morning." The book went on to discuss the different forms taken by energy and how it is transferred among people, machines, and nature. I added examples that Rex could relate to. "You need energy to run. And when you run, you use up your energy, so you're tired and you're breathing hard, huffing and puffing, and you say, 'Mommy, I need to stop running. I need to rest to get more energy so I can run some more.'" A few more examples, to try to drive home the concept, and I summed up. "So Rex, like the title says, *Energy Makes Things Happen*. Do you understand?"

"Yes, Mommy, you understand!" With that I kissed him good-night, having no idea if he had grasped any of the energy concept.

Then came morning. My seven-year-old boy got out of bed a little groggy, and as I pulled his pants and shirt from his dresser, he walked into the bathroom, as he did every morning. But then I heard him calling out to me, all tiredness suddenly gone from his voice. "Mommy, Mommy!"

"What is it, sweetie?" I asked, already heading for the bathroom, fearing a faulty aim and a soggy floor.

Just as I reached the door to see my bare-bottomed boy standing proudly in front of the toilet and bubbling with excitement, he announced, "Look, Mommy, I'm using my energy to pee!"

I'm using my energy to pee!!! Yes! And quite an energetic arc it was, perfectly aimed, descending straight down into the toilet bowl!

He got such a kick out of himself when he knew he got things right. And I got such a kick out of him because he was Rex, the one and only original, doing things his way and in his time. He was beautifully guileless, and I wondered if he would always have that pure, childlike spirit. I hoped so, because it seemed to me that it was in the depths of that innocence that God had chosen to infuse His grace. Sometimes it was cute, just like this bathroom scene—a snapshot, as if He was winking at me through my son's blind eyes, letting me know He was there. And sometimes it hit me straight in the heart.

IT WAS a pristine Saturday morning, and Rex and I were walking along our sandy beach, hand in hand. The tide was out, but instead of focusing on the tide pools and all the sea life the receding waters had left strewn about, I was giving all my attention to the little boy at my side. His personality was pushing through more and more. Ever since the day he had shown he understood what energy was, we'd been using it. In fact, it had become one of his favorite words that could be thrown into a variety of situations: "Look, Mommy, I'm playing the piano with good energy!" Followed by a big smile and a lively beat. Or, "We're going to the gas station so our car has energy to go to school. Vroom! Vroom!"

Walking in the sand, we were now learning to nuance it. "Rex, we're using our energy to walk, but if we walk faster we'll use more energy," I said picking up the pace. Moving into a slight jog, I added, "And if we run, we will use . . . ?" I paused, waiting for him to fill in the blank.

"More energy!" he shouted.

"Yes, but if we run too much, we won't have any energy left and we'll have to stop and . . . ?"

"Rest!" Rex was very good at filling in appropriate responses, which helped him follow and build logical sequences.

"So we can get . . . ?"

"More energy to run some more!" Rex said, tugging at my arm. But he was out of breath.

"That's it, sweetie. But I'm a little tired. So why don't we sit here and rest for a moment?"

Rex agreed, using my sentence, and turning it into his own question. "Mommy, shall we sit here and rest for a moment?"

"Good idea, Rex!" I sat down, and he plopped into the sand. There wasn't another soul anywhere on our stretch of beach, and I felt the glow of the sun warming me, the sound of waves soothing. "Rex, do you hear the waves?"

"The waves are crashing!" he said, excited. "I'd like to tell a story about a little boy named Rex who goes to the beach."

Putting himself into adventures was his favorite thing to do. We told stories a lot, in order to help him develop an imagination, as well as work on language. The storyline always had to be concrete and related to activities from his life, but then we could intermingle characters from the vast wealth of audio books he listened to. Since Rex's world revolved around Rex, in the manner of a very young child, the stories we told normally had him as the hero, going to battle against such foes as Captain Hook or Shere Khan, the great tiger of *Jungle Book* fame.

"Go ahead Rex, tell me a story," I said, despite knowing he meant he wanted me to tell him the story. Normally I would begin and then craft it into a team effort, cueing him up for his turn with a question or a blank to fill in. Soon, I believed, he would be able to sequence a whole story on his own. I felt it coming. There was a lot locked up in my little boy that just needed to be pulled out . . . creatively.

"I want Mommy to tell you a story about Rex," he said, right on cue.

I couldn't help smiling. Sometimes it was my son's predictability that filled me with love, and sometimes it was just the opposite—that jaw-dropping surprise you didn't see coming . . .

I began. "Once upon a time, there was a little boy named . . ."

"Rex," he jumped in.

"And what was Rex doing?" I asked.

"Rex was running on the beach . . . with good energy!" he said proudly.

"Yeah. That's right. Rex was running on the beach. And then there was a wave. Way out in the ocean. A big, giant wave. And what was the wave doing, Rex?"

"The wave was crashing, Mommy!"

"Yes, and where was it crashing?"

"The wave went *crash!*" he said. Then, laughing, added, "The wave was crashing on Rex's back. And Rex fell down, and he was smashed by the waves."

"No! He can't be smashed! Our hero Rex must be saved, to come back another day. So who saved Rex? Was it the Little Mermaid?"

"No!" said Rex.

"Was it Hercules? Who could have saved Rex?" I asked, expecting the Herculean nod, or perhaps his current favorite, Robin Hood.

Rex had his own idea. "It was Mommy. Mommy saved Rex!"

He turned to me and threw his arms around me. I squeezed back, hard, not wanting to let go, knowing only the depths of love I had for this child and, on occasions like this, how safe that love made me feel. "And you saved me, Rex. You did. We're a family. We take care of each other."

Rex pulled out of the hug, too soon for me, but it looked as though he had something on his mind. I thought he wanted to go on with the story, but he said only, "Mommy?"

His face was pointed at mine with such intensity that it looked almost as though he could see me. "What is it, Rex?" I asked.

He was trying to process something. I could tell by his concentrated look that it was hard. "Mommy?" was all he could get out again.

Trying to coax whatever it was out of him, I said encouragingly, "You have to tell me what you're thinking."

The struggle continued as my son rocked back and forth in the sand. "Mommy?" he said. I waited. "Mommy?" he repeated, louder, like he was trying to get enough energy, revving up an internal motor to get the momentum to get his thought out. "Mommy?"

"Rex?" I said, giving a slight nudge to pull his thought forward.

"I love you, Mommy!" he burst out, triumphant, his face mirroring his words, telling me how real they were.

I love you, Mommy! The four words I'd been waiting so long to hear, not knowing if they'd ever come, or if they did, that they'd be truly felt. Those four words took my breath away . . . but then pumped it right back into me, fuller and more alive. How many specialists had wondered about my son's ability to feel complex emotions? Sure, he played emotions like happy and sad on his piano. But what about emotions like anger, friendship . . . or love? As I threw my arms around my son, I knew that he was the one who had just saved me from all those crashing, smashing waves.

> *As I threw my arms around my son, I knew that he was the one who had just saved me from all those crashing, smashing waves.*

REX FINALLY got his computer at school. It had been a ten-week wait, but that was because he had first gotten the software, which didn't work on any of the current classroom computers. That, of course, meant he would need a new computer. So, more red tape and waiting. But now at least he was equipped. In the meantime, his teacher of the visually impaired had ceased and desisted with the Braille, which meant Rex wasn't exhausted and apathetic all the time. I believe that fact alone helped him to make his real breakthroughs, such as grasping an abstract concept like energy or expressing the true emotion in "I love you." Gone were those draining Braille sessions! Over the next couple of weeks, it became obvious Rex began to look forward to the days when he would see his vision teacher and the work they did together on his new computer. I knew this from his morning spiel, which had now changed to include events he anticipated, such as, "Today is Tuesday, and I'm going to see Karen and work on the computer." His big smile said things were turning around. Yet, in spite of the progress in some areas of his education, I wondered what was being done to promote Rex's interaction with his peers. Hadn't that been a priority? Yet, to date, I hadn't had much feedback in that critical area. Had all my words been wasted, falling on deaf ears? Or ears that were too busy to really hear?

Sitting at my own computer one night, with Rex tucked into bed, I was reflecting on his dependence on the people around him—starting with me and then his piano teachers. But that was an easy dependence, because I was dependable where he was concerned and he was musically gifted. But what about his reliance on his teachers at school where he was anything but gifted? His dependence on the system? The fact was simple—there weren't enough teachers of the visually impaired (TVIs) to go around.

Blindness was a low-incidence disability, and so not enough people had gone into the field. Before they had hired Karen, our district had no one to work with the blind students for almost an entire school year. There were just no applicants, no one qualified. Learning about the deficit of specialists in the area of blindness, I had made a big personal decision. I wouldn't just complain about the system and its problems; I would get inside it. That meant going back to school myself and becoming trained. How many other children were out there floundering in the system because they were misunderstood or misplaced? How many parents didn't know any better? How many other parents felt lonely and cut off from noncommunicative teachers?

I felt the call to lend a hand and bring parental perspective into the classroom by earning a credential. The law gave me parental rights, but a credential would give me equal professional footing to assure my rights would be adhered to. The inspiration couldn't have come at a better time. I would need to get back into work life soon anyway, and I'd want to do something I was passionate about. Just as I was clicking on the Web site of the only university program in Southern California to train specialists in the education of the visually impaired, the phone rang.

"Hi, it's Pat Cairns," said the voice. I had never received a call at home from my son's principal, so I hoped it wasn't bad news. "I just had an idea for Rex—how to help him mix with other students. Do you think he would like to play his piano for our yearly talent show?"

I had a vision of an auditorium full of kids watching my son's amazing gift at the piano and said, "Yes. That's a wonderful idea."

"It would give more kids the chance to hear Rex play, and parents too. I think it would be great for everybody," Pat said. "It might just be the bridge we're looking for."

"Yes, thank you," I said, at a loss for words. "Thank you. Yes, I'll look into it."

The auditions for the talent show had already been held. But I took Rex to a rehearsal to try to get him into the roster after the fact. The mother who was organizing the show took one look at the blond boy feeling his way with his cane and said, "Of course, he can play something." His audition not only got him in the show but won him the spot right at the end of the program, the coveted finale. "Just what we needed," she said, after he'd played and sung a bluesy version of one of his Beatles favorites "When

I'm 64." "A good closer!" She had a smile of wonder on her face, the look of one who'd discovered a hidden pearl, and I had a smile in my heart.

Vocalists, pianists, skits, and dancers. The students in Rex's school had many varied talents. And they were supportive of one another, encouraging, clapping. But the other kids all knew each other and were friends. They knew Rex, too, but only as that little blind boy—the one they saw on the playground with his cane and his adult aide. Sure, some of them went up and greeted him, but they rarely stayed to play. He wasn't really their friend. So how would this group react when Rex took the stage?

There was a hush in the audience as I walked Rex to the piano. There had been talk that the little blind boy could play the piano, but what did they think that meant? "Mary Had a Little Lamb"? Or were they expecting a duet? Mommy plays the hard part, then son pipes in a few notes, as we did with our storytelling?

I helped him center himself on the piano bench, helped position his mike, then stepped aside. His schoolmates were all sitting in the front rows with parents behind as he began. But began what? This wasn't the song he'd planned. Was this God winking again? Rex broke his script, surprising us all as he began to sing the blackbird's song.

His sweet voice floated wistfully over the room, asking for eyes that could see and wings that could soar, as he wove Bach-like trills into the musical line, giving the piece lightness and air.

There was a collective, spontaneous gasp from the audience, parents and kids alike. This was not what they'd been expecting. Not at all.

There were no more sounds from the audience, and, except for Rex's pure soprano gliding atop his chrystalline piano notes, the room was so quiet, it was almost solemn. No shifting or shuffling, no sideways whispers, just reverence, as if they were listening to a prayer. Was this my son's prayer? Did he want it for himself as much as I did for him?

I can do it! As though he were willing himself to fly alongside the blackbird. His fingers and voice were now in full flight, soaring beyond limits, beyond disability. And with the spotlight hitting his blond locks, like a light from heaven, his cry for freedom sang out into the room. *I can fly, Mommy!*

Into the light of the dark, black night.

There was a pause, a suspension of disbelief as the notes trailed off. And the kids were the first to shout. "Rex! Rex! Bravo! Great job!" And the parents were the first on their feet. And all were clapping, heartfelt and real. And Rex felt all of it, how special everybody thought he was. I looked back and forth from my son jumping up and down on stage to his fellow schoolmates, my eyes clouded by tears. Then I glanced to the back corner of the auditorium, where the principal stood nodding. She was smiling as I caught her eye, as if to say, "We just got it right."

WE WERE planning a trip to an amusement park, and we had invited a friend whose high school daughter, Jessie, babysat Rex from time to time. The daughter would come and so would her brother, Brian, who was a year older than Rex and had always treated him very well. I thought it would be great to have a peer near Rex's age come and spend some time with us. However, boys will be boys, and they have their pals. So Brian asked if it was okay if he brought along another friend as well. Thinking the day might be even better with a couple of boys, I gave my okay. We would all go in one car, my friend's family-sized silver Suburban.

The morning came, and the big Suburban lumbered into our driveway. Rex and I walked out, equipped with our backpacks filled with all the necessities for such an outing, most importantly, the "food support" his ongoing feeding issues required, but also a Walkman equipped with noise-cancelling headphones in case the clanging and clanking and overall hullabaloo became too much for him. My friend was smiling out the car window, and so was her daughter.

"Rex, are you ready for a fun day?" Jessie asked.

"You're ready for a fun day," Rex said eagerly, loving all those spinning, twisting, jerking rides he knew were awaiting him.

The two boys were in the back. I could make out Brian, but I couldn't see the other boy's face until I opened the door to the car to get us in. My heart stopped when I saw the face looming from the back seat. Not him! He was older, but I couldn't mistake that face. I could see that same face, laughing and smirking at my son, while he and his buddy waved their hands in front of his unseeing eyes. That bully from two years ago! The awful scene flooded my consciousness, and my stomach knotted as I steadied myself for yet another confrontation, when Brian said, "This is my friend, Drew."

"Hello, Drew," I said icily, not acknowledging our prior run-in. "I'm sure you know Rex," I added, with a steely look. *Why was this boy being forced on us?* I didn't have long to wait for the answer, but it wasn't what I expected.

"Yes, I know Rex," he said, and then spoke not to me but to my boy. "Hi, Rex. Do you like to go on rides?"

"You like to go on rides," Rex answered.

Drew was smiling. Was he going to ridicule Rex's pronoun confusion? I was ready to stop any such thing dead in its tracks, but what happened next did just that to me instead.

The boy's voice was full of respect as he said, "That's cool,

Rex! I like rides, too, especially roller coasters. Maybe we could go on some rides together."

I looked from Drew to Rex, trying to assess what was going on here, as I helped my boy climb into the car. "Well, we'll see," I said, not trusting this boy. Brian climbed into the far back of the Suburban to leave room for Rex and me on the middle seat next to Drew.

The boy reached over to help Rex with his seat belt and said, "I thought you were great in the talent show, Rex. You're a great pianist!"

"Thank you," Rex said, beaming. How my child came alive when he was praised and appreciated! That was it! This boy had seen another side of Rex in the talent show, so now my son was a person and not just "that blind kid."

"I play the drums," Drew threw out to Rex. Then he added, "Maybe we could get together sometime and jam!"

Rex remained silent, not answering. But it didn't diminish the offer . . . the potential . . . and the wonder of it.

Mean-spirited bully turned potential friend? How could that be? Was I dreaming? Or had God heard a prayer in Rex's song?

CHAPTER THIRTEEN

Musically Speaking

*One has to find a balance between what people need
from you and what you need for yourself.*

—Jessye Norman, opera singer

Rex's piano teacher Richard Morton heard something altogether different in Rex's song. In fact, not just in "Blackbird," but in every note my son played. Perhaps he allowed that God was playing a minor role, but to him Rex was first and foremost a scientific mystery, an intellectual teaser, a limitless source of fascination, frustration, and overall awe. Ever since the day he had used the word *savant* to describe Rex, his obsession with Rex had been growing. In fact, Richard insisted on spending so much time with him, to develop his genius, that our forays up the magical musical mountain to work with his other piano teacher Lynn, became fewer and fewer until they stopped entirely. Richard's increasing domination of Rex didn't leave us the time for other teachers. As a result, the balance we had found previously between science and God in Rex's two piano teachers began shifting dangerously out of balance.

A prodigious musical savant! I hated the label that reduced the beauty of my child to a sort of scientific anomaly. Yet, at the same time, this man was devoting himself to developing Rex's piano music. I couldn't deny that. So I found myself compliant the day he said, "Would it be okay if I brought a cameraman to film a lesson with Rex?" He wanted to begin a sort of "running record" of my son's music, and presumably his own role in that development. I found myself raising my eyebrows but only voicing minor reservations the day he announced, "I've been nominated as a Volvo hero for my work with Rex." He explained that someone through his "savant network" had put his name into a national contest to award everyday heroes. Then a couple of months later, he won third place in the same contest, and I congratulated him but had an uneasy feeling about the whole thing. However, when I learned he was discussing my little boy's life and development, in addition to his music, with a variety of scientists and researchers in the field of musicology, I took him to task.

"Not only is it unprofessional," I said, struggling to keep my voice level, "but you're not qualified to understand Rex's development." The idea of my son being reduced to a science project was repugnant and abhorrent, and it left me cold. So, like a musical crescendo, what had begun as a whisper of unease began to resonate louder and louder until it was booming in my heart as a resounding internal conflict. Conflict between my duty to help develop this precious gift God had given my son, and my duty to protect him in the process. It was a conflict ready to explode.

So when Richard came to the door for his lesson with Rex, looking like the cat who'd swallowed the mouse, I immediately wondered what else was in the works. I didn't have long to wait. "I've been contacted by a producer from 60 Minutes who heard about my work with Rex," he said, trying to act nonchalant, but his excitement was nonetheless bubbling out at the seams. "So I sent off the videos I had filmed."

"You did that without asking me?" I said, annoyance trumping any amazement that Richard had been able to spread word of Rex's existence so far and so fast.

A flush swept up his face from his warp-speed networking jaw to his balding half moon. "Well it all happened so fast," he said, in lame excuse. "This is all going too fast for me," he added, like he'd set some automatic process in motion over which he now had no control. Like he was the victim and not the perpetrator. "I didn't think, didn't want . . ." He was stammering under my steely gaze. "But you know people are going to want—"

"What?" I cut in. "What are people going to want?"

Not answering my question, he shrugged his bearlike shoulders and tried a helpless grin. "Well, you know it's imminent. It was going to happen sooner or later." Like he'd been swept innocently into the destiny of it all! "Rex is just so . . . interesting." He was smiling sheepishly.

"Of course, he's interesting," I said, softening just a touch at the thought of my extraordinary boy. Then I threw out a warning. "But he's also a beautiful child, and not a science project."

In appeal, he said, "The world should know about Rex." He paused, clearly trying to sell me, and said, "A lot of incredible things could come out of it for him. It's sort of mind-boggling, when you think about it." A coy grin tugged at the corners of his mouth.

Of course I wanted good things for my son. I paused briefly, but in a way that must have told him I was backing down, and so he let everything out. "The producer is already planning on calling Susan Rancer and Dr. Treffert after she speaks with me again," he said, referring to the perfect pitch expert he'd been consulting with and the world-renowned savant expert, Dr. Darold Treffert, who had first described a savant as having "an island of genius in a sea of disability."

Furious now, I snapped. "No! Did you hear what I just said?" I challenged. But then seeing my son out of the corner of my eye, I caught myself . . . and Richard. Practically pushing this man into another room, I said, "Rex, honey, I have to talk to Richard for just a second. I'll be right back." I had one tone for my son, quite another for this man, and the second we were out of Rex's earshot, my honey tone turned back to carefully measured ice. "I'm going to say it again. Rex is a child . . . not an experiment. And I won't allow a bunch of scientists who don't even know him to gather around some media table to discuss him. Do you think I want the world to view my son as an oddity?"

My eyes were boring through him now, and his pink flush turned deep crimson as he began stammering anew. "Well it probably won't . . . I mean it wasn't sure . . . She might not want . . . It was really about my techniques . . ."

I cut him short, too angry to listen anymore. "We're going to skip our lesson today. You'd better go now. I don't want Rex getting as upset as I am. Rex's music is for him, and I don't want to discuss this anymore."

The door shut, and I took a deep breath, knowing I would cancel Rex's piano lessons for a week or two, or maybe a month, I wasn't sure. We just needed a break from the storm I felt brewing.

A couple of weeks later, lacking a babysitter, I took Rex with me to a committee meeting for a fund-raiser for the Blind Children's Center. Wanting to give back to the school that had given Rex his start in life, I had joined the planning committee for the annual Tom Sullivan Blind Children's Center Celebrity Golf Classic. Several committee members were seated around a large table chitchatting, while we waited for the tournament host, Tom Sullivan, to arrive. I took Rex to the piano in the corner of the room so he could play for a few minutes before the meeting began. Well, it didn't take long. A little Mozart, a touch of Bach with a Beethoven swirl, and the room had fallen silent. The man we were waiting for walked into the room, but no one interrupted, and Tom himself stopped still to listen. Since Tom was also blind, he didn't immediately know who was playing. But being a musician himself, he was captivated by the sound. The director of the

Center got up and whispered in Tom's ear. I watched as a grin instantly spread the expanse of his face.

"Rex! My man! That was great!" He was still smiling as the director guided him in our direction. "And I have an idea, Rex. So I'm just going to talk to your mom for a minute here." I loved the way this man spoke to my son, not around him or about him right in front of his face as if he were deaf instead of blind. Tom knew what being blind was, and he knew what respecting a blind child meant. "Cathleen, I don't know what you and your son feel about this idea, but we would be honored if Rex would consider playing some piano for the tournament. If he would . . . I think it would make the day really special."

It was a decision for my son, not me. When asked if he wanted to perform, he remembered the applause he'd gotten at the talent show and said, "Everybody will clap so loudly!" That was his answer. Yes, he would do it.

After a couple of weeks' break in his lessons, Richard began coming back to our home to work with Rex on a set for the event. He would be performing four songs—three vocals his teacher had arranged and one instrumental. The door had just closed on a lesson when our phone rang. It was a woman. "Hello. My name is Shari Finkelstein, and I'm a producer for *60 Minutes*." I was a bit defensive, not knowing exactly what Richard Morton had said, or not said, with regard to my son, but I found myself warmed by the tone of this woman, who turned out to be a new mother herself. "I watched a video of your son, and I have to tell you, I had to show it to my husband, which I normally never do. But this was so amazing and cute I even found myself telling him, 'Oh you have to see this part,' or 'Wait till you see what he's going to do now.'"

All of a sudden, speaking mother to mother with the producer, the proposed *60 Minutes* project seemed more a human interest story about an extraordinary child than a freaky science study, and we set up an exploratory conference call with an associate producer to speak more in depth. During that call, it was in speaking about the stuff of Rex's life, the astounding extremes that had become our norms, that I found myself living our lives through external eyes. "That's incredible" and "fascinating" were the reactions that drew me back into the intrigue of my son's being. Shari asked if Rex ever performed. In a small, somewhat-hesitant voice, I said, "Actually, he will be performing for a Blind Children's Center fund-raiser in a couple of weeks." At that, she said she might like to film the event. But that would be contingent on her first getting a go-ahead on the piece from her boss, correspondent Lesley Stahl.

I wondered how the famous correspondent would respond to Rex. Would she be as captivated by my son as Shari seemed to be? The response came a couple of days later, when Shari called to tell me Lesley had answered her project proposal with an e-mail, which contained only three words—"I Love Rex!" Those three words confirmed my own decision to allow the project to move forward. I trusted these two women to get it right.

THE DAY of the tournament arrived. And I panicked, wondering what I'd allowed Rex to get us into, since he had all but refused to practice the songs for the evening's event in the week leading up to this day. He had never had to work on a song repeatedly, to polish it so that it was performance ready, let alone four songs. The downside of his genius was a reluctance to play a song over and over, craving new input for his brain, preferring to play something he'd just heard. So, when he'd played the songs as a rehearsal, it had been half-hearted and lackadaisical, causing his fingers to fumble and make mistakes. Okay, so there we were! I didn't have any idea what his hands would produce that evening. Then, too, he had been clearing his throat constantly lately, leading me to believe he had some undiagnosed allergies. And that might signal death to his vocals. So, with both piano and voice as unknowns, things didn't bode well for the evening's musical presentation as I arrived at the tournament in the morning to help set up Rex's piano. What we had left was the child himself, the glowing smile, that hearty laugh. It took just one screeching feedback sound from a microphone we were setting up for Rex's piano to realize how much at risk that was too. Maybe my son's whole being was too fragile for any of this. Right now, I felt I was too.

The golfers were arriving, checking in and hurrying out to the putting greens and driving range for some last-minute practice. I walked out to watch a couple of putts and air my brain for a minute. The event host, Tom Sullivan, was there lining up a twelve-foot putt, aided by his coach who would serve as his eyes. Tom would be playing this whole eighteen-hole course blind. This amazing man, who exuded confidence and optimism, liked to quip, "Golf is easier when you've never seen a water hazard or a sand trap." Maybe that's what I needed to do, close my eyes and trust. Tom tapped the ball. It was veering to the left but slowed down just as it approached the hole, which allowed the slant of the green to nudge it ever so slightly to the right. And *clink!* Tom smiled as he heard it drop into the cup.

"Great putt, Tom!" I exclaimed.

"Cathleen!" He recognized my voice instantly. "How's my boy doing?"

"He's at school for a couple of hours, but he's looking forward to tonight," I said, lacking conviction in my voice.

Tom picked up on it immediately. "Just let Rex enjoy the evening," he encouraged. "That's the important thing. There's no pressure."

No pressure? Three hundred guests, golfers, and wives sitting in an elegantly set banquet room, with all eyes on my son? *Just close your eyes and trust*. Trust! *I can do it*, I thought, heading back to the dining room.

That trust lasted all of five minutes, until the van carrying the *60 Minutes* television cameras arrived. They would be poised that evening to catch Rex's every move, every sound, bringing my child's performance into the homes of people across the country. The rest of the morning was a blur. I met Shari, the producer for the *60 Minutes* piece, who had flown across the country for the event. The soundman and cameraman were both setting up equipment—cameras, lights—while Rex's piano teacher, Richard, was supervising piano positioning. We argued about it. He thought more of the audience should see Rex's hands; I thought more should see his face. Mechanics versus the child—old issues I didn't want to mar the day. *Everything will be okay*, I told myself as I walked back outside to get a break from the tension. The golfers were heading down to their golf carts. Only Tom Sullivan would not use a cart. He would walk the course himself, with his golf coach. That way he could get the feel of the course, its slopes, its angles. As host, Tom would kick off the tournament with his first drive. And so as the last of the majestically sung tenor notes of the National Anthem floated over the line of golf carts, I watched Tom's coach line him up for the shot. I heard the sharp crack and saw the ball flying straight down the fairway. And Tom was off with his athletic stride to track the ball. *Close your eyes and trust.*

THE SILENT auction hall had come alive—golfers were coming in off the course as their guests were already busy drinking cocktails and socializing, while marking down names and figures on the bidding sheets attached to auction items. Soon the party would shift into the dining room. Rex had arrived that afternoon dressed in a white dress shirt and off-white pants. He didn't have a dress jacket, and even if he did, given his sensitivities, it would have been too confining for his arms, inhibiting the arm movements he needed to play the piano. Unfortunately, the cameras and lights didn't like white. Shari explained to me that white would cause Rex's face to be washed out. So now he was sporting a red sweater that matched the casual golfing attire of the players. And I did notice the healthy color in his face when he said, "I want to see Grandpa."

My eyes scanned the room, looking for my dad and the other members of our party. "He'll be here soon, sweetie. And who else is coming to hear you play?"

"Aunt Roz . . . and Daddy!" Rex said beaming.

"That's right, Rex, your daddy will come to hear your beautiful music. So, your daddy and my daddy will both be here."

"And Jenny and Raffaella too," Rex added, knowing his full list of personal attendees.

"That's right. We have a lot of people coming, don't we? And, of course, Richard will be here."

"They're coming to see *me!*" he said proudly.

"They sure are, along with a lot of other people," I said surveying the room. I caught sight of my father and Aunt Roz skirting their way toward us through the throng. My father was handsome in a dark blue sports coat and my aunt Roz looked her usual elegant self, as they grinned their way to us. I hugged them each in turn, as did Rex, and I felt the warmth of knowing that my son and I would have an entourage tonight—the support of those closest to us.

"So Rex, are you ready for your big night?" my father asked.

"I'm *ready*, Grandpa!" Rex said it with a certainty in his voice I didn't feel.

The other members of our party arrived, and after greetings and hugs, I left them to browse the auction tables while I took Rex in to check on his piano and do a sound check. We needed to make sure the sound level was right not only for the room but for the future television audience.

The banquet room had been transformed—the tables all impeccably primped and preened. The stage was adorned with colorful, decorative awards baskets and live-auction items. And there in the center, sitting aglow in a pool of light, stood Rex's piano. The CBS cameras now flanked it on all sides—his every move, every gesture would be captured. Nothing could be dissimulated, hidden. The soundman would place a microphone on Rex. Then nothing he said, no note he sang or sound he made would be left unheard either. The moment of truth was upon us. Would Rex play half-heartedly as he'd done for the past week, not wanting to put in the work it took to polish his pieces? He'd been the epitome of a seven-year-old who'd set his eyes on the prize of audience applause without consideration for the work he needed to put into getting there. Or would the audience change that, giving him that good energy, the adrenaline his body needed, to execute his piano pieces cleanly?

The room began filling with people, and the evening's festivities were set to shift into high gear. I was vaguely aware of smiles in our direction as I focused my attention on my son. Rex needed to be comfortable, not overwhelmed by external stimuli, in order to optimize his potential for success. I had brought some tapes with our noise-reduction headphones just in case. Richard was trying hard to maintain a calm exterior, but the beads of sweat on his forehead betrayed his anxiety. Shari was smiling at me, encouraging, and I appreciated it. Once again, I wondered what we'd gotten ourselves into. More than that, I wondered if this was the right thing for my son. Sure, he thought he wanted to do it, but he hadn't appreciated the process one bit. Nor had I. It had been a lot of work . . . and worry. If this was right, shouldn't I be swept over by a wave of peace by now?

All the diners were seated, and Tom Sullivan took the podium. That was my signal to begin my move with Rex to the stage. "We have a very special musician here with us tonight who's going to make you forget all those bunkers you visited today," Tom ribbed. "In fact, this young man, Rex, might even make you forget a hole in one."

I guided my son lightly as he walked sure-footed up the steps of the stage. "I'm going to share with my friends, Mommy," Rex said as I helped him onto the piano bench. *Share! What a wonderful way of thinking of it.*

"You sure are, sweetheart. There are a lot of people here to see you play," I said softly, feeling more than seeing the hundreds of curious, expectant eyes trained on our every move. There was a sudden hush in the room—all dinner chatter aborted as the crowd wondered what they were in store for. I sat down next to Rex, knowing his performance was out of my hands, like so much of his life. All I could do was support him to the best of my ability; the rest was up to him—as always. I looked up to see Tom smiling at us from the podium on the other end of the stage. I could still hear the resolute crack of his opening drive down the fairway, and see its graceful arc as it took off. Now it was Rex's turn.

"So Rex, what would you like to play for your friends?" I asked him into the microphone.

"'When I'm 64,'" he said, announcing the Beatles song Richard had worked into a jazzy number for him. The one he hadn't played for his talent show.

He played and sang the first verse with the audience hanging on each note. He was holding his own. I took a breath, and that's when I heard the beginning of an agonizingly drawn-out, throaty sound, amplified unmercifully for all to hear—Rex clearing his throat. He'd been doing it so much lately; I'd had nightmares of him battling the insurgent phlegm all the way through his performance. I cringed but knew there was nothing I could do. Miraculously, his fingers didn't miss a beat as the unforgiving microphone caught the particularly slow and guttural sound at the end of the verse. That sparked a wave of laughter in the audience, perhaps because of the reminder that Rex was just a child, with seven-year-old habits in spite of the sophistication of his music.

Then applause followed, either to encourage or because they thought the song was ending. Would it throw Rex? Disturb his timing in the second verse—the one he had struggled with during practice because of the large jumps it required his tiny hands to make? I glanced discretely at my son as he played through both laughter and applause, not at all distracted. On the contrary, it sparked him on. His face lit up at the sound—the laughter was joy to him, and the applause was the fuel he craved. That's the way his body worked, as an energy sponge. His hands became stronger, more commanding, as he struck the keys with greater precision and his voice sang out with increased vigor. He now knew how many people were watching him and how enthusiastic they were! And he loved it! As he reached the end of the third verse, to which Richard had added a rousing blues finale, the whole audience was clapping along to the final beats. It spurred Rex on to the final, "Will you still need me, Will you still feed me . . . . cause I get *hungry* . . . when I'm 64? Yeeaaah!"

The applause was so thunderous that I thought Rex might fall backward off his bench. His eyes went round with exuberance, and his teeth shone bright in the spotlights as he leaned back on his tailbone and started flapping his arms rapidly in his gesture that said excitement was overwhelming his nervous system. He was laughing with such abandon, I wanted to just let it go. But I knew he needed to reign in his emotions to a manageable level, in order to continue, so I put my arm tenderly around his shoulder, in a gesture to calm.

The apathy of the previous few weeks was clearly a dead issue. Now we were tipping the scale to the opposite extreme as Rex began the only classical piece on the program, Beethoven's Sonatina in F. It required speed and precision, with the left and right hands playing against each other. He played the piece as though he had pressed the "automatic" button on his hands, setting them loose, while his mind remained caught up in the audience response. His eyes were still alight and far away, not encapsulated in the music, and he punctuated intermittent phrases of the melody with laughter. It was fun. It was funny. It was joyous. No one had ever had such a good time playing that Sonatina. It was like he couldn't believe himself what was happening to him. As he laughed his way into the final notes, the crowd roared, loving the child and his unconstrained joy even more than the music, with spectators and performer feeding off each other in a sort of escalating response crescendo.

The expression on my son's face beaming in the spotlight, sparkling like a rare and priceless diamond, swept over me like a heavenly torrent, a revelation. Music was Rex's heart, his soul, the special gift God had given him to communicate like no other. It was his language—his grace. I would keep fighting the external battles of our lives, trying to push back the clouds of our existence, but his was an internal battle, and the look on his face said his spirit was winning.

CHAPTER FOURTEEN

Beyond the Music

*Hope is that thing with feathers that perches in the soul
and sings the tune without the words and never stops . . . At all.*

—Emily Dickinson, poet

I don't know where Rex's music is going in the future. Hopefully as far as possible. But I think the most important thing is that it connects him to the world, that it gives him a sense of who he is, that it helps him to socialize. You know, he loves the applause. It really hooks him into the rest of the world." My words, answering Lesley Stahl's question, said it all. They also brought Rex's *60 Minutes* profile, "Musically Speaking," to a close as the logo clock ticked in the station break.

Rex's classmates clapped, shouting, "Great job, Rex!"

"Thank you very much," said Rex, laughing, on a high from watching himself on TV.

His principal, Pat Cairns, who had been so supportive ever since he'd entered her school, walked over to where we sat on the couch and said, "That was beautiful." She was beaming. I felt relief that the profile had truly caught the beauty of my child, and that I'd been right to trust the filming to go forward. We had gathered at a classmate's home for a "pool and viewing" party so that Rex could be with his peers as we watched his profile air on the year's season premiere for *60 Minutes*.

But after months of excitement surrounding this profile, I

wanted our lives to return to a semblance of normalcy. Inevitably that meant a change of piano teachers, a change from Richard's obsession with the science of "savant" back to the purity of the child, great composers, and the music. Fortunately, this also came at a time when Richard, who was a piano teacher only by passion and not profession, was struggling to keep up with the infinity of Rex's musical brain, feeling the weight of his charge.

Chance led us to a brilliant, somewhat-eccentric man who had been a concert pianist and who, incidentally, had vast experience working with the blind. His name was David Pinto, and he knew how to teach Rex from day one. His own quirkiness and originality was the perfect match for Rex's own. He met Rex on his own level—bringing his own creative genius to whatever childlike need Rex had at any given moment (and this from a man in his late fifties).

By the time we met David, Rex's hand's had desensitized enough to not only touch, but actually seek out the "soothing" feel of edges and cracks and seams in different surfaces, whether wood, concrete or fabric. It was another repetitive, obsessive movement, but one that was discrete, and which also seemed to calm Rex and provide him with a sense of order. When he was "feeling seams" as I called it, I knew how hard it was to get his attention, and David learned quickly. During his first lesson with his new teacher David said he needed to work one-on-one with my son. So I planted myself a little hesitantly, but silently (as requested) in a distant corner of the room, and watched my eight-year old son dash off a few notes on the piano. But then as David started to say something, Rex removed his right hand from the keys, dropping it to explore the leg of the piano bench, and discovered grooves carved in wood! He couldn't pull his hand away as his index finger circled the leg again and again. And what David had intended to say faded in Rex's unhearing ear to "blah, blah, blah," a voice with no meaning to the autistic brain intent on feeling piano bench grooves. Well instead of attempting to instruct Rex to get his hands back on the piano, which Rex would have heard as more "blah," this clever man sat down cross-legged on the floor next to my son and said, "these grooves do feel pretty good, shall we count them together?" After joining Rex in counting piano bench grooves he moved the numeric idea along to beats in a measure. And moved Rex's hand back to the keys, from mindless repetition back to piano notes.

In Rex's entire life I had never met a teaching professional of any kind who could establish an instant rapport with my son. He had been able to keep him captivated and involved from the very instant they met, and all without any input from me. And so David Pinto became the undisputed master of helping Rex learn not just music, but musicianship through creative fun. He was in the process of founding the Academy of Music for the Blind, which would incorporate other skills, such as rhythm and dance and social skills, along with piano, to develop the whole child.

What could be better than this ingenious and holistic approach of learning to tango and tap-dance in addition to piano? But the problem was the sixty-mile commute through heavy Los Angeles traffic it took to get to his establishment. We could go on Saturdays before the traffic hit, but we also needed to be practical. And that meant finding a suitable local teacher who also placed the child before the science. I hoped we could find local support from his original teacher, Lynn Marzulli. Regretfully, this man, who had described my son's gift as a touch of the Divine, could no longer help us. As with Richard Morton, Rex had moved beyond Lynn's skills to teach since Lynn was primarily a composer, not a teacher. But he told us about a woman who could sight-read even the most complex musical scores, assuring us she could stay beyond Rex for a good many years. Her name was Sara Banta, and she was the head of instrumental music at Pepperdine University, right next to our home.

We made an appointment to meet her in a music rehearsal

room on campus, where we found the woman alongside two massive Steinway concert grand pianos. I saw kindness in her eyes as she smiled at us in welcome. "I watched the *60 Minutes* piece, and I'm happy to give it a try," she said, then added, "but I'm afraid I don't know anything about teaching a blind child to play the piano."

"Don't worry, Sara. All you really need to know about Rex you'll learn from being with him, not from a bunch of reports. Rex's two former piano teachers didn't have any experience teaching a blind child either. The training comes in the doing."

Sara invited Rex to sit down. I helped my son position himself at the nearby piano as she went around to the second piano. He had begun testing the notes before he was even seated and immediately began improvising, loving this big, resonant instrument.

Sara had an uncertain, questioning look on her face, not really knowing where to begin or whether she should cut in on his melody. But he wasn't about to stop, so finally she suggested, "Would you like to play something for me, Rex?" His voice remained silent. He hadn't even heard her. Only the depth and resonance of this Steinway could speak to him.

"I don't think he heard you," I said, already beginning the Rex education. She would teach him piano, and in return, she would be required to learn about this special boy.

Sara probably wasn't used to students ignoring her, but she caught on quickly. She watched for an opening, a break in his notes, and then jumped in on her own piano, mimicking his melancholic style for a few measures. That got his attention, and he listened, intrigued now. She let him back in. Then after he'd played his own measures, he stopped, expectant.

Sara's fingers turned melancholy to lightness and cheer, calling it a "Mozart style," with trills and runs up and down the keys. Cheery was good, and Rex giggled, hardly able to wait for his turn. He practically fell on the keys when she stopped. The dialogue had begun.

Her eyes widened as she watched him play back to her. Then she shook her head at the speed and creativity of my son's responses. "None of my college students can respond that quickly, that intuitively," she said. She began nodding her head now, effusively, and smiling broadly. And as her hands jumped back to the keys with extra vigor, she added, "This is going to be fun!"

And with that, Rex and I found what would become our new musical home at Pepperdine University, with a lovely woman named Sara. It was a wonderful feeling, having his musical development in her capable and caring hands along with those of David Pinto and his academy. It allowed me a new sense of peace, having found two solid sources of musical input for Rex. And his music began moving forward at an accelerated pace.

Meanwhile, I felt the need to find other ways to connect him to life, to keep all the rest moving forward as well. As his sensory system matured, allowing him to progressively overcome his touch and sound aversions, the world was becoming increasingly accessible. This allowed us to accept some invitations for Rex to perform his music at various educational and inspirational venues, requiring travel. I thought his music provided a means for Rex to have new and varied experiences that taught him more about the world beyond the music—a means to an end, a connector to life.

"Get ready for takeoff," he would shout excitedly at the new experience of an airplane. Or, "Touchdown," followed by "Put on the brakes," as the plane would land and come sliding to a halt. Or, "Make the fire go whoosh," as our hot-air balloon soared over the same desert, after performing his piano at a YPO (Young Presidents Organization) educational conference. Rex's cry for adventure was obvious in his appeals to others—to pilots and drivers. But there was another cry I felt even stronger—a cry to do for himself, a cry for freedom—the cry of the blackbird.

Rex's father, William, lived in Utah, a stone's throw from various ski resorts, and so it was the perfect opportunity to get Rex on skis. As luck would have it, the Park City Ski Resort was the home of a ski school for the disabled, the National Ability Center. I'd booked him a couple of two-hour ski lessons during our stay with his dad. "I'm going to bomb down the ski slope," he announced the morning of his first lesson. He was using his father's words and didn't yet know their meaning. Same thing for his parka and powder pants. He wondered why he was wearing these fluffy, awkward clothes that made him stiff and robotic as he tried to walk to the car.

We drove to the Center, which was located right at the base of the mountain. We'd been told they'd have skis and boots there for Rex, as well as gloves and goggles. Rex was excited as we walked through the door and were introduced to a well-tanned ski instructor named Don who would be giving him his lesson. "I'm going to bomb down the ski slope," Rex stated once again to the man.

"I'm sure you will, but first we have to get you all suited up in your bombing-down-the-mountain gear, okay?" the instructor said, not missing a beat.

"Okay, Don," Rex said confidently.

"First, I'm going to slip a little vest over your head, Rex, just as a little precaution," he announced, tying the side straps to secure the bright orange vest, stamped with glaring black letters, which said, "Blind Skier." Catching my eye, he explained, "It's for safety."

Meanwhile I was struggling to get his ski boots on. "I don't want to go skiing," he cried out suddenly, his previous anticipation now obliterated by very real hypersensitivity, as the first boot grabbed and squeezed his foot. His free foot started kicking forward to avoid the other torturous boot.

"It's just a ski boot that will help you bomb down the mountain," I said, praying his still-sensitive feet and hands would not put a stop to the whole thing, right then and there.

"You'll see, Rex. You'll have a blast," Don promised in a confident, relaxed voice that calmed Rex's foot long enough for me to slip the other boot on. "You'll need some gloves too, Rex," the instructor said matter-of-factly, picking through a box until he came across a pair that looked about my son's size.

However, feet were one thing, hands quite another. He batted and flailed, not letting the thing on, until I grabbed his hands, saying, "You won't be able to ski without gloves to keep your hands from freezing, Rex." But reason was useless in the face of this kind of autistic sensitivity, and his fingers crumbled up into a ball and simply refused to be pushed into the gloves. Don raised his eyebrows—for a first time—but went back to the box. This time he chose a pair of mittens that opened up with a zipper on the back. That might do the trick. So I uncoiled my son's fingers, flattened his hand, encased it in the mitten, and zipped before he could refuse. Same process with the other hand, and he was protected from the cold. His hands stuck straight out like rods, as though getting his hands as far away from his body as possible would also distance him from the mittens. And he was now completely stiff as he stood up.

"All right, Rex, looks like we just need some glasses or goggles and we're good to go," Don said.

But on that one, my son laid down the "law of Rex." "Take the glasses off!" he wailed, shaking his head violently once I'd stuck them on.

"Okay, okay, Rex, you don't need to wear glasses," I assured him, removing them quickly, seeing my son at his limit. "It's not that sunny today, so you can just wear your hat." I popped his baseball cap onto his head, hoping it would be enough to protect his sensitive eyes. Once again, I found myself in that balancing act between what I knew Rex needed for his health and safety and what his sensory system would allow. There he was, fighting that incessant internal battle of his own, fighting autism's relentless grasp on his brain, needing to overcome his own body to get the freedom that was so easily attainable for others. And I had only one recourse in it all—to maneuver the external, attempting, as always, to pave the way for him.

But how far should I push? I asked myself as I watched my son seeming to withdraw into the shell of his equipment. He didn't even know what skiing was. It had all been my idea of something he'd enjoy, knowing his love of physical movement and fast and jerky sensations, but maybe he wouldn't like it, maybe it was way too much. An outsider looking on might consider I was torturing my son, forcing this on him. But remembering back, the same could have been said when I was smearing food on his refusing lips to get him to eat or forcing him to straighten and strengthen his spaghetti legs when all he wanted to do was collapse. And now he was a hearty eater and had strong, capable legs. This was the same thing. I felt God asking me once again to step out in faith. *Walk by faith, not by sight.* I had to push forward, trusting, or we'd never know, even though I acknowledged a fundamental difference between eating and walking, and skiing. Before, it had been for my son's very survival that I had been unrelenting, and now it was so he could get the extras. I felt a lump growing in my throat as I remembered how far we'd come. Then I clutched my son's stiff hand, led him haltingly out the door of the Center, down a small ramp, and onto the snow, leading him beyond mere survival toward "quality of life."

Don was taking it all in stride as he witnessed the extreme reticence that had replaced his student's prior enthusiasm. Rex was taken aback when he touched the "crunchy" snow. He hadn't known what it would be like, even though I'd tried to explain it to him. He had to experience it himself. "It's a little crunchier, but it's soft like sand, isn't it, Rex?"

"Yes," he said, but he didn't look convinced as he plodded tentatively forward to where Don had placed his skis in the snow.

"Rex, I've got your skis here, and I'm gonna just help you put your right foot in," the instructor said. "Just hold on to your mom." With me clutching hold of my son, since his ski mittens made it impossible for him to grab anything, Don lifted his foot, placing the toe into the ski binding. "Now stomp your heel down, Rex."

And after repeating the same process for the other foot, he was all set, although he looked even more concerned now that his feet were completely imprisoned in skis as well as boots. What had he gotten himself into?

Don placed a clip on the front of Rex's skis, which connected them. "This is to keep his skis together," he explained. "And I'm going to place a tether on your skis, Rex. It's a sort of strap to make sure you don't get away from me up there on the slopes." The instructor winked at me and said to Rex, "I know you're probably going to want to leave me behind, but we can't let that happen just yet."

At this point my son didn't have an ounce of his "bomb down the slopes" bravado left, but I was hoping once he got to moving on the skis, that might trend back.

"I'm going to move you forward just a little, so we can get you used to the feel of sliding on the snow," Don said, pulling on the tethers.

Rex's face registered shock at the sudden slipping movement, his hands moving up and to his sides, an automatic balance reflex. "Good, Rex. That's exactly what you need to do to balance," the instructor said.

Don pulled some more. Rex shifted his body to maintain his balance, but his face looked frozen with fear. "Okay, Rex, now try to slide your own feet." He couldn't do it, until the instructor took hold of his hips from behind and helped him glide one leg forward, then the other.

Rex had a good sense of balance, but he looked so scared slipping around on this unknown surface. I was seriously beginning to doubt the whole endeavor. That's when Don gave a strong tug on the tethers, jerking Rex forward too quickly. He lost his balance, and with my automatic maternal reaction mode always turned on, I dove to catch him before he fell into the snow. The weight of my falling son threw me down instead, with his own fall cushioned by my body.

Just as I was feeling proud of my fast reaction, I caught the instructor's look, as he watched mother and son lying in a heap. He had a smile tugging at his lips, as he raised his eyebrows once again. "I wanted Rex to fall," he explained, extending a hand to help us up. "So that he will know what it is—and so he'll know it won't hurt. That's the only way he'll be able to ski without fear."

I stood back, then, to allow the instructor to do his job. He was the expert in teaching children of all abilities to do this. He promptly caused Rex to lose his balance again. But this time, even though it went against my mother's instinct, I just watched my son fall. And as he plunged into the soft, cold snow, I braced myself for him to say that was it, that he was done with skiing now. But he did no such thing. In fact, it was just the opposite. To my utter amazement, he squealed with delight, laughing, his tension broken by the fall. The relief made me laugh as well.

"Did you like crashing into the snow?" I asked, thrilled, helping him back to his feet.

All fear was gone from his face, replaced by new wonder and anticipation of what lie ahead. "I want to crash into the snow some more," he said. This time, I was the one who raised my eyebrows!

There were many different aspects of skiing that made Rex temporarily freeze up again, and naturally so. It was all unknowns he couldn't see. He was being asked to trust, to step out in faith during each step of the process. Boarding ski lifts, exiting the lifts with a fast sliding motion, the first small descents when he felt as though his skis were out of control. But he learned that Don's command of "weight on the left foot" meant he would turn to the right, while "weight on the right foot" would make him go left; and he began to feel the control he could exert on his own skis, slowing his speed down. By the end of the two-hour lesson, the tethers were there just as insurance.

It was on our last run, suitably called "Home Run," after we had followed a cat track for some time, that Don had Rex ski down a sharper and steeper corner than he had on the previous runs. My son's face lit up, and the slopes suddenly resounded in his laughter. "Rev up the motor!" I shouted, adding fuel to his joy fire.

"I want to go faster," he said, still laughing as the slope flattened and slowed him down, all remnants of robotic Rex now dead and buried. Don looked to me, as though for permission to grant my son his request.

I motioned back to my boy as if to say, "He's the boss."

"All right, Rex, you're in charge on this last run. You know how to make your turns, and how that slows you down. So I'm not going to call out turns to you unless we get in trouble. Okay?"

"Okay, Don."

"Are you ready, Rex?" he asked.

"I'm ready!" And he was. Clearly. Ready to take control, whatever that meant. On his own skis, feeling the exhilaration of speed, his body flew down the slope unchecked by the tethers that were there just for insurance and remained slack in his instructor's hands. As I skied by his side, his face was alight with the thrill and excitement of it all. And I felt it too. Gone was my own fear and reticence. This was about really living.

"I'm bombing down the ski slope!" he shouted to the world as he flew faster and faster. This reminded me of the day Rex had first taken off running, the exhilaration of breaking free from his chains. That is, until I realized just how fast we were going and how close we were to the Center. A man who saw the "Blind Skier" label on Rex's chest removed himself quickly from my son's path, just as Don was about to pull on the tethers. But taking my son's freedom was his last recourse, and instead, he shouted, "Turn to the right, Rex," just as we approached our destination.

Rex delayed a second, two, maybe even three, not wanting to have his wings clipped, wanting only to keep soaring. I watched a momentary struggle between heart and mind as his mind was following orders, applying pressure to his left foot, but his heart was still flying free, bombing down the mountain. I knew what was going to happen in the split second before it did, but I could do nothing to stop it. His internal hesitation sent him pitching over his skis to tumble into the snow. I heard muffled sounds coming from him as he lay face down in the snow.

Popping my own skis off, I bounded to him, not able to bear his tears. I pulled him up, already berating myself once again for allowing the whole thing to happen, for pushing too hard for real life. But that's when I realized that the sound wasn't crying, it was laughter, breathless and choppy, but escalating as I sat him up. "I bombed down the ski slope, Mommy, and landed with a crash!" he said, laughter racking his body now. "I want to bomb down the mountain again!"

He not only survived the crash landing but was begging for more. I felt my heart swelling. I knew Rex would have many more ski days—hopefully he would learn to execute a more controlled "bombing down the mountain." But I also knew, as my son reached out toward normalcy, there would be many other arenas where he would need to learn to fall. Don had gotten it right, because that was the only way he would ever be able to fly.

CHAPTER FIFTEEN

Meeting Derek

Friendship is born at that moment when one person says to another:
"What! You, too? Thought I was the only one."

—C.S. Lewis, author

J ust two years after the filming of "Musically Speaking," when Rex was nine years old, the mystery of Rex's gift, and fascination surrounding it, led to a follow-up profile by Lesley Stahl and the *60 Minutes* crew. The segment was simply called "Rex" this time, and as with his first profile, it included an older, now twenty-six-year-old British savant named Derek Paravicini, as a sort of bookend, a glimpse of where Rex might possibly end up as an adult. This young man was described as "a human iPod" for his ability to store in his brain every piece of music he'd ever heard. Derek was an extraordinary jazz musician, blind, and even more cognitively impaired than Rex, as demonstrated by his inability to show what the number three meant, or any number for that matter. He was also blond and handsome, a chiseled, older version of my son's cherubic and childlike beauty.

A boy and a young man leading parallel lives—separated by sixteen years and an ocean—had never met. Then came an invitation to meet Derek. Rex was ten when he was asked to come to London to meet his older counterpart as part of a British production called "The Musical Genius" for the series *Extraordinary People*, produced in conjunction with Discovery Health, which would air the episode in the States under the title "Musical Savants." It was a chance to gaze into the looking glass of my son's future, his musicality of course, but also into his being. How far had this twenty-six-year old made it down life's road emotionally and socially? Might not Derek provide me with a benchmark for Rex?

As chance would have it, Rex and I would be in Germany in the spring of his tenth year to receive the Winspiration Award for his inspiration in helping others to take whatever hand they'd been dealt in life and using it to win. That enabled us to make only a minor adjustment to our travel plans and make the Channel leap to meet the British musician. At the same time, Shari Finkelstein from 60 Minutes was flying in from New York to film the meeting of the two musical savants for the first time, presumably to be used for the next episode of the "Rex" savant saga on CBS. By policy and philosophy, 60 Minutes didn't orchestrate the displacement of the subjects of their segments, but if the people displaced themselves into newsworthy meetings, they would happily have cameras there to film.

In preparation for meeting Derek, who was renowned for his jazz, Rex began dipping his fingers into the genre, which had previously been a bit too free-form for his classical brain. To date, he had only been able to take it in small doses before requesting a Beethoven break or some other such classical brain reset. But he had been given George Gershwin's "I've Got Rhythm" to work on in anticipation of the meeting, so the two musicians could play together and eventually collaborate for the culminating documentary piece, which would be a jazz performance featuring the two pianists at the Mandalay Bay Hotel in Las Vegas, a mere ten days after their initial meeting.

With two sets of cameras rolling, the British documentary team and CBS, Rex and I walked into the Belsize piano studio in the north of London where Derek would be waiting with his piano teacher and mentor, Adam Ockelford. I had visions of Schroeder, from the *Peanuts* comic strip, when we entered the room. The young man was bent over his piano, his white shirtsleeves billowing out as his arms rose and fell with such intensity and concentration that I wondered if he even realized we were there. But as soon as Adam signaled our arrival to him, he stood up, and with his teacher's assistance, moved in our direction and extended his hand. "I'm Derek. Hello, Rex. I'm Derek." He was outgoing but seemed repetitive and a bit disoriented away from the piano keys. Like Rex, this young man needed grounding in his piano, almost as if he got his balance from the keys, the notes. "Would you like to play some piano, Rex?" he asked, already moving back to his instrument.

"Sure, Derek," replied my son to the invitation. Rex played "I've Got Rhythm" just as he had learned it. But when the older musician took over the same piece, playing it in a more flamboyant style, Rex covered his ears and protested. At twenty-six, music had clearly become a social vessel for Derek, enabling him to play with other musicians, either jamming at the piano or as part of an ensemble; but for my ten-year-old son, it was still mostly his private domain. He struggled when asked to listen to a different musician playing an alternative version of a song he already knew. On the other hand, Rex could take a song and mix it up, playing it in a variety of styles. He even liked to quip, "I can turn a sonata into a waltz, or Mozart into Chopin, or even a Russian dance."

Rex demonstrated a similar aversion to another musician invading his space later in the day upon a visit to the famous Beatles studio, Abbey Road Studios, when Derek began singing my son's beloved "When I'm 64." Rex again covered his ears with a plaintive, "Stop singing, Derek!"

Musically, Derek was prolific and commanding, seeming to feel a deep need to fill the silence in any room with myriad notes, and two questions popped to my mind within the first few minutes with this young man: Would my little boy be able to hold his own in a collaboration with such a powerhouse? And how would the musical Derek translate into Derek the person and social skills?

The first question was answered when Adam suggested a new ragtime tune to Rex, one that Derek had been playing for twenty years, Scott Joplin's "The Entertainer." Since this was a song my son had never played before, not only did he not have any proprietary claim to a certain version of it, but he clearly had his own deep need to get his fingers into it. Adam played it one time, and Rex had to jump in, unable to contain that need. With this new song, he had no problem allowing Derek and all his substantial George Shearing chords into the mix as Adam set the tempo on still a third piano. "Shall we swing it now?" the piano teacher suggested.

As I watched the intent twenty-six-year-old sweep the piece up into quick-stepping jazz moves, Rex refused to be left behind by the more experienced jazz pianist. "It's bluesy, baby!" Rex exclaimed, kicking it into a higher gear himself. And what a "meet and greet" it was, the room coming alive to the beat, with the bodies of the two musicians moving as much as the music, with Rex bouncing up and down on his piano bench while Derek rocked his head from side to side. A true audio and visual jam session!

"Fantastic, Adam and Derek!" Rex exclaimed as they finished, with a sparkle in his eye, which boded well for the music these two would share over the upcoming ten days. What remained unknown was how the two would relate on a personal level. Would there be any meeting place for them beyond the music?

Following our initial meeting with Derek in London, he followed us back to our home in Malibu along with his piano teacher and film crew. It was during this visit that we got to know the British musician better, and he answered my question about how his music translated into his person. If Rex was reticent to share his music with Derek, it was not the same with his musical world. And this world Rex happily shared with the young man, first taking him to Pepperdine University, where he had been studying music for the past two years, and then to the Academy of Music for the Blind, where he also studied piano along with dance and got to play with other gifted and blind youngsters. Wherever we went, as soon as Derek touched a piano, he took control of the room. But what was even more interesting for me to observe was his ability to interact socially. It was that ability that really came as a surprise to me. He had a clear grasp of social etiquette, polite forms, and such—thrusting his hand out as if he was drawing a sword each time he met a new person, accompanied by a rather starched and British, "Hello, I'm Derek." But, in addition, I watched him sustain conversations, something that had been, until now, impossible for Rex.

Adam Ockelford explained it to me. "Derek has learned all the forms and conventions of communication in much the same way he has with music. So he mixes them up and varies them and, presto, out comes conversation." I found the analogy fascinating. Even more enlightening was the fact that back home, as Derek had gotten older, he had found another activity he actually preferred to music. I was stunned when Adam said, "He doesn't play as much piano as he used to because he likes to go out with friends and just hang out." I'm not sure whether my jaw actually dropped upon hearing those words, or if it did so only in my mind, but my heart yearned to be able to say the same thing of Rex. Would his genius be a conduit to normalcy, or would it keep him locked up in his exceptional extremes?

Derek and Rex were both sitting around a lunch table full of adults and children at the Academy of Music for the Blind. Derek was garrulous and involved; Rex was silent and withdrawn. In contrast to the Brit, too many people talking shut my son down. He needed to listen so intently in order to process and be able to interject anything into the mix that he normally just refrained in such a setting. That is, unless he felt like throwing in a particular concern that was completely out of context. For example, when the group was discussing foods, Rex threw in, "Adam, are you Derek's piano teacher?" He was drawing from the *60 Minutes* piece he knew so well, and then he asked, "And did you work daily with Derek for more than ten years?" Perhaps in time Rex would reach Derek's level of social interaction.

However, the truth of Derek's communication wasn't immediately apparent. It was revealed at the end of that lunch, when I remarked wistfully to the British cameraman, "I love the way Derek can engage in a sustained conversation with people."

The man responded with a smile. "It is fascinating, I agree, and Derek is a lot of fun." He then added, "But you never know what to believe of what he says. He will spin a totally believable yarn and get you going. And then you find out none of it is true." He shook his head at the incorrigible Derek, who seemed full of surprises indeed.

"What do you mean?" I asked.

The explanation was fascinating. Derek's words were without comprehension; his conversations had a form and continuity but didn't mean anything to one of the participants. I was determined to pay more attention to the content of what Derek said after that. The young man would throw in inflections, sometimes questioning, but speaking with certainty in his voice that commanded not only a response but belief he knew what he was talking about.

I wanted to see for myself. So I asked, "Derek, will you come to our house and go swimming in the ocean?"

"I would love to, Cathleen! I would love swimming in the ocean!" I caught a dubious look on Adam's face as Derek continued. "I swim in the ocean back home."

"You do, Derek? That's great! Well, there will be a lot of surfers in our ocean!"

"A lot of surfers, yes! I love surfing too. Riding on the waves, you know. I love to ride on the waves."

"You're a surfer, Derek?" I asked, playing his conversation game.

"Yes, Cathleen. I am! Can we surf in the ocean at your house, Cathleen? I would love to ride on some waves like I do back home in England." He threw in enthusiasm to match his words. "When can we go surfing in the ocean, Cathleen?"

A conversation with Derek was like storytelling with Rex. He just made things up and fit it in, turning fantasy to fact. But he loved it, and people enjoyed his company. It was his way of being involved, apparently as far as his own mental development would take him. Adam said it best: "Rex is so much more cognitively connected than Derek." That was the difference. Rex never made things up. Conversation was still a laborious process, not at all automatic as it seemed with Derek. But what he said was real, and that was why his words were few in comparison.

Ask Rex what he would like to get his mother as a present, and he would answer, "I don't know." The truth. I asked Derek that same question one day during a break in our filming, while we were strolling through an outdoor marketplace wandering among eateries and boutiques. "Derek, would you like to buy your mother a gift while you're here in Malibu?"

Derek paused for just a second, before responding in an ingenuous, reflective way, "Why, yes. I think I'd like to buy Mary Ann [his mother] a glass of wine!"

It was cute and rather charming, coming from this aristocratically handsome young man with his upper-crust British accent, even telling of his mother's tastes, but it was, of course, completely out of context.

During the course of the week we spent together, my fascination with Derek grew, and I found myself wondering how much of what I was seeing would actually be my son in a few years. Derek and Rex had been assigned the same highly unique label of prodigious musical savant, as if they'd gained entry into a club with only a handful of members worldwide. And yet they were individuals. While Derek's neurological system seemed to border on hypertense, conveying almost manic energy at times that he pumped into his endless runs up and down the piano keyboard, Rex's neurology tipped the scale at the other end of the spectrum. He was hypotonic, and it was a struggle to maintain his energy levels. Too much noise and mania around him caused him to shut down and become nonresponsive. Both boys found their balance in the piano—Derek using the instrument to calm and drain nervousness, and Rex using it to infuse energy and creativity into his body.

The two musicians spent the week together collaborating for the biggest performance of their lives, in front of an expected audience of ten thousand at the Mandalay Bay Hotel in Las Vegas. But it wasn't the gloss of Las Vegas or the prospect of such a big event that became my snapshot for that week. It was the day Derek and Adam came to our home in Malibu, and we all took a walk down to the beach. That was the first time I saw Derek's personality really shine through. While in London, it had all been about the music and playing piano together. And I'd never seen the young man smile, let alone laugh. He seemed to be the epitome of the dry, overly serious Brit, which was perhaps even accentuated by the mix of disability and genius—not what I wanted my son to become. But back in Malibu I saw quite a different young man in Derek unplugged.

The skies were gray in Malibu—not at all the image the British had of springtime in California, the land of endless sun—but the surf was pounding. Surfers were out in force on the Point, just north of our home, and with documentary cameras in tow, I led Derek and Rex and entourage down to the sand. "It gives atmosphere," Derek's piano teacher Adam assured me, when I apologized for the overcast skies.

Derek climbed down seventeen steps to the waterline. He counted the steps as he went, as Rex did, which made me think he did, in fact, have an awareness of numbers. Adam assured me his counting was rote and that he didn't understand the underlying concept. I wouldn't let it go, knowing how Rex was just the opposite with numbers, possessing an ability to count silently even such things as the number of times you moved the toothbrush back and forth in his mouth. It had to be exactly twenty in each quadrant. Accidently brush twenty-one times or nineteen, and you were in trouble! "That was twenty-one, not twenty," he would say through clenched teeth.

Given Derek's numeric sense in his music, I felt compelled to give him my own test. "Derek, could you clap five times?" Rex could do that in his sleep.

He began clapping as he counted, "One, two, three—" I interrupted. "No, Derek. Do you think you could clap five times for me without counting out loud?"

"I can do that," he assured me. And began . . . clap, clap, clap, clap, clap, clap, clap . . . Adam looked at me with a smile as if to say, "Satisfied?"

Yes, I was satisfied. I knew my son and Derek were different beings, with unique challenges, in spite of their unique commonalities. But what came to define Derek for me went past the music and past the disability. The young man touched the sand. "Cathleen, I think I'd like to take a walk on the sand. Would Rex like to take a walk on the sand?"

"Rex, what do you think? Are you ready to show Derek your beach?" I asked.

"I'm ready!" Rex said, loving the beach and the adventure of Derek.

Rex was used to walking this beach, but Derek seemed a little reticent and off balance at first. We were all walking arm in arm—Adam, Derek, me, and Rex—trudging in partially wet sand, when I wondered what Derek would be like if I threw some unreserved California energy at him, as I did with Rex all the time. "Derek, shall we run into the surf?" I asked.

"I think I'd like to run into the surf," he responded in a rote manner, not knowing what was in the works.

"So let's go!" I said with urgency that spoke as loud as the words. I moved Rex around so he was facing the water, obliging the others to follow suit, then charged forward. "Into the surf!" I cried out, pulling the trio forward as water splashed around our calves.

"Into the surf!" Rex repeated my chant, laughing as the water encircled his legs. Adam appeared a bit dubious but followed suit. We moved forward and back, advancing into the waves and then pulling back. "Into the surf, Adam and Derek!" Rex shouted again.

Derek was cracking a smile. It encouraged me to push for more. I wanted to see Derek really unplugged. I laughed along with Rex, pulling everyone forward again. "Derek, isn't this fun running into the surf?" This time, a slightly larger wave rolled in to clip the bottom of the young man's rolled-up trousers.

His smile broke into a laugh, which was hesitant at first but began escalating with our movements. "Yes, Cathleen! This is fun running into the surf!" he responded, using echolalia laced with excitement. I didn't know Derek had laughter in him, but once it broke loose, it became infectious.

I looked out on our ocean to see three different surfers jumping atop their boards just in time to catch a long, rolling wave. They were at one with nature and their sport, and it all looked effortless, a seamless choreography dictated by the waves—dip and lean, shift, straighten.

Adam saw the surfers, too, and made a suggestion. "Derek, since we're in California, would you like to sing some Beach Boys?"

Still laughing, Derek said, "Why yes, Adam. I think I'd like to sing some Beach Boys."

And before I even had a chance to wonder how Rex would do with the older British boy singing the classic sun-drenched vacation songs, Derek and Adam had begun "Surfin' Safari."

"It's a song about surfing on the waves, Rex," I explained, and joined the singing.

With the three of us singing the California beach classic, Rex shouted, "Into the surf one last time," as he tugged on my arm.

Rex had picked up the chorus, and as "Come on a safari with me . . ." trailed off, Derek shouted, "I love the Beach Boys!" His accent held a touch of British restraint, but his enthusiasm was cut loose, signature California, so reminiscent of his wild, take-no-prisoners improvisations on the piano.

"I love the Beach Boys too!" Rex mimicked, suddenly sounding British himself. And they both burst out laughing, with Derek's head and torso bobbing forward and back and Rex jumping up and down in the sand. I looked from my little boy to this charming young man, who had so much life inside him to be brought out, and was filled with hope for the future.

At the end of our week together, Rex and Derek miraculously pulled off their performance at the Mandalay Bay Hotel stadium in Las Vegas. It was big and glitzy and glamorous, and they played beautifully together, but what I remember best about our week with our British friends was conversations with Derek—the yarns he would spin, manipulating words like music to keep the communication going and connect to others—and that day at the beach, laughing and singing and charging forward into the surf, experiencing life.

CHAPTER SIXTEEN

Rex's Time

I know the plans I have for you, declares the LORD, plans to prosper you
and not to harm you, plans to give you hope and a future.

—Jeremiah 29:11

Musical collaboration with Derek opened an important door for Rex, which came at the same time he finished fifth grade and graduated from elementary school. Over the next months, his musical speech took on new depth. In addition to his numerous solo performances around the country, he began playing with other musicians in his new middle school. Meaning his school peers! This was what I had been hoping for all along, but it hadn't been easy, and was still a work in progress.

Middle school presented a lot of new challenges to Rex . . . and sources of potential anxiety for Mom—bigger, noisier campus, bigger, tougher kids, changing classrooms throughout the day. But Rex's musical experiences, and life experiences, and with all the travel and newness, had paved the way for these new daily challenges to his body and mind. He was ready to take on middle school! And by the time we approached the end of his first year of middle school, I had to acknowledge just how much had changed for Rex—in his music, his life, and now at school. Educational issues which had continued to gnaw at me from one degree to another throughout his elementary years, from academics to opportunities to his mixing with other kids, now seemed mostly moot with his entry into middle school and two teachers who really got it . . . and got him.

The first was his special education classroom teacher Lisa Szilagyi, affectionately known as Lisa S. She was his "base camp (or classroom) teacher where he spent a couple of periods a day, working on special skills, from which he then traveled out to other selective "mainstream" classes. Lisa S. redefined "excellence in special education" by working creatively . . . and collaboratively (yes!) . . . to bring out the essence of Rex. She made sure he got numerous opportunities to use his gift to bridge social and educational gaps. And she was able to create that appropriate education (meaning relevant to his life) the law had promised him all along, but which, if truth be told, his elementary school teachers had never quite managed to give him, in spite of the support he had always gotten from caring one-on-one aides. As a result, instead of coming home exhausted by this new, more challenging environment, he seemed to be infused with energy. I'd collect him off the special education bus, which he rode to and from school each day now, and on many a day, he would quite literally be singing (well, let's say humming) as he stepped from the bus.

Secondly, there was his Period 1 teacher, Bill Bixler, who taught concert band and who was instrumental in affirming Rex in his new school setting. I saw the immediate connection between the two at the very beginning of the year. It was Back to School night, and being new to the middle school "changing classes thing," Rex and I were running late in finding classrooms. By the time we got to band, the teacher was introducing himself to a room full of parents, sitting wedged between percussion, keyboards, and music stands. "I'm Bill Bixler" he was saying as Rex tromped into the room, with his white cane leading the way past an impressive set of drums. Hearing his teacher's voice my son confidently announced to all, "Well, I'll just call you Bill!" Parents couldn't help smiling, and the band teacher chuckled at the interruption, saying, "It's nice to see you Rex. And I'm looking forward to your playing piano with us this year."

His concert band teacher encouraged Rex's participation in his class, understanding just how important this would be for his life. However, in the beginning of the year, Rex could barely tolerate all the other instruments and the kids in the class, who might be playing wrong notes, or tuning their instruments, or who might simply be in "his musical space"! He would ram his fingers in those sensitive ears, flap his hands to distraction, or just need to leave the room. Rex had made tremendous progress in desensitizing other sensory issues, but music was his sensitivity stronghold. His gift played against him in this area with his musical brain too finely tuned. It seemed his genius had created a level of intolerance that was unbridgeable. But his band teacher took it all in stride, countering any inflexibility in Rex with his own easygoing flexibility, and ability to go with the "Rex flow." And over the months, the miraculous once again began to unfold—my son's "sense of affront" began to change. That frustrating brain rigidity, born of autism, was being dealt just enough of a daily blow to progressively stretch it out (without breaking Rex in the process). This created much greater flexibility and a huge increase in what he tolerated. And as a result, the year saw Rex's dramatic transformation from a child who could barely tolerate musical exchange, even with a brilliant musician like Derek, into a young man who was emerging as a collaborative musician. And yet, I did need to admit that "emerging" was the operative word here.

The defining moment was at the Malibu High School spring instrumental concert, where he would be performing Mozart's Eighth Piano Concerto, backed up by the school orchestra. Rex's band teacher had given him an invaluable opportunity and demonstrated confidence that his student would rise to the occasion of being a team player in front of an auditorium full of parents. Playing with a whole stage full of other musician peers would show how music could help him connect to others. At twenty-six, Derek had been described by his teacher as a bomb proof performer. This event would put now eleven-year old Rex to that same test.

I was sitting in the audience, surrounded by friends I had asked to come to support my son and me, and I felt the nerves of life upon me. Would Rex trip up the orchestra if his fingers fumbled? A whole orchestra of kids was counting on him to play flawlessly. And what about them? Would they trip him up with lack of synchronization? His piano had delivered him to a group of peers who were dependent on him and on whom he depended—critical interdependence, so essential for life. Yet, I acknowledged, like so many times before, my son and I were way outside our comfort zones. And so, as the conductor raised his baton and began the orchestral intro of the thirty-six measures Rex had automatically counted, with my special child bouncing up and down on his piano bench while flapping his hands, my prayer was that God would just sit down next to my boy. *Hold his hands as he plays . . . and mine as well, while You're at it.*

Rex, get ready! I implored silently, my stomach clutching. As if he'd heard my thoughts, he settled down by the end of the intro and entered perfectly, playing his section with dexterity and tonicity. I finally took a breath. But then the orchestra played a section without the piano, freeing my son's hands once again. He was battling to keep them near the keys, waiting and ready for his next section, as we had worked on; but the excitement overwhelmed him, and they popped back up, like they were breaking free from societal constraint, and the rapid hand flapping began again.

No, Rex! Your hands need to be ready, sweetheart! How in the world could he land his hands from a mid-air flap in unknown space onto any specific key in a mere instant? He was blind, for goodness' sake!

Here comes your beat, Rex. Your hands, please. I was willing him to hear my thoughts. But his hands kept at it, as if they were playing a game of chicken, up and down, until he had the tiniest fraction of a second to respond. But . . . by the grace of God . . . that was all it took! Reacting with lightning speed, with his arms in full upward extension, his flapping motor jerked to a stop. Then his hands, possessed by the music and knowing exactly where they needed to be, plunged down onto the keys in a free fall! I heard gasps from the audience as he struck the keys with exact precision right on his entry beat. Catastrophe averted, miraculously.

I relaxed again, but he wasn't about to let me off lightly. He was determined to test my faith—in him and in God—for the same scene repeated each time the orchestra would take over the score. For the duration of the concerto, he would enter his piano section each time from some new random position in mid-flight. But he didn't miss a note, and didn't miss a beat, as though God were grabbing his hands and landing them home in perfect time.

Four beats to a measure. Four-four time. Also known musically as "common time." Common time! That's what Mozart had written, but Rex's time was anything but.

"Uncanny," came the response from a friend sitting next to me. I also heard "Unbelievable" and "Incredible," but as I lifted my heart in silent thanks, my own thoughts were, *Otherworldly.*

As the applause rang out for a stunning performance, I watched a boy in the row in front of us shut off his camcorder. Nathan. He was but a year older than Rex and was a piano prodigy

> *Then his hands, possessed by the music and knowing exactly where they needed to be, plunged down onto the keys in a free fall! I heard gasps from the audience as he struck the keys with exact precision right on his entry beat.*

himself, and he aspired to be a concert pianist. Nathan's mother was sitting next to him, and she turned to ask me how long it had taken Rex to learn the concerto. She shook her head in disbelief when I said, "Three weeks."

I was suddenly struck with an idea. "Wouldn't it be great if Rex and Nathan could play something together?"

Nathan turned around in his seat. "That would be fun," he said. "I played a concerto this year too . . . Beethoven. But it took me three months to learn it."

In spite of how far Rex had come, he still never had playdates, hadn't shown a desire to connect to his peers. They were open to him like Drew at the amusement park. They sought him out at school and elsewhere, but he showed no interest. *Why?* I wondered. Was it because kids his own age didn't have the patience it took to sustain communication with him? And if so, would this boy, who spoke the same musical language, be just the one to break that barrier? I knew that Nathan was being homeschooled so he could work on his piano during the day. "Where do you all live?" I asked his mother.

Mother and son exchanged amused looks. "We just rented out our home for the summer because we're going to be traveling. But for this month [June], while we're still here, we've moved into a condo on the beach, just north of Pepperdine."

If I'd been looking to God for some sort of sign, encouraging me, that would have been it. It turned out they were living just a couple of doors down in our very own condominium! Wow! Yet another wink from God!

Rex was a little tired from school on the day Nathan was coming to play, so I hoped he would allow the musical interchange I had set up. Facilitating Rex's interaction with another child was harder than facilitating a performance. And yet, Nathan was a pianist and a bright, energetic boy, who I hoped wouldn't be intimidated if my son was less than enthusiastic with their time together. He was beaming as he walked through the door, excited to see Rex play up close and personal and excited to play himself. Nathan said he'd like to hear Rex first. The older boy listened with true appreciation to my son's new Debussy "Arabesque." Then when he took his turn, he spoke to Rex directly, instead of to me, as was often the case. "Rex, I'd like to play you the Chopin Etude I've been working on."

The piece was nicknamed the "Torrent," and it was indeed a torrential flooding of notes he played with flamboyance and virtuosity, which made my son squeal and jump out of his chair. He had never heard a peer play with such prodigious skill! Nathan then played a Chopin Impromptu and got the same reaction.

Seeing Rex's interest, I had the longing again that he and Nathan should collaborate on a piece of music and work together. Remembering this boy had seemed open to just that, I tried following through. "Nathan, how would you like to study a piece of music that you and Rex could play together sometime?"

"Sure," he said without hesitation.

"You know, Rex learns pieces very quickly. If you'd like to see, maybe you could teach him part of the Chopin Impromptu you just played."

"Okay," Nathan said, although I suspect he doubted what he would get back. He played a melodic part, and Rex played it back instantly, to the boy's fascination. "Amazing," he said. Wanting to keep the interaction going, I suggested Rex play back the same part in another key, changing it from A-Flat to D.

"He can do that?" Nathan asked, incredulous.

"I think he can," I said, but in my pride as his mother, I'd spoken for my son.

Rex spoke for himself now. "No," he said, refusing.

I wouldn't give up, so I countered with an easier key change, speaking to him and not around him, like I berated others for doing. "Well, how about B-Flat, then, sweetheart? I think you can do that, Rex, can't you?" I coaxed.

Once again he had his own ideas, exerting his personality, his will. This time it was to pick the harder challenge, and he said, "D. I'll play it in D." It was an astounding transposition that left Nathan smiling, saying he wished he could have some of Rex's brain. But just as my heart was swelling with visions of these two boys as friends, Rex deflated my hopes, saying, "Nathan has to go now."

I knew that meant Rex had suddenly reached his limit. That's why he didn't have playdates. But I tried to deflect my son's meaning by saying, "No, sweetheart, I don't think he has to go yet, or do you, Nathan?"

"Yes, Nathan has to go," Rex repeated, his own independence suddenly becoming my foil.

The boy looked taken aback for a moment, since he was thoroughly enjoying his time playing music with Rex, but as he looked at his watch, he realized he'd been here past the time he'd told his mother, and said with a chuckle, "Well, actually, I do have to leave. But that was really fun, Rex."

The door shut to the sound of Rex playing what sounded like a nocturne, knowing he was improvising in that haunting, melancholic style. He seemed content but far away, removed from Nathan, removed from me, in that place of his own deep within, where only music could reach. "Rex, did you have fun with Nathan?" I asked, trying to pull him back, wanting him with me, not in some other world I couldn't access.

He answered me only with notes. They were beautiful and sad, wistfully fluttering, suspended in space, longing for completion before spiraling downward. My heart ached with a longing of my own—to reach my child. "Rex, did you have fun with Nathan?"

I asked again, more urgently, hoping, yearning. But we were in separate worlds.

We'd come so far together. His personality had begun emerging, and he was asserting himself. That was good, but I didn't want it to keep him separate. I wanted it to connect him to the world. Yet what I had yearned for all these years remained elusive. Would he ever become truly interactive, needing and desiring the company and companionship of a peer? Derek's example had given me hope. If he could get there with even greater cognitive limitations than Rex, so could my son. And so I had pushed forward with Nathan. But right when it looked like it would happen, Rex shut down. My letdown was intense, all the more so because Rex seemed to be able to just fly away on a nocturne and leave me alone in my frustration. And yet, I couldn't be all alone. That was what faith was all about. God had access to my son even deep within the music. And He had to be with me now, even though it didn't seem like it. Even if it seemed He was as deaf to me as my son was just then.

The next day, Rex and I went to the beach. And it was there, with the infinite horizon staring me in the face, that my son finally answered my question. "Mom, that was fun playing piano with Nathan!" In Rex's time. *Oh, you of little faith! Why do you doubt?* Everything in his life happened in his own time, that's the way my son worked. I couldn't push him past what he was ready for himself. Why hadn't I learned it yet? Waiting on God meant waiting on Rex. He dipped his feet into the surf, as he'd done with Derek, and said, "I will tell Nathan the water in the ocean is really cold!"

"You do that, sweetheart; you do that!" I said, my voice breaking with emotion.

"Nathan will come knocking on our door, and I will say, 'Come in Nathan,' and I will tell him."

YES! I cried to myself.

Two days later, there was a knock on the door. "Come in,

Nathan!" Rex shouted, with excitement, fulfilling his own prophecy. The door opened.

"Hi, Rex. How are you?" Nathan asked politely, walking in.

"I'm fine. And yourself?" Rex answered.

"I'm good. I've been thinking about a piece we could work on together, Rex. There are some Beethoven concertos that have different piano parts we could do," he said.

Just as I was about to jump in and say, "Good idea," effectively exerting my own desires on my son, I stopped myself, practically biting my lip, remembering, *In Rex's time*. Seconds can be an eternity when you're waiting for something life-altering to happen.

A beat. Two. Three. Then, enter a new measure altogether. "Nathan, I'd like to play a Beethoven concerto!"

YES! I cried again, silently.

I sat myself down in the living room, leaving the two boys to play together without Mom interfering. That's the way it would be. Facilitator, not interposer. After playing new pieces for each other, they had begun playing back and forth on the piano in a sort of musical conversation. Rex called it "question and answer," a musical game he'd learned at Pepperdine, where one would play a musical phrase in the style of a certain composer that would elicit an "answer" back, with each participant having to think quickly and creatively to keep the interaction going. This was Rex's language. But Nathan had mastered the tongue as well, and both boys were verbose. And both were having fun.

"How about some Russian, Rex? This is a Stravinsky style," Nathan said.

Rex smiled. He loved Russian. Tchaikovsky, Rachmaninoff. I knew he'd have much to say.

As I watched the two boys talking back and forth—never at a loss for words in Russian or Mozart or Chopin—I didn't know what the future held. Would Nathan become a friend? Maybe. But if not, there would be someone else, because I knew my son was reaching out, using music as a foothold as he'd always done. The door that had opened to let Nathan come in was just one more door opening in our lives. I gave thanks for it, knowing just how big it was, and I knew that if I would just trust, there would be many more to come. Trusting God meant trusting Rex and following his lead. I could provide him with opportunities as I always had, but I needed to lighten my touch and allow him to move forward at his own pace, in his own time.

Rex laughed as he shot back a Beethoven answer with such confidence and joy that it made Nathan laugh as well. As the notes filled the air, I had no doubt the future would be filled with work, hard work . . . for my son and for me. It was a complex road we were traveling. With his body and mind as the meeting place of such extremes of genius and disability, how could it be otherwise? And yet there in the mix of laughter and music I suddenly saw the truth unveiled. What I'd caught in glimpses throughout Rex's life—snippets, as God kept winking at me, sustaining me with just enough grace—was suddenly stark naked. The parts had become whole. And it really wasn't complicated at all; in fact it was beautiful and awe-inspiring in its simplicity. I'd write it on a Post-it to remind myself in the future, in a month or a year when I might forget . . . or doubt . . . or be buried once again by circumstance.

The whole fact is—Rex loves his life, every second, minute, hour, month, year. He's like a living revelation, the unlikely embodiment of grace—a touch of the Divine. My son knows that it *is* a wonderful life! And through my faith and love for a little boy, so do I.

The other day the bumps became words, and the words had meaning,
and the meaning was . . stories! Rex was reading Braille! Almost five years
after his mother gave up on his fingers ever being able to make sense
of those hated "bumps on a page," Rex was showing her once again to
never say never where he was concerned. Or where God was concerned.

L ater that night, I was sitting in the living room, thinking about Rex and Braille and the mystery of life and grace. The sliding doors to the terrace were fully open and I could almost touch the heady smell of salt and ocean in the humid night air. Mixed with the scent of the jasmine bushes, which grew in abundance directly below the terrace window, the evening air became an intoxicating perfume enveloping my senses. Add to that, the gentle waves rhythmically caressing my mind along with the shore, and I felt myself drifting into a peaceful trance. Beyond the ocean, all was silent, with Rex safely tucked in his bed, sleeping peacefully. Suddenly, breaking the silence, snapping me instantly from my sensory trance, I heard giggles coming from his bedroom. By the time I got to his bedside to check on him, he was chuckling to himself, apparently having a good time in his dreams. He has started that of late, sometimes even during the waking hours, he drifts off into his own thoughts, laughing. Sometimes it's giggles, other times it's a deeper, more sustained sound, and once in a while it escalates to include laughter in his body movements as well as sound. I've asked him on different occasions, "What's so funny, Rex"? He will invariably answer, "Mom, I'm not sure." Personally I think the laughter is his punctuation to all his miraculous break- throughs, and how he keeps proving doubters wrong (even when it's Mom). *So you really thought I'd never read Braille, Mom?* But then, the laughter is even more than that. It demonstrates how joy is at the very core of his being. It would have to be to inhabit his sleep that way, and to seep into his subconscious wakefulness. Listening to that sound, and admittedly joining him in laughter on many occasions, just "for the fun of it," has made me realize that there needs to be an afterward to his story. So here are a few more thoughts.

The basics are simple. *Rex is joy and I want what he has.* But the process is not. So let's go back in time.

Just like Rex was living in a dark, lonely world before he found his voice through music, so I was living in the dark before I found God, or rather, before He found me. Of course, I didn't know I was in the dark, since my world was filled with motion, and I was living in the City of Lights—Paris. How could there possibly be darkness there in the exciting world of fashion where I worked as a model or in a career in high finance? And yet, in the stillness, when the movement would stop for a moment, there was a vague feeling of emptiness that would seep in, in spite of all the "things" in that world. Back then, I would "cure" it by making myself busier.

I didn't know back then that I was living with a hole in my heart that simply couldn't be filled with things. And I certainly didn't know what it would take to fill that hole. Before Rex, I never could have dreamed him up. But that's what God specializes in—the outrageous, the unexpected, and the knock 'em down, out-of-this world unbelievable! Not to mention our own unspoken need . . . or unacknowledged need.

As I look back at the portrait of the young woman I was back then, I see how firmly I was grasping the wheel of my life. I was willful and stubborn, sure that I knew what I wanted and what was best, conditioned by my environment. I was trying to measure up, and uncertainty wasn't a trait admired at Stanford, nor was lack of conviction the stuff of a successful currency trader. I was enmeshed in the standards of the world around me, and bowing to ideals and exigencies of daily life.

Then came Rex! A steely bond of love gripped my heart when I looked into my baby's eyes. Unshakeable, unbreakable, beyond any emotion I'd ever felt! Little did I know, those beautifully innocent baby blues were the eyes of the perfect storm that would bring down the world as I knew it. Conditioning, expectations, standards. Rex's whole being was about uncertainty and lack of guarantee. I could have no expectations . . . not even the most basic for the child I loved so intensely! Devastated by grief and without any point of reference from my life experience, Rex's birth plunged me into confusion, despair, and utter hopelessness. He was a hurricane wrapped in a baby blanket, smashing the foundation of my existence, a tornado pushing me this way and that, leaving me spinning in unknown space, clinging only to my baby boy, hanging on for our lives. The only thing I knew back then was that I couldn't let go of my child. I was his mother, and that bond of love seemed the only absolute I could trust. And his daily existence was suffering, upset, and sensitivity. He couldn't live in the world as it was . . . or as he was. And it was living the picture of my two-year-old child, the tortured prisoner of his own dysfunctional body, that brought me to my knees and led me to God. Little did I know back then that what I was seeking from God went far beyond my son and my life since his birth. But God is bigger than our own imagination and He is a very clever Creator indeed!

I hadn't grown up in the church, so hearing words of God's redemptive grace sounded like a foreign language at first, especially

given what I was living with Rex. And so, it was all the more surprising when I found my heart changing, even as my son's condition
didn't change. I had attended church for a whole year, praying for
nothing but healing for Rex. For him to walk, and talk. Yet, without
any of those prayers for physical healing of the son being answered,
God had begun to heal the mother. Me! He had begun to instill faith
in my heart, which was far beyond my own understanding. It was
like the words of hope from the Bible bypassed my mind, refuted
the evidence in front of my eyes, and took root directly in my heart.
How could I have hope in my heart when our plight seemed utterly
without hope? The answer is I couldn't. Not without faith. And so,
for me that was the first miracle that touched our lives, a good year
before the physical miracles began to manifest in Rex's walking and
speaking and piano gift. By that miracle of faith that God was
growing in me I came to know He did have a plan for Rex's life . . .
and mine. I see in retrospect that plan had to begin with me and my
own change of heart. Maybe He had no use for me as I had been.
Maybe I had no use for me as I had been!

In the years since that first seedling of faith was laid in my
heart, it hasn't exactly been a quiet and even keeled "walk of
faith." It's been more like a tug-of-war with God—pitching this
way and that, digging in my heels, or loosening my grasp because
His grasp on me was too constraining, and the way He was leading was too frightening!

How many times did I forget reverence and just scream at Him
to listen to me! Was He uncaring . . . or just plain deaf? Or . . .
did He hear beyond my words, beyond my own momentary
agenda or concern to the big picture of our lives? Living in a constant state of uncertainty for so long grows new trusting muscles,
helping to pry loose old agendas and conditioning. You either let
go and trust or your body and mind fall apart over time. One thing
is sure—God left Rex and me in the mucky mess (miry pit) for an

interminably long time. (Sometimes it even seems we're back there.) But in all the erratic life and faith swings that I've encountered during the course of Rex's life, I've come to understand that God has allowed me to maintain a thread of hope through it all, without which all would have been lost. And coming out the other side of pain and darkness has refined my vision so that even a dim light shines like a jewel.

So much of Rex's life simply can't be explained by books or reason. I used to try to analyze, quantify, and assess ramifications of things that were beyond explanation and beyond my control. The result was a mind in turmoil—I was pulling away from God. Each time that would happen, when I looked beyond God for answers, I would come back blank. Blank and confused and upset.

Then I would hear Rex's piano music, and it would take my breath away . . . and take my mind out of the equation. I would know beyond any reason that God was present, and the rest of the world would fade away. It was like He was telling me to look past my own mind, and just trust. *Hear My voice in the music. Hear each note. Don't worry about where it's going. Just hear the sound and know that it's beautiful . . . And know that I am God.* Trust. That was hard for someone who had grown up believing that success came from working the mind. I mean, think about it. I'd pushed myself to get straight A's and high test scores in high school in order to get into a top college, which I managed in Stanford. Then after college, the financial markets were all about analysis—facts and data. As a currency options trader I lived and breathed economic indicators and chart analysis to get a fix on short-term or long-term movements. I was conditioned by reason.

Trust. If it wasn't the piano, it was Rex's laugh, straight from the belly that went beyond reason, transcendent. And I knew I wanted what he had. Joy that was just joy, all in the moment, which defied his disability and spoke of a direct connection to God. Before

Rex, I don't believe I even knew what joy was. That's because any happiness I had felt before was always modulated and conditional. Back then I would wonder if I was really happy or why I was happy, or even when "happy" would end. Ah, the elusive and short-lived happy! Like most people, I did want happiness to endure, so I was searching for what I felt would do the trick in a myriad of ways—living the Paris adventure, professional success, novelty, romantic love. Like analysis, that search took me away from God, hopping from one thing to another. I was definitely seeking something in my youthful restlessness. I just didn't know what. But God knew, and He gave me Rex—the child who would not only lead me into the "refiner's fire" of transformation by crushing my previous life structure, but who would also show me, by living it, that true joy is inside and doesn't come from things or conditions. And so, the birth of a new, more solid structure. A structure of purpose. Purpose.

Old desires became obsolete. Speak to me of market trends or cutting losses now and I'd probably look at you like you were speaking Swahili—it simply doesn't register. Not that there is anything wrong with my old profession, it just gives me no sense of purpose for living. Rex's birth gave me purpose, and now that has led me to a new life purpose—sharing the miracle of what I've lived with Rex in any way it might help others. Now I'm passionate about working with children with visual impairments or multiple disabilities, as I've became a fully Certified Educational Specialist in the field, or using my experience as a parent to help other parents cope with the emotional impact of their child's disability. I'm passionate about extending outwards, offering up my personal foibles, the wisdom I've gained through my own mistakes or misconceptions to others, whether it's speaking one-on-one with someone, or in the forum of a motivational speech, as Rex and I have been honored to share our lives with educational groups around the country and world. Now in writing this book, my hope is that it can help others gain encouragement and perspective in whatever their own personal struggles might be, that I might offer the blessing I've found in my son back to the world.

Not only does God work in unexpected ways, but I believe He is a master of irony! Ah yes, indeed. I went abroad to discover and experience the world. Travel! Paris! The glamorous city of lights! Yet it was through Rex and staying home with a little boy whose body and mind were under daily assault, that the whole world came to me. God delivered it right to my very doorstep!

Let me explain. Firstly, it was the intensity of Rex's needs that slammed the door shut on any outside distractions, effectively getting my attention. I see now how God had whispered to me through a seed of instability for many years prior to Rex, but those whisperings had been lost in the din of life. Then came Rex's birth. That birth was not just a loud cry, but a resonating scream that pierced my soul and wouldn't go away. And then, once I was really looking and listening (this took some time, mind you), I began to see God's truth revealed. Initially vaporous and blurred, that truth gained clarity in the emergence of Rex's spirit, pure and beautiful, from out of the darkness of his own imprisoned body and mind. *The whole world* (the one I'd been seeking before through perpetual motion in my conviction that it was "just a step away") *is with me at all times . . . and before my eyes at any given moment . . . if I choose to see it.* If I choose to see it! I've been conditioned for many years to believe the opposite, but God has given me Rex, the daily reminder that keeps me on track.

I still enjoy the adventure of travel, all the more so because I couldn't do any for so many years, having been held hostage by Rex's autistic sensitivities. But now when I experience life with my son, whether it's traveling or homebound, my senses are more attuned. My eyes have clearer vision, and the world seems fresher and more in focus, perhaps because I don't look everywhere at once like I used to. And being Rex's mother has given me ears to hear a beautiful song, even in the chaotic confusion of the world, because now I can filter out the static. And now I love stillness. It's in the same stillness that used to unsettle me that I really feel my heart at peace. That's when I can smell life's subtle hint of jasmine layered on an ocean breeze or reach out and actually touch the air. I hear life's symphony there now—deep in the stillness—my son chuckles, or giggles or unleashes that breathtaking belly laugh. I hear my son's piano notes fluttering over the gentle rhythm of waves outside our window and know that all of life's longings have found completion. That's when I can hear all the notes, even the subtle harmonies . . . with each note resonating His truth.

Acknowledgments

First of all, a very special acknowledgment to CBS's *60 Minutes* for believing in the exceptionality of Rex's life, and for opening up so many doors for Rex and me by shining a national light on our daily trials (and triumphs) To the incredible correspondent Lesley Stahl for "loving" Rex from the get go, and for seeing the mother side of it all. And to our amazingly talented producer Shari Finkelstein for "getting it right—"for blending humanity and scientific intrigue to create a beautiful "running portrait" of our lives.

I would like to express my gratitude to the numerous people that helped make this book possible:

To Tom Sullivan, my dear friend, who has always believed we had a story that needed to be told and that I was the one to tell it. Thanks for your vision and persistent belief in Rex and me, without which this book would not have been brought into being— not to mention the inspiration of your friendship and creative guidance throughout this project.

To our literary agents Jan Miller and Nena Madonia of Dupree Miller & Associates for your encouragement and your wise advice throughout this process.

I am very thankful for my entire Thomas Nelson team, who believed in REX.

To Victor Oliver, for taking your belief in our book proposal and my abilities as a writer to the Thomas Nelson Editorial Board and recommending publication. And to the Thomas Nelson Editorial Board for taking a chance on a first time author

To Kristen Parrish and Heather Skelton, my wonderful editors—you've both encouraged me and walked me through the very exciting and personal process of bringing our book to publication.

To Joel Miller for your commitment to this project and understanding that it is about "sharing the miracle of Rex."

To Dave Schroeder for your personal touch in connecting us to the entire Thomas Nelson team, even as your own first baby was about to kick her way into creation!

To Scott Harris and Curt Harding for your understanding of the value of Rex's smile and laugh in any marketing or publicity plan, and for helping to give that smile a forum.

To the many select individuals, who have helped Rex and me along the way:

To Gail Davis and all the ladies at Gail Davis and Associates for being the perfect caring representation we need to expand Rex's experiences in a speech/performance forum, in order to share the miracle of Rex. You are "off the charts."

To the caring staff of the Blind Childrens Center, who helped Rex and me gain a foothold in life.

To my brother Alan, for pointing me to church and to God. And to Malibu Presbyterian Church for becoming the home where I would find God and the faith to get me through. It remains my church home, even in the ashes of the fires that burned the structure to the ground this year.

To the heroes of Rex's school days, from Kindergarten to seventh grade, 6 exceptional one-on-one aides. Without your singular caring commitment to Rex throughout his "hard school days," he wouldn't be where he is today. KD (Khadevis Robinson)—the national running champion, who moonlighted as Rex's devoted school pal, and my friend, during the toughest of times. Ari, your incomparable sweetness was a light to my heart. Nanette, your tireless discipline and commitment to helping Rex was endless.

Caroline—your artsy creativity brought life to Rex. Catherine, thanks for seeing my mother's needs as well as Rex's. And Rex's current school aide and pal, the incomparable Jim O Neil, you make school not just learning, but fun for Rex, and who but you to take him out surfing to catch 3 long, amazing rides into the shore?

To Rex's piano teachers :

Sara Banta at Pepperdine for your loving guidance in Rex's music, and creative genius in producing brilliant improvisations on the spot, and for being the light behind Rex's performance music.

David Pinto, you bring magic and laughter to Rex's music every Saturday at your wonderful Academy of Music for the Blind. An extra special thank you for getting Rex to read Braille when I had given up. And to David's wife Gayle for your loving and patient persistence in pushing Rex further in other disciplines, such as computer skills and Braille reading. Thanks to both David and Gayle for trying "Braille" one more time, even though Mom had given up.

Lynn Marzulli for nurturing Rex's "touch of the Divine."

To Angela Rasmussen Rex's voice teacher, who went with Rex on his precocious and vertiginous voice slide at 11, helping him land his little boy's soprano into a surprising and resonant tenor/baritone just months later.

To Gloria Terry Knutson and Jennifer Jackson, Rex's two first loves (other than Mom). You gave me crucial hours of respite and peace knowing Rex was in your loving hands.

To my dear friend Raffaella, who stood by my side through each hospitalization and helped to hold me up. To Naomi for your prayers. To Susan for caring and never forgetting a Rex birthday or Christmas!

To my family for your prayers, and for being my family.

About the Author

Cathleen Lewis spent a home-grown Southern California childhood in the rustic, throwback Ojai Valley. Then at 15, she went to cosmopolitan Rio de Janeiro with a Brazilian exchange student from her high school for a summer, and a need to leave home and see the world was born. She went on to earn a B.A. at Stanford University in International Relations with her eyes on travel and life beyond the "Ojai orange groves."

After graduation, a summer in Paris, a chance encounter with the head of a Parisian modeling agency, and Cathleen decided to "stay for a while." That summer turned into 12 years of living in Paris. During that time she initially worked in the glamorous world of fashion as a model, then returned to school to earn a French Business Degree, which she applied in the financial markets when she was given the mission to create a currency options trading desk at the large French bank. After 7 years of the challenging and fast-paced currency markets, the demise of the European Monetary System coincided with an extreme urge to "return home," and the author returned to California.

But after so many years abroad, California didn't quite feel like "home" anymore. Another chance encounter, this time in Los Angeles, and Cathleen met the man she would marry. Since Rex's birth, her life has been consumed by the love and responsibility for her son. The break-up of her marriage only served to reinforce that absolute commitment. Her struggles to advocate for Rex in the public school system made her aware of a great lack of vision specialists in the system, and especially those with expertise in autism. Cathleen's passion for her son, and desire to help other kids like him, along with their parents, led her back to school once again, this time to earn a credential as an Educational Specialist in Visual Impairments.

Cathleen lives in Malibu, California, where she currently divides her time between her work as a Vision Specialist, the demands of her life as a single mom, raising her complex son, and travel around the world to select speaking/piano playing engagements with her son, where he can share his gift, and she can share the miracle and beauty of Rex and what it's like to finally "come home."